AQA GCSE

COMPUTER SCIENCE

Steve Cushing

Approval message from AQA

This textbook has been approved by AQA for use with our qualification. This means that we have checked that it broadly covers the specification and we are satisfied with the overall quality. Full details of our approval process can be found on our website.

We approve textbooks because we know how important it is for teachers and students to have the right resources to support their teaching and learning. However, the publisher is ultimately responsible for the editorial control and quality of this book.

Please note that when teaching the *AQA GCSE Computer Science* course, you must refer to AQA's specification as your definitive source of information. While this book has been written to match the specification, it does not provide complete coverage of every aspect of the course.

A wide range of other useful resources can be found on the relevant subject pages of our website: www.aqa.org.uk.

HODDER
EDUCATION
AN HACHETTE UK COMPANY

The Publishers would like to thank the following for permission to reproduce copyright material:

Photo credits

p. 3 t © TfL from the London Transport Museum collection, b © TfL from the London Transport Museum collection; **p. 83** © Photodisc/Getty Images; **p. 126** © Robert Gray; **p. 238** © Robert Gray; **p. 240** © Godfried Edelman/iStockphoto; **p. 246** © Jwrodgers CC licence: http://creativecommons.org/licenses/by-sa/3.0

Acknowledgements

Every effort has been made to trace all copyright holders, but if any have been inadvertently overlooked the Publishers will be pleased to make the necessary arrangements at the first opportunity.

Although every effort has been made to ensure that website addresses are correct at time of going to press, Hodder Education cannot be held responsible for the content of any website mentioned in this book. It is sometimes possible to find a relocated web page by typing in the address of the home page for a website in the URL window of your browser.

Hachette UK's policy is to use papers that are natural, renewable and recyclable products and made from wood grown in sustainable forests. The logging and manufacturing processes are expected to conform to the environmental regulations of the country of origin.

Orders: please contact Bookpoint Ltd, 130 Milton Park, Abingdon, Oxon OX14 4SB. Telephone: +44 (0)1235 827720. Fax: +44 (0)1235 400454. Lines are open 9.00a.m.–5.00p.m., Monday to Saturday, with a 24-hour message answering service. Visit our website at www.hoddereducation.co.uk

First published in 2016 by

Hodder Education,
An Hachette UK Company
Carmelite House
50 Victoria Embankment
London EC4Y 0DZ

Impression number   10 9 8 7 6 5 4 3 2 1

Year   2020 2019 2018 2017 2016

Cover photo © Vladyslav Otsiatsia/Thinkstock/Getty Images

Typeset in India by Aptara, Inc.

Printed in Italy

A catalogue record for this title is available from the British Library

ISBN 978 1 4718 6619 7

Contents

Contents

Contents

Summary of features

3 Using Pseudo-code

When you fully document your code with comment tags, you're answering two questions (at least):

1 Why did I do that?
2 What does this code do?

No matter how simple, concise, and clear your code may end up being, it's impossible for code to be completely self-documenting. Even with very good code it can only tell the viewer how [it works, but it] can also say why it works.

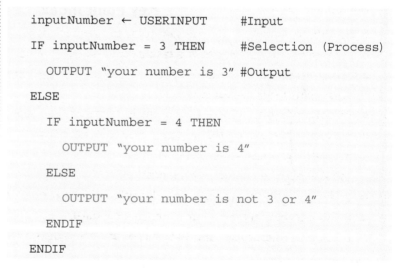

Practice Tasks will help build students' coding, programming and problem-solving skills

TASK

Describe the main reasons why a programmer would wish to annotate or add comments to their code.

KEY POINT

A comment is explanatory text for the human reader.

Key Points clarify significant information for students to be able to process and recall easily and include Key Terms to help students develop computing language skills to facilitate greater subject understanding

Adding selection

As we discovered in the last chapter on flowcharts, another important aspect of programming is selection. If we want to write pseudo-code that tells a user to enter a number to a variable and then we want the code to see if the number they entered is a 3 or a 4 we could write a selection algorithm in pseudo-code that could look like this:

```
inputNumber ← USERINPUT      #Input
IF inputNumber = 3 THEN       #Selection (Process)
   OUTPUT "your number is 3" #Output
ELSE
   IF inputNumber = 4 THEN
      OUTPUT "your number is 4"
   ELSE
      OUTPUT "your number is not 3 or 4"
   ENDIF
ENDIF
```

QUESTION

What is a comment?

Regular questions test topic understanding to assess progress

Clear Examples show students computational approaches to problem-solving

EXAMPLE

Say we want to input two numbers, add them together and show the answer on the screen.

Table 1.1

Input	Process	Output
Two numbers	Add the first number to the second	The new number

We could write this as the following sequence:

INPUT first number   # input stage
INPUT second number   # input stage
ADD first and second number together and
STORE as total   # process stage
OUTPUT total   # output stage

Each chapter concludes with a Review of key information to assess and consolidate topic knowledge and understanding

CHAPTER REVIEW

In this chapter we have explored pseudo-code and how to use it to show program flow and decision making.

We also explored the importance of syntax and how to comment on your code.

Remember before tackling any computer science task or question on this topic you must:

- be able to work out the steps or rules for getting things done;
- manage the complexity of the task by focusing on the key details;
- use a systematic approach to problem solving and algorithm creation representing those algorithms using pseudo-code;
- be able to explain simple algorithms in terms of their inputs, processing and outputs;
- be able to determine the purpose of simple algorithms;
- record your ideas using pseudo-code;
- think about the correct syntax needed;
- understand that more than one algorithm can be used to solve the same problem;
- be able to obtain user input from the keyboard;
- be able to output data and information from a program to the computer display.

Cross Referencing

Paper 1	Papers 1 & 2	Paper 2	Non-exam assessment

AQA Computer Science GCSE Specification content			Book chapters
1 Fundamentals of Algorithms			
1.1	Representing algorithms	Understand and explain the term algorithm.	1
		Understand and explain the term decomposition.	1
		Understand and explain the term abstraction.	1
		Use a systematic approach to problem solving and algorithm creation representing those algorithms using pseudo-code and flowcharts.	2, 3
		Explain simple algorithms in terms of their inputs, processing and outputs.	2, 3
		Determine the purpose of simple algorithms.	2, 3
1.2	Efficiency of algorithms	Understand that more than one algorithm can be used to solve the same problem.	1, 2, 22, 23
		Compare the efficiency of algorithms explaining how some algorithms are more efficient than others in solving the same problem.	1, 2, 22, 23
1.3	Searching algorithms	Understand and explain how the linear search algorithm works.	22
		Understand and explain how the binary search algorithm works.	22
		Compare and contrast linear and binary search algorithms.	22
1.4	Sorting algorithms	Understand and explain how the merge sort algorithm works.	22
		Understand and explain how the bubble sort algorithm works.	22
		Compare and contrast merge sort and bubble sort algorithms.	22
2 Programming			
2.1	Data types	Understand the concept of a data type.	17
		Understand and use the following appropriately: ● integer ● real ● Boolean ● character ● string.	17

AQA Computer Science GCSE Specification content			Book chapters
2.2	Programming concepts	Use, understand and know how the following statement types can be combined in programs: ○ variable declaration ○ constant declaration ○ assignment ○ iteration ○ selection ○ subroutine (procedure/function).	6, 7, 8, 11, 12
		Use definite and indefinite iteration, including indefinite iteration with the condition(s) at the start or the end of the iterative structure.	8
		Use nested selection and nested iteration structures.	9
		Use meaningful identifier names and know why it is important to use them.	6
2.3	Arithmetic operations in a programming language	Be familiar with and be able to use: ○ addition ○ subtraction ○ multiplication ○ real division ○ integer division, including remainders.	4, 10
2.4	Relational operations in a programming language	Be familiar with and be able to use: ○ equal to ○ not equal to ○ less than ○ greater than ○ less than or equal to ○ greater than or equal to.	4
2.5	Boolean operations in a programming language	Be familiar with and be able to use: ○ NOT ○ AND ○ OR.	4, 5
2.6	Data structures	Understand the concept of data structures.	17, 18
		Use arrays (or equivalent) in the design of solutions to simple problems.	10, 18
		Use records (or equivalent) in the design of solutions to simple problems.	18

Cross Referencing

AQA Computer Science GCSE Specification content			Book chapters
2.7	Input/output and file handling	Be able to obtain user input from the keyboard.	3, 4, 6, 7
		Be able to output data and information from a program to the computer display.	3, 4, 6, 7
		Be able to read/write from/to a text file.	20
2.8	String handling operations in a programming language	Understand and be able to use: ⊙ length ⊙ position ⊙ substring ⊙ concatenation ⊙ convert character to character code ⊙ convert character code to character ⊙ string conversion operations.	7, 15, 17
2.9	Random number generation in a programming language	Be able to use random number generation.	4
2.10	Subroutines (procedures and functions)	Understand the concept of subroutines.	11
		Explain the advantages of using subroutines in programs.	11
		Describe the use of parameters to pass data within programs.	11
		Use subroutines that return values to the calling routine.	11
		Know that subroutines may declare their own variables, called local variables, and that local variables usually: ⊙ only exist while the subroutine is executing ⊙ are only accessible within the subroutine.	11, 12
		Use local variables and explain why it is good practice to do so.	12
2.11	Structured programming	Describe the structured approach to programming.	1, 12
		Explain the advantages of the structured approach.	1, 12
2.12	Robust and secure programming	Be able to write simple data validation routines.	19
		Be able to write simple authentication routines.	19
		Be able to select suitable test data that covers normal (typical), boundary (extreme) and erroneous data. Be able to justify the choice of test data.	24

AQA Computer Science GCSE Specification content			Book chapters
2.13	Classification of programming languages	Know that there are different levels of programming language: ◉ low-level language ◉ high-level language.	14
		Explain the main differences between low-level and high-level languages.	14
		Know that machine code and assembly language are considered to be low-level languages and explain the differences between them.	14
		Understand that ultimately all programming code written in high-level or assembly languages must be translated into machine code. Understand that machine code is expressed in binary and is specific to a processor or family of processors.	14
		Understand the advantages and disadvantages of low-level language programming compared with high-level language programming.	14
		Understand that there are three common types of program translator: ◉ interpreter ◉ compiler ◉ assembler. Explain the main differences between these three types of translator. Understand when it would be appropriate to use each type of translator.	14

Cross Referencing

AQA Computer Science GCSE Specification content			Book chapters
3 Fundamentals of Data Representation			
3.1	Number bases	Understand the following number bases: ◉ decimal (base 10) ◉ binary (base 2) ◉ hexadecimal (base 16).	13
		Understand that computers use binary to represent all data and instructions.	13
		Explain why hexadecimal is often used in computer science.	13
3.2	Converting between number bases	Understand how binary can be used to represent whole numbers.	13
		Understand how hexadecimal can be used to represent whole numbers.	13
		Be able to convert in both directions between: ◉ binary and decimal ◉ binary and hexadecimal ◉ decimal and hexadecimal.	13
3.3	Units of information	Know that: ◉ a bit is the fundamental unit of information ◉ a byte is a group of eight bits.	15
		Know that quantities of bytes can be described using prefixes. Know the names, symbols and corresponding values for the decimal prefixes: ◉ kilo, 1 kB is 1,000 bytes ◉ mega, 1 MB is 1,000 kilobytes ◉ giga, 1 GB is 1,000 Megabytes ◉ tera, 1 TB is 1,000 Gigabytes	15
3.4	Binary arithmetic	Be able to add together up to three binary numbers.	13
		Be able to apply a binary shift to a binary number.	13
		Describe situations where binary shifts can be used.	13
3.5	Character encoding	Understand what a character set is and be able to describe the following character encoding methods: ◉ 7-bit ASCII ◉ Unicode.	15
		Understand that character codes are commonly grouped and run in sequence within encoded tables.	15
		Describe the purpose of Unicode and the advantages of Unicode over ASCII. Know that Unicode uses the same codes as ASCII up to 127.	15

AQA Computer Science GCSE Specification content			Book chapters
3.6	Representing images	Understand what a pixel is and be able to describe how pixels relate to an image and the way images are displayed.	15
		Describe the following for bitmaps: ◉ size in pixels ◉ colour depth.	15
		Describe how a bitmap represents an image using pixels and colour depth.	15
		Describe, using examples, how the number of pixels and colour depth can affect the file size of a bitmap image.	15
		Calculate bitmap image file sizes based on the number of pixels and colour depth.	15
		Convert binary data into a black-and-white image.	15
		Convert a black-and-white image into binary data.	15
3.7	Representing sound	Understand that sound is analogue and that it must be converted to a digital form for storage and processing in a computer.	15
		Understand that sound waves are sampled to create the digital version of sound.	15
		Describe the digital representation of sound in terms of: ◉ sampling rate ◉ sample resolution.	15
		Calculate sound file sizes based on the sampling rate and the sampling resolution.	15
3.8	Data compression	Explain how data can be compressed using Huffman coding.	21
		Be able to interpret Huffman trees.	21
		Be able to calculate the number of bits required to store a piece of data compressed using Huffman coding. Be able to calculate the number of bits required to store a piece of uncompressed data in ASCII.	21
		Explain how data can be compressed using run-length encoding (RLE).	16
		Represent data in RLE frequency/data pairs.	16
		Understand why data are often compressed.	16

Cross Referencing

AQA Computer Science GCSE Specification content			Book chapters
		4 Computer Systems	
4.1	Hardware and software	Define the terms hardware and software and understand the relationship between them.	25, 34
4.2	Boolean logic	Construct truth tables for the following logic gates: ◉ NOT ◉ AND ◉ OR.	5
		Construct truth tables for simple logic circuits.	5
		Interpret the results of simple truth tables.	5
		Create, modify and interpret simple logic circuit diagrams.	5
4.3	Software classification	Explain what is meant by: ◉ system software ◉ application software. Give examples of both types of software.	34
		Understand the need for, and functions of, operating systems (OS) and utility programs.	34
		Understand that the OS handles management of the: ◉ processor(s) ◉ memory ◉ I/O devices ◉ applications ◉ security.	34
4.4	Systems architectures	Explain the von Neumann architecture.	25
		Explain the role and operation of main memory and the following major components of a CPU: ◉ arithmetic logic unit ◉ control unit ◉ clock ◉ bus.	25

AQA Computer Science GCSE Specification content			Book chapters
		Explain the effect of the following on the performance of the CPU: ◦ clock speed ◦ number of processor cores ◦ cache size ◦ cache type.	25
		Understand and explain the fetch-execute cycle.	29
		Understand the differences between main memory and secondary storage.	27
		Understand the differences between RAM and ROM.	27
		Understand why secondary storage is required.	28
		Be aware of different types of secondary storage (solid state, optical and magnetic).	28
		Explain the operation of solid state, optical and magnetic storage.	28
		Discuss the advantages and disadvantages of solid state, optical and magnetic storage.	28
		Explain the term cloud storage.	28
		Explain the advantages and disadvantages of cloud storage when compared to local storage.	28
		Understand the term 'embedded system' and explain how an embedded system differs from a non-embedded system.	26
5 Fundamentals of computer networks			
		Define what a computer network is.	35
		Discuss the benefits and risks of computer networks.	35
		Describe the main types of network including: ◦ personal area network (PAN) ◦ local area network (LAN) ◦ wide area network (WAN)	35
		Understand that networks can be wired or wireless.	35

Cross Referencing

AQA Computer Science GCSE Specification content			Book chapters
		Discuss the benefits and risks of wireless networks as opposed to wired networks.	35
		Explain the following common network topologies: ○ star ○ bus.	35
		Define the term 'network protocol'.	36
		Explain the purpose and use of common network protocols including: ○ Ethernet ○ WiFi ○ TCP ○ UDP ○ IP ○ HTTP ○ HTTPS ○ FTP ○ email protocols – SMTP – IMAP.	36
		Understand the need for, and importance of, network security.	31, 32
		Explain the following methods of network security: ○ authentication ○ encryption ○ firewall ○ MAC address filtering.	30, 31, 32
		Describe the four-layer TCP/IP model: ○ application layer ○ transport layer ○ network layer ○ link layer.	36
		Understand that the HTTP, HTTPS, SMTP, IMAP and FTP protocols operate at the application layer.	36
		Understand that the TCP and UDP protocols operate at the transport layer.	36
		Understand that the IP protocol operates at the network layer.	36

AQA Computer Science GCSE Specification content			Book chapters
6 Fundamentals of Cyber Security			
		Be able to define the term cyber security and be able to describe the main purposes of cyber security.	32
6.1	Cyber security threats	Understand and be able to explain the following cyber security threats: ● social engineering techniques ● malicious code ● weak and default passwords ● misconfigured access rights ● removable media ● unpatched and/or outdated software.	32
		Explain what penetration testing is and what it is used for.	32
6.1.1	Social engineering	Define the term 'social engineering'.	32
		Describe what social engineering is and how it can be protected against.	32
		Explain the following forms of social engineering: ● blagging ● phishing ● pharming ● shouldering (or shoulder surfing).	32
6.1.2	Malicious code	Define the term 'malware'.	31, 32
		Describe what malware is and how it can be protected against.	31, 32
		Describe the following forms of malware: ● computer virus ● Trojan ● spyware ● adware.	31, 32
6.2	Methods to detect and prevent cyber security threats	Understand and be able to explain the following security measures: ● biometric measures (particularly for mobile devices) ● password systems ● CAPTCHA (or similar) ● using email confirmations to confirm a user's identity ● automatic software updates.	31, 32

Cross Referencing

AQA Computer Science GCSE Specification content			Book chapters
7 Ethical, Legal and Environmental Impacts of Digital Technology on Wider Society, Including Issues of Privacy			
		Explain the current ethical, legal and environmental impacts and risks of digital technology on society. Where data privacy issues arise these should be considered.	26, 28, 33
8 Aspects of Software Development			
		Design Be aware that before constructing a solution, the solution should be designed, for example planning data structures for the data model, designing algorithms, designing an appropriate modular structure for the solution and designing the user interface.	37
		Implementation Be aware that the models and algorithms need to be implemented in the form of data structures and code (instructions) that a computer can understand.	37
		Testing Be aware that the implementation must be tested for the presence of errors, using selected test data covering normal (typical), boundary (extreme) and erroneous data.	24, 37
		Evaluation/refining Be aware that code created during implementation will often require refining as a result of testing. Be aware of the importance of assessing how well the solution meets the requirements of the problem and how the solution could be improved if the problem were to be revisited.	37

1 Computational Thinking

KEY POINT !

Computational thinking involves applying a set of problem-solving skills and techniques that are used by computer programmers to write programs.

KEY POINTS !

Problem-solving skills and techniques refer to the designing of systems, and understanding concepts such as decomposition and abstraction which are fundamental to computer science.

Output is anything that a computer produces.

Logical reasoning is the process or method of using a rational and systematic approach to solving a problem. It will often be based on mathematical assumptions and procedures.

Before you can succeed in computer science you must learn about what is called 'computational thinking'. Computational thinking involves applying a set of **problem-solving skills and techniques** that are used by computer programmers to write programs. Computational thinking is not thinking about computers or even thinking like a computer. Computers don't think for themselves. If you give ten computers the same instructions and the same input, they will give exactly the same **output**. Computers are predictable.

Computer scientists use **logical reasoning** to work out exactly what a program or computer will do. Computational thinking involves thinking about a problem in a logical way, and enabling a computer to solve it. This logical reasoning is the essential building block of computer science, so first we need to fully understand the techniques involved and how we start with a problem and end up with the programming code.

Two important techniques used in computational thinking are:

- **Decomposition**: This is breaking any given task or problem into simple logical steps or parts.

- **Abstraction**: This is the process of taking away or removing characteristics from something in order to reduce it to something simpler to understand. In computer science, abstraction is often used for managing the complexity of computer systems.

We will explore each of these in detail later in the book but let's start with a simple example of decomposition and abstraction as they relate to problem solving.

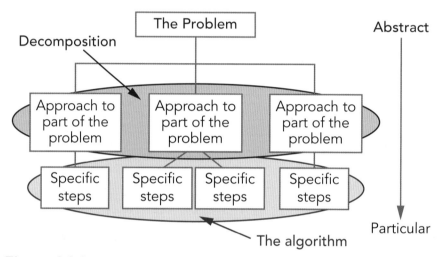

Figure 1.1 *Decomposition and abstraction*

Decomposition

When a chef writes a recipe for a meal, that chef is creating a set of instructions that others can then follow to replicate the meal. Each part of the recipe is listed separately. The overall meal is decomposed into separate dishes, and these are often decomposed further, for example making the pastry and the filling.

Abstraction

You may have come across the term 'Abstract Art', where a painting is a set of shapes representing the scene. A good example of the use of abstraction for technical purposes is the London tube map. It is the brainchild of an electrical draughtsman named Harry Beck.

Rather than emphasising the real distances and geographical location of all the tube lines, Beck stripped away the sprawling tube network by abstracting just the information needed by travellers. He then used this to create an easy-to-read diagram of coloured, criss-crossing lines common in electrical diagrams.

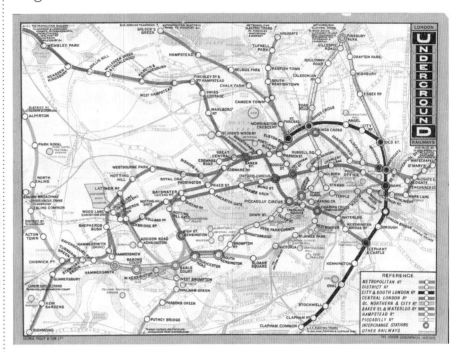

Figure 1.2 *A geographical map of the London underground stations*

KEY POINT

In abstraction we remove unnecessary details from a problem until the problem is represented in a way that is possible to solve.

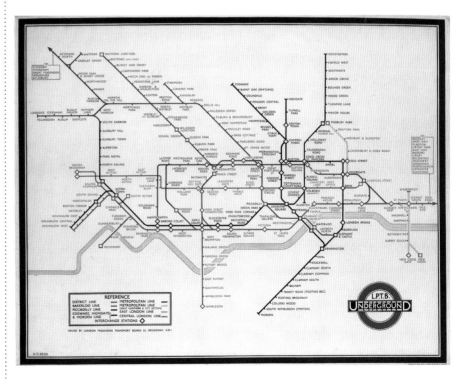

Figure 1.3 *An original abstracted map of the London underground*

Let us look at a simple example of abstraction.

EXAMPLE

Figure 1.4 *Fred wants to cross a river*

A man called Fred wishes to cross a 10 metre wide river with a wolf, a white goat and a bail of newly cut hay. He has a small blue boat and oars, but unfortunately he can only take one thing across at a time. The problem is, if he leaves the wolf and the goat alone together, the wolf will eat the goat, and if he leaves the goat with the hay, the goat will eat the hay. They are currently all together on one side of the river, which we will call bank B, and they want to get to the other side, called bank A.

How does he do it?

There is a simple computational approach for solving this problem.

Of course, you could simply try all possible combinations of items that may be rowed back and forth across the river. Trying all possible solutions to a given problem is referred to in computer science as a **brute force approach**. But logical thinking will bring about a better solution.

Only the relevant aspects of the problem need to be represented, all the **irrelevant** details can be ignored. A representation that leaves out details of what is being represented

is a form of abstraction. So what can we leave out?

```
Is the man's name relevant?
Is the width of the river
relevant?
Is the colour of the boat
relevant?
```

> ### KEY POINT ....
> A representation that leaves out unnecessary details of what is being represented is a form of abstraction.

```
We can start with the following
bits of information:
```
- River banks are A and B
- Goat = G
- Hay = H
- Wolf = W
- Man = M

So to start with we have:

```
    A              B
                   G H W M
```
But we need to end up with:
```
    A              B
    G H W M
```
Each step we show needs to correspond to the man rowing a particular object across the river (or the man rowing alone).

Let's look at the first step:
```
    A              B
    G M            H W
```
The man (M) has taken the goat (G) to the other side of the river.

TASK

Solve the rest of the river-crossing problem.

KEY POINTS

- Abstraction is the process of removing unnecessary detail from a problem.
- Abstraction draws out the essence of a problem. By solving it we can also see what other problems can be solved using the same techniques.

More than one solution to any problem

There will often be more than one solution to the same problem, but you always need to create **ordered steps** to achieve any of these solutions. Let's look at another simple problem.

Imagine a map; you are given a starting point and the point you wish to arrive at. The map contains a grid to help navigation. The map grid has numbers in the vertical axis, and letters in the horizontal axis. Let's say we start at 10 C and want to arrive at 15 L.

Figure 1.5 shows four possible pathways. There are of course many more. We could take a very complicated route, but we want to be efficient and take as few moves as possible.

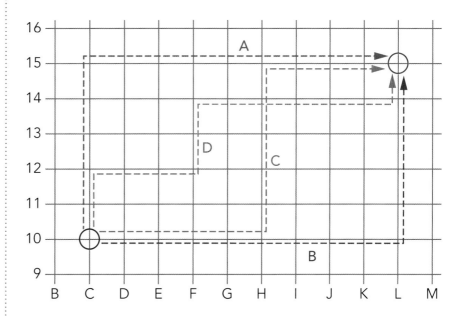

Figure 1.5 *Four possible pathways*

We could describe each of these pathways using words. Pathway 'A', for example, could say move north until you reach map reference 15, then turn right 90°, now move forward to map reference L.

We can also describe the path using distances rather than the grid positions. For example, move forward five, turn right 90°, move forward nine.

Of course both of these directions will only work if people follow them exactly. We have abstracted the problem as an example. We could make the directions better by **refining the instructions** and adding more detail, perhaps by informing the user what to do if they go wrong. We could add a **position check**. If you can understand these concepts, you are well on the way to being able to write computer programs.

Choosing the best solution

So we know there can often be many answers to the same problem, but we need to determine what makes the best solution and would lead to the best algorithm.

The first set of criteria we need to consider are:

- does the solution work?
- does the solution complete its task in a finite amount of time (within set boundaries)?

We have lots of solutions to our problem and each, whilst very different, satisfies these two criteria. Therefore, the next step is to determine which of our solutions is 'best'.

There are generally two criteria used to determine whether one computer algorithm is 'better' than another. These are:

- the **space requirements** (i.e. how much memory is needed to complete the task)
- the **time requirements** (i.e. how much time will it take to complete the task).

Another criterion that we can consider is the cost of **human coding time**. This is the time it will take us to develop and maintain the program. A clever **coding** system may improve the space and/or time requirements but result in a loss of program **readability** and an increase in the human cost to maintain the program.

What is an algorithm?

The word '**algorithm**' comes from the ninth-century Arab mathematician, Al-Khwarizmi, who worked on 'written processes to achieve some goal'. The term 'algebra' also comes from the term 'al-jabr', which he introduced.

Algorithms are at the very heart of computer science. An algorithm is simply a set of steps that defines how a task is performed. For example, there are algorithms for cooking (called recipes), algorithms for finding your way through a strange city (directions), and algorithms for operating washing machines (manuals). There are even algorithms for playing music (sheet music).

A scientific description of an algorithm would be:

> *'a series of unambiguous steps to complete a given task in a finite amount of time.'*

An algorithm has input data, and is expected to produce output data after carrying out a process which is the actions taken to achieve the required outcome. You will need to understand this input–process–output model, as much of what you will learn in computer science is founded upon this model.

TASK

What is an algorithm?

The input–process–output model

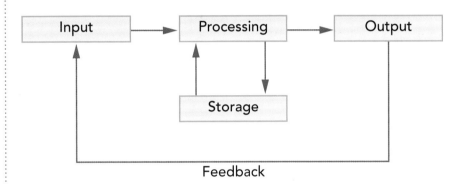

Figure 1.6 *The input–process–output model*

A computer can be described using a simple model, as shown in Figure 1.6.

The INPUT stage represents the flow of data into the process from outside the system.

The PROCESSING stage includes all the tasks required to affect a transformation of the inputs.

The OUTPUT stage is where the data and the information flow out of the transformation process.

You will notice that we have added two new parts to the model: storage and feedback.

The STORAGE stage keeps the data until it is needed.

FEEDBACK occurs when outputs of a system are fed back as inputs and so form a circuit or loop.

In solving any problem, you must follow this model. First you define the problem, then you define what the solution must be,

KEY POINT

You must be able to identify where inputs, processing and outputs are taking place within an algorithm.

RESEARCH TASK

Use this book and other sources such as the internet to research how to analyse a problem, investigate requirements (inputs, outputs, processing, initialisation) and design solutions.

and finally you work on the transformation (process) to achieve the desired solution.

Sometimes programmers even plan out their code using these headings.

Sequences

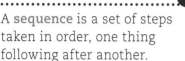

KEY POINT

A **sequence** is a set of steps taken in order, one thing following after another.

To solve a problem there must be a **sequence**. In computer science, a sequential algorithm is an algorithm that is executed sequentially, one step at a time from start to finish. It does this without any other processes executing. Most standard computer algorithms are sequential.

EXAMPLE

Say we want to input two numbers, add them together and show the answer on the screen.

Input	Process	Output
Two numbers	Add the first number to the second	The new number

We could write this as the following sequence:

INPUT first number   # input stage
INPUT second number   # input stage
ADD first and second number together and
STORE as total   # process stage
OUTPUT total   # output stage

Saving an INPUT with a name – for example, in this instance we input a number and called it 'first number', then we input another number and called it 'second number' – is called **assignment**. It is called this because we 'assign' a value to the variable. In computer programming, an assignment statement sets and/or re-sets the value stored in a storage location. We will explore this in more detail later in the book.

Why are sequences so important?

In computer programming you have to first work out the correct sequence of the commands. This may sound simple but let's look at an example to show how careful you need to be. If you write down your friend's address it may look like this:

John Smith
22 Holly Road
Hempton
London
AB12 3CD

You know that this is the order that you should write an address, but this is the exact opposite of the way that the postal system works. There are millions of John Smiths. There may be hundreds of Holly Roads, many of them with a number 22. The postal system needs to know the address in the logical task order, meaning the order that you carry out to find the address. In this case that is London first, followed by the area, then the road and finally the number.

In some countries the conventional order follows the logical task order. In Russia, letters are addressed in exactly the opposite order to the UK, with the city first.

For your programming to work correctly, all the commands have to be there *and* they need to be in the correct sequence. Sequencing is extremely important in programming.

Decomposition and sequences

Let's look at a simple problem in terms of input, process and output.

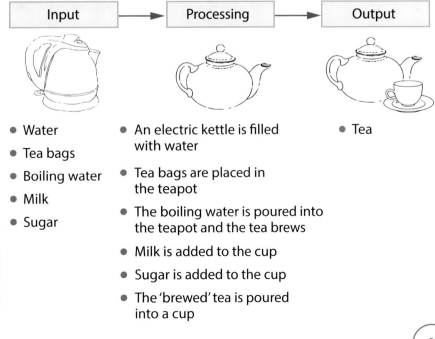

- Water
- Tea bags
- Boiling water
- Milk
- Sugar

- An electric kettle is filled with water
- Tea bags are placed in the teapot
- The boiling water is poured into the teapot and the tea brews
- Milk is added to the cup
- Sugar is added to the cup
- The 'brewed' tea is poured into a cup

- Tea

KEY POINT

Many computer programmers label their files using the date format year, month, day as this is the logical way to automatically list them, the year being the first piece of data required, the month the next and the day last. This is because there can be 12 files with the same day number in a single year.

RESEARCH TASK

Use this book and other sources such as the internet to research how to decompose a problem into smaller sub-problems.

Figure 1.7 *A sample system diagram*

Let's say we want to make a cup of tea using tea bags and a kettle.

The sequence could look like this:

Input	Process	Output
● Water ● Tea bags ● Boiling water ● Milk ● Sugar	● An electric kettle is filled with water ● Tea bags are placed in the teapot ● The boiling water is poured into the teapot and the tea brews ● Milk is added to the cup ● Sugar is added to the cup ● The 'brewed' tea is poured into a cup	● Tea

We would do the same to make more than one cup of tea but we would only fill the kettle and boil it once. We could divide the sequence into two parts.

Sequence one

```
Count the number of people wanting tea    #input
Fill the kettle with enough water         #input and process
Boil the water                            #process
Put tea bag in pot                        #input and process
Pour on water                             #input and process
Allow tea to brew                         #process
```

Sequence two

```
For each person wanting tea    #requires input from first sequence
   Pour brewed tea from pot
   to cup                      #process
   Add sugar to cup            #input and process
   Add milk to cup             #input and process
Serve tea                      #output and process
```

Indents have been used to show the parts of the sequence we would repeat.

We would need to carry the number of people wanting tea from the first sequence to the next sequence so we can repeat the second sequence of the task in order to make a cup of tea

KEY POINT

A **variable** is a value that can be changed.

for each person. We could do this by creating what is called a **variable**.

```
Count the number of people wanting tea

Store answer in a variable called teaCount

Fill the kettle with enough water

Boil the water

Put tea bag in pot

Pour on water

Allow tea to brew

Repeat the following steps for the number stored
in the variable called teaCount

    Add sugar

    Add milk

End Repeat

Serve
```

We could of course extend this by asking who wants sugar or milk. This is called an **IF** statement construct.

```
Do you require sugar?

If answer is yes

    Add sugar

End If

Do you require milk?

If answer is yes

    Add milk

End If
```

We could also run parts of the task in parallel. For example, whilst the kettle is boiling we could add the teabags to the cups, and we would almost certainly add all the teabags to the cups before adding the water. We would not add one teabag, then add the water to that cup before adding the next teabag.

Explore all these possibilities and represent them as simple English sentences. If you do this you have just decomposed a problem and have started to create a program. We will explore all of the concepts you need such as 'loops' and 'if' statements in more detail later in the book. For now, you just need to understand how to break a problem down into simple steps and how to group these steps into separate parts of the task.

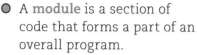

Modularity

There are several advantages to designing solutions in a structured manner. One is that it reduces the complexity, as each set of steps can act as a separate **module**. **Modularity** allows the programmer to tackle problems in a logical fashion. Modules can also be reused.

To develop modules the programmer needs to carry out what is called decomposition. This is to break down a problem into easy-to-understand steps.

Because modules can be re-used many times, it saves time and reduces complexity, as well as increasing reliability as the modules will have already been tested in another program. It also offers an easier method to update or fix the program by replacing individual modules rather than larger amounts of code. Modular programming (also called structured programming) avoids the increased possibility of data corruption often caused by using a large number of lines of code. It ensures that there is a logical structure in the program being written, which makes the code more efficient and easier to understand and modify.

Structured programming makes extensive use of subroutines, block structures and 'for' and 'while' loops. We will explore all of these later in the book.

Algorithms and code

Each instruction should be carried out in a finite amount of time. An algorithm, given the same input, will always produce the same output. During the processing the underlying code will always pass through the same sequence of states.

Since we can only input, store, process and output data on a computer, the instructions in our algorithms will always be limited to these functions.

First, we must not only fully understand the problem but give each item a name before solving it:

- Identify and name each Input/Given
- Identify and name each Output/Result
- Assign a name to our algorithm (Name)

- Combine the previous three pieces of information into a formal statement (Definition)
- Results = Name (Givens)

Recording your ideas

Once we have abstracted the necessary data and understood the sequences involved, rather than writing long text explaining the problem and its solution, we need to find a way to record our thinking and the method we will use to solve the problem. The most effective way is to use either a flowchart or pseudo-code.

> **KEY POINTS**
>
> Flowcharts show a sequence of events or movements involved in a complex activity or process.
>
> Pseudo-code is an easy-to read language to help with the development of coded solutions.

CHAPTER REVIEW

In this chapter we have explored computational thinking including decomposition and abstraction. We also looked at the input, process and output model and explored the importance of sequences.

Remember, before tackling any computer science task or question on this topic you must:

- be able to take a complex problem and break it down into smaller problems
- be able to work out the sequences needed
- understand and explain the terms algorithm and decomposition
- understand and explain the term abstraction and manage the complexity of the task by abstracting the key details.

2 Using Flowcharts

There are a lot of different design procedures and techniques for building large software projects. The technique discussed in this chapter, however, is for smaller coding projects and is referred to by the term 'top down, structured flowchart methodology'. We will explore how to take a task and represent it using a flowchart. A flowchart puts the sentences from a sequence into shaped boxes. The shapes indicate the action.

You will know from the last chapter that a sequence is where a set of instructions or actions are ordered, meaning that each action follows the previous action.

Flowchart advantages

- Flowcharts are a graphical way of writing an algorithm.
- They are standardised: they all agree on the symbols and their meaning.
- They are very visual.

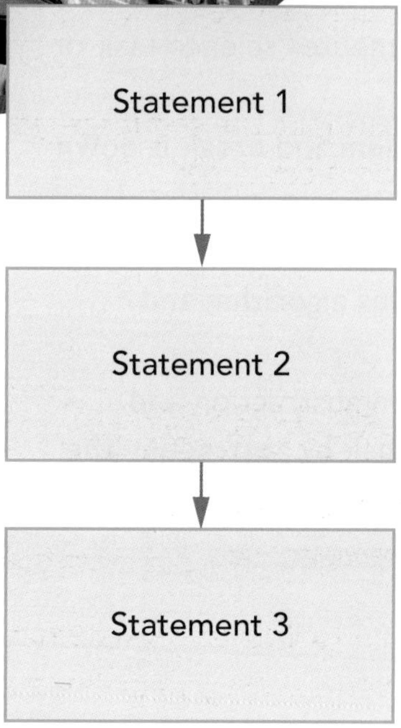

Statement 1

Statement 2

Statement 3

Figure 2.1 *A flowchart*

Flowchart disadvantages

- They are hard to modify and can be time consuming.
- They need special software for symbols, although some software has these built in.

General rules for flowcharts

- All symbols of the flowchart are connected by flow lines (these must have arrows, not lines, to show direction).
- Flow lines enter the top of the symbol and exit out of the bottom, except for the Decision symbol, which can have flow lines exiting from the bottom or the sides.
- Flowcharts are drawn so that flow generally goes from top to bottom of the page.
- The beginning and the end of the flowchart is indicated using the Terminal symbol.

Let's look at a simple sequence. Say we want to add A to B, where A = 200 and B = 400.

```
Start
A = 200 B = 400
Add = 200 + 400
Output = 600
End
```

We could create a simple flowchart, like the one shown in Figure 2.2.

Let's look at another sequence. For example, the sequence you carry out each morning in the bathroom could be:

- Brush your teeth.
- Wash your face.
- Comb your hair.

TASK

Produce a sequence to show how to brush your teeth.

As you can see, sequences are a useful tool for showing what happens, and in what logical order each step happens. But each step, for example 'brush teeth', needs to be defined in more detail to be carried out.

KEY POINTS !

- An algorithm is a sequence of steps that can be followed to complete a task.
- A sequence is where a set of instructions or actions are ordered, meaning that each action follows the previous action.
- Flowcharts must have flow lines with arrows to show the direction.

QUESTION

What is a sequence?

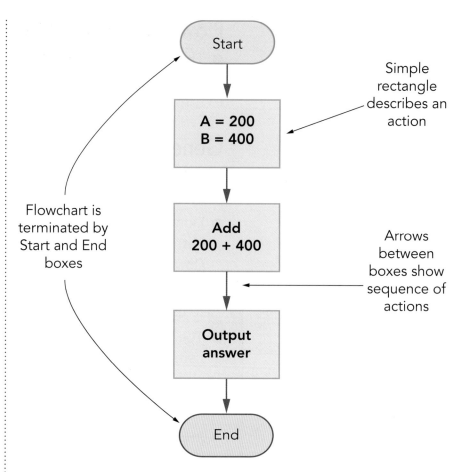

Figure 2.2 *A flowchart showing a simple sequence*

Once we have picked up our brush, turned on the tap and added the toothpaste we can put the brush in our mouth and brush. The act of actually brushing your teeth could be recorded in a linear way: press, brush up, brush down, brush up, brush down etc. But it would be much simpler to explain the brushing once and then tell the user to repeat the same action x amount of times. We will explore this later when we consider looping, but for now let us explore how we can use a flowchart to represent simple sequences. First we need a few more elements.

QUESTION

What is an input/output?

KEY POINT

Cleaning your teeth is called a procedure in coding. You perform the same action every day, for example pick up brush, put toothpaste on brush, brush teeth for two minutes, spit out, clean brush. These actions could be given a procedure name: 'Brushing Teeth'.

Basic elements of flowcharts

The flowchart symbols denoting the basic building blocks of programming are shown in Figure 2.3. Text inside a symbol is called a label.

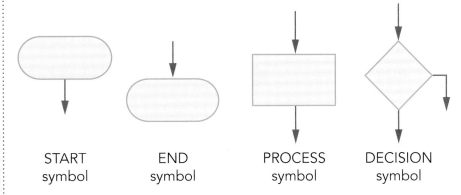

| START | END | PROCESS | DECISION |
| symbol | symbol | symbol | symbol |

Figure 2.3 *Basic elements of a flowchart*

The START symbol represents the start of a process. The PROCESS symbol is labelled with a brief description of the process carried out by the flowchart. The END symbol represents the end of a process. It contains either END or RETURN depending on its function in the overall process of the flowchart. A DECISION symbol is used when there are two options (Yes/No, 1/0, etc.).

Representing a process

A 'Process' symbol is representative of some operation that is carried out on an element of data. It usually contains a brief description of the process being carried out on the data. It is possible that the process could even be further broken down into simpler steps by another complete flowchart representing that process. If this is the case, the flowchart that represents the process will have the same label in the 'Start' symbol as the description in the process symbol at the higher level. A 'Process' box always has exactly one line going into it and one line going out.

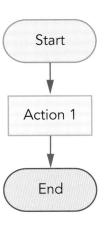

Figure 2.4 *A flowchart showing a process*

In practice, sequences are not a simple line. Often the next action depends on the last decision. This is called selection. In a selection, one statement within a set of program statements is executed depending on the state of the program at that instance. We ask a question and choose one of two possible actions based upon that decision.

Representing a decision

A 'Decision/selection' symbol always makes a Boolean choice, i.e. a choice between two options. We will explore Boolean logic in more detail later in the book. But the label in a 'Decision' symbol should be a question that clearly has only two possible answers to select from.

The 'Decision' symbol will have exactly one line going into it, and two lines coming out of it. The two lines coming out of it will be labelled with the two answers to the question in order to show the direction of the logic flow depending upon the selection made.

Selections are usually expressed as 'decision' key words such as IF, THEN, ELSE, ENDIF, SWITCH or CASE. They are at the heart of all programming.

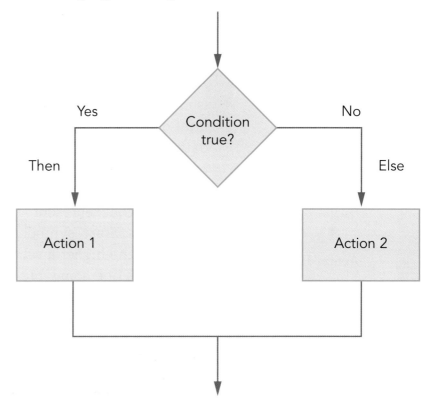

Figure 2.5 *A flowchart representing selection*

In flowcharts you use the following symbols:

Symbol	Purpose	Use
↓	Flow line	The lines show the sequence of operations
⬭	Terminal (Start/Stop)	Denotes the start and end of an algorithm
▭	Processing	Denotes a process to be carried out.
◇	Decision	Used to represent the operation in which there are two alternatives, true and false.

We can use a decision to create a flowchart of what happens in the morning on school days.

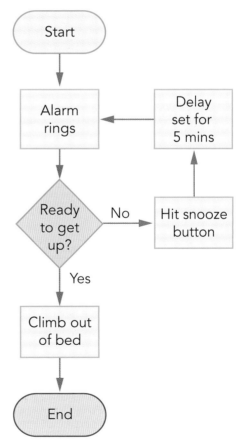

Figure 2.6 *A flowchart for what happens in the morning on a school day*

We also explored selections a little when we looked at the sequence of making tea. We explored using IF someone wants sugar and IF someone wants milk. The process of making the tea differed according to their answer to these questions.

The flowchart below shows a different process for making tea and adds two decision boxes.

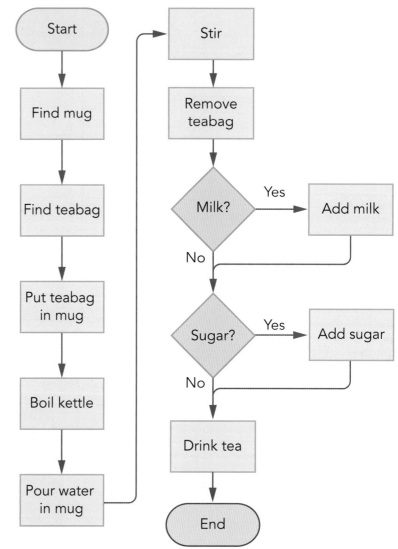

Figure 2.7 *A flowchart for making a cup of tea*

If we wanted to show how to play the game of snakes and ladders we could explain how to play the game in English as follows:

```
Start game
Throw the dice: the number indicated by dice is x
Move your counter: x squares on the board and check:
    Have you landed on snake head?: no/yes
        If yes slide down snake to its tail
        If no check next statement
```

```
Have you landed on the bottom of a ladder?: no/yes
    If yes move up the ladder
Have you reached the last block of the game?: no/yes
    If yes Output "you are the winner"
    If no Give the dice to the next player
Repeat until someone reaches the last block of the game
End
```

We have more decisions in this example and could show the game with the following flowchart.

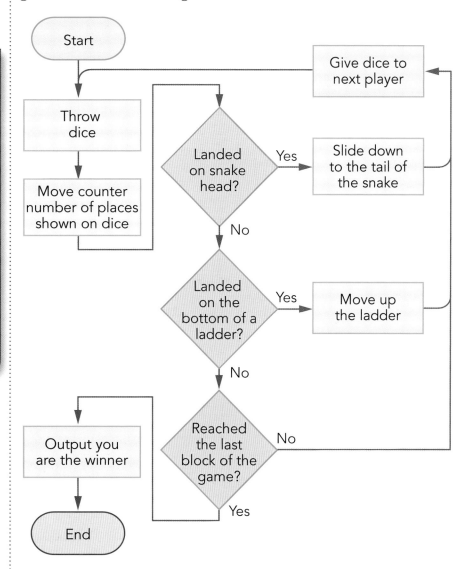

Figure 2.8 *A flowchart for playing snakes and ladders*

Other structures we will use are shown in Figure 2.9.

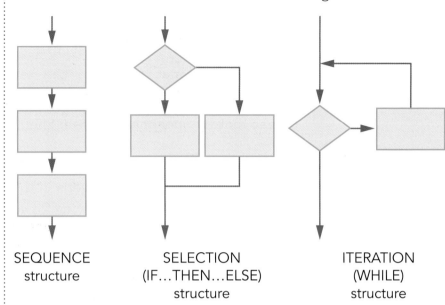

SEQUENCE
structure

SELECTION
(IF…THEN…ELSE)
structure

ITERATION
(WHILE)
structure

Figure 2.9 *Other structures we will use in this book*

On-page and off-page 'Connectors' may also appear in some flowcharts. This occurs when a flowchart goes over more than one page. For the purpose of this chapter we will only explore flowcharts that can be represented on a single page. If a flowchart is so big it needs to go on to another page, you should split into subprocesses.

Subprocesses

We can also use subprocesses in flowcharts using the symbol shown in Figure 2.10.

Subprocesses are useful because:

- they help with the modularisation of complex programs
- they provide a way of simplifying programs by making common processes available to a wide number of programs
- they lead to more reliable programs, since once a process is tested and works it can be made into a subprocess and need not be tested again.

In flowcharts subprocesses are also useful in dealing with the flowcharting rule that a flowchart should fit on a single page.

Figure 2.11 shows an example of the main page of a flowchart. It contains two 'Subprocess' symbols. Each symbol contains text which describes briefly what the subprocess does.

Subprocess

Figure 2.10 *The subprocess symbol*

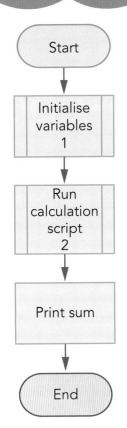

Figure 2.11 *The main page of a flowchart*

Each 'Subprocess' symbol also contains a page reference where the flowchart for the subprocess will exist.

CHAPTER REVIEW

In this chapter we built upon the last chapter to explore sequences in more detail and how we can show these using flowcharts.

We looked at the basic elements of flowcharts and introduced the concept of decisions and how these can be represented.

Remember before tackling any computer science task or question on this topic you must:

- work out the steps or rules for getting things done
- use a systematic approach to problem solving and algorithm creation, representing those algorithms using flowcharts (More on this topic in chapter 3.)
- be able to explain simple algorithms in terms of their inputs, processing and outputs
- understand the concept of selection and the concept of subprocesses
- be able to record your ideas using flow diagrams
- be able to describe the structured approach to programming (More on this topic in chapter 3.)
- be able to explain the advantages of the structured approach. (More on this topic in chapter 3.)

3 Using Pseudo-code

Pseudo-code

Pseudo-code is another way to develop an algorithm. It consists of natural language-like statements that precisely describe the steps required.

Pseudo-code must:

- contain statements which describe actions
- focus on the logic of the algorithm or program
- avoid language-specific elements
- be written at a level so that the desired programming code can be generated almost automatically from each statement
- contain steps. Subordinate numbers and/or indentation are used for dependent statements in selection and repetition structures.

KEY POINTS ❗

- Pseudo-code is a language designed to express algorithms in an easy-to-follow form.
- Pseudo-code is an easy-to-read language to help with the development of coded solutions.

Pseudo-code advantages

- Pseudo-code is similar to everyday English.
- It helps programmers to plan an algorithm.
- It can be done easily on a word processor.
- It is easily modified.
- It implements structured concepts well.

Pseudo-code disadvantages

- Pseudo-code is not visual like flowcharts.
- There is no accepted standard, so it varies widely.
- It is not an actual programming language.
- It is an artificial and informal language.

The importance of syntax

Syntax is the set of rules, principles and processes that enable us to understand a programming language. The syntax rules of a programming language define the spelling and grammar and, as with natural human languages, each language has its own rules. Computers are very inflexible and understand what you write only if you state what you want in the exact syntax that the computer expects and understands.

Each programming language has its own rules and specialist syntax including the words the computer understands, which combinations of words are meaningful, and what punctuation is necessary to be correctly structured. Whilst pseudo-code does not have a fixed syntax, you will need to understand the syntax used in AQA pseudo-code. Understanding the importance of syntax is also vital when you start using a programming language.

Symbols

When we write code in English we also use symbols in the form of punctuation and special characters. For example, – is a symbol, and so is #. We will explore these later in the book. Symbols are used as they are human-readable, but they are important as they also have an effect in your code.

Symbols can also be used as what are called identifiers. In some programming languages, they can be called atoms rather than symbols.

The symbols ←, <<, <- are often used as what are called '**assignment** operators'.

```
Examples
Name ← USERINPUT
or
LengthOfJourney ← USERINPUT
or
YesNo ← USERINPUT
```

Common action keywords

Several keywords are often used to indicate common input, output and processing operations.

● Input: READ, OBTAIN, GET, USERINPUT
● Output: PRINT, DISPLAY, SHOW, RETURN, OUTPUT
● Process/compute: COMPUTE, CALCULATE, DETERMINE
● Initialise: SET, INIT
● Add one: INCREMENT, BUMP

```
In AQA pseudo-code you use the following
syntax to send output to the screen. The red
brackets < > are only to show where you add
something; you don't need to put them in your
code
Syntax:
OUTPUT <add expression here>
Example:
OUTPUT 'Have a good day.'
```

Whilst there is no common way of writing pseudo-code, in this book we have written the commands in capital letters to differentiate them from the examples in Python and to help you understand what the command words are.

Some of the pseudo-code words used by AQA involving code are:

```
ELSE                 USERINPUT
ENDFOR               OUTPUT
ENDIF                REPEAT
ENDWHILE             RETURN
FOR                  THEN
IF                   WHILE
```

Commenting on your code

Good code is not only well written but should also be well annotated. There are programmers who argue that comments are not necessary if the code is written well, but remember that you are telling a third party what your code does and why.

You will find many examples of commented code in this book. Comments are shown using either // or #. Different programming languages have different ways to tell the computer that this is a comment *not* the code. You can make all the code you write in pseudo-code a comment when you write the actual code using your chosen language. This is considered good practice when learning to code. You can also comment out bits of code to find errors but we will explore this later.

The following pseudo-code syntax may be used in code for comments:

```
#some text
```

Multiple comments will show the hash # for each separate comment line.

```
#some text
#some more text on a new line
```

Comment tags remind you why you included certain functions. They also make maintenance easier for you later.

Have you ever tried to work with someone else's complex spreadsheet or database? It's not easy. Imagine how difficult it is if you're looking at someone else's programming code.

KEY POINT

Good code is well written and well annotated.

When you fully document your code with comment tags, you're answering two questions (at least):

1 Why did I do that?
2 What does this code do?

No matter how simple, concise and clear your code may end up being, it's impossible for code to be completely self-documenting. Even with very good code it can only tell the viewer how the program works; comments can also say why it works.

KEY POINT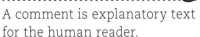

A comment is explanatory text for the human reader.

QUESTION

What is a comment?

TASK

Describe the main reasons why a programmer would wish to annotate or add comments to their code.

Adding selection

As we discovered in the last chapter on flowcharts, another important aspect of programming is selection. If we want to write pseudo-code that tells a user to enter a number to a variable and then we want the code to see if the number they entered is a 3 or a 4 we could write a selection algorithm in pseudo-code that could look like this:

```
inputNumber ← USERINPUT       #Input
IF inputNumber = 3 THEN       #Selection (Process)
   OUTPUT 'your number is 3' #Output
ELSE
   IF inputNumber = 4 THEN
     OUTPUT 'your number is 4'
   ELSE
     OUTPUT 'your number is not 3 or 4'
   ENDIF
ENDIF
```

The colours are used to show the level of indentation.

If we remove the comments, then the code would look like this:

```
inputNumber ← USERINPUT

IF inputNumber = 3 THEN

    OUTPUT 'your number is 3'

ELSE

    IF inputNumber = 4 THEN

        OUTPUT 'your number is 4'

    ELSE

        OUTPUT 'your number is not 3 or 4'

    ENDIF

ENDIF
```

CHAPTER REVIEW

In this chapter we have explored pseudo-code and how to use it to show program flow and decision making.

We also explored the importance of syntax and how to comment on your code.

Remember before tackling any computer science task or question on this topic you must:

- be able to work out the steps or rules for getting things done
- manage the complexity of the task by focusing on the key details
- use a systematic approach to problem solving and algorithm creation representing those algorithms using pseudo-code (More on this topic in chapter 2.)
- be able to explain simple algorithms in terms of their inputs, processing and outputs (More on this topic in chapter 2.)
- be able to determine the purpose of simple pseudo-code algorithms (More on this topic in chapter 2.)
- record your ideas using pseudo-code
- think about the correct syntax needed
- understand that more than one algorithm can be used to solve the same problem (More on this topic in chapters 1, 2, 7, 23.)
- be able to obtain user input from the keyboard
- be able to output data and information from a program to the computer display.

4 Algorithms in Mathematics

The study of algorithms did not start with the invention of computers. The example we have used so far in the book, of adding two numbers together, is a mathematical problem. We need to also understand how algorithms work in mathematics. When the term algorithm is used in mathematics, it refers to a set of steps used to solve a mathematical problem. The algorithm for performing long division or multiplication is a good example.

EXAMPLE

To carry out a long division for 52 divided by 3 you would have the following specific sequence of steps and their outcomes:
- How many times does 3 go into 52? **17 (3 × 17 = 51)**
- How many are left over? **1**
- How many times does 3 go into 1? **0 with 1 left over**
- And, of course, the answer becomes **17.3333333...**

The step-by-step process used to do the long division is called a long division algorithm.

Algorithms are used a lot in mathematics, especially in algebra.

Modules

A module is a software component or part of a program that contains one or more **routines**. Grouping related code into modules makes the code easier to understand and use. We will look at modules in more detail in chapter 12, but one of the advantages of modules is that some of them are already written for you and many relate to mathematical operations, so you will need to understand what they can do.

A number of very useful modules exist in Python, normally in a file named <modulename>.py. You can use any Python file as a module by using an import statement.

The import for a module has the following syntax:

```
import <module name>
```

Here's how these statements and functions work:

import <module name> imports the module named and creates a reference to that module. After you have done this, say you have imported module A, you can use A.name to refer to things defined in the imported module A.

This textbook is divided in chapters and paragraphs. In a computer program, we now know that specific functionality can be divided up into modules. Programs often use blocks of code and modules that have already been created in other projects. In a computer program these modules are parts of a program that we want to re-use or repeat. Modules often contain functions which take input values and produce some output. We will explore these in more detail later.

```
In AQA pseudo-code, you use the following
syntax to define a function. The red brackets
< > are only to show where you add something
(you don't need to put them in your code).
Syntax:
SUBROUTINE <id> (<add parameter here>, ...)
   <add command here>
   RETURN <add expression here>
```

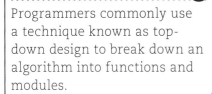

KEY POINT

Programmers commonly use a technique known as top-down design to break down an algorithm into functions and modules.

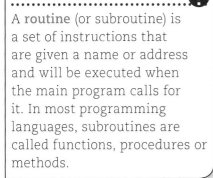

KEY POINT

A **routine** (or subroutine) is a set of instructions that are given a name or address and will be executed when the main program calls for it. In most programming languages, subroutines are called functions, procedures or methods.

4 Algorithms in Mathematics

```
ENDSUBROUTINE
Example:
SUBROUTINE myMarks (Mark1, Mark2, Mark3)
   avTotal ← (Mark1 + Mark2 + Mark3)/3
   RETURN avTotal
ENDSUBROUTINE
```

You can also use from <module name> import *. This imports the module and then you can use the plain name of things defined in the module instead of <module name>.name. You can even call the module by coding from <module name> import a, b, c. This imports the module and creates references to the specified objects in the module. In other words, you can then use a, b and c in your program.

In Python, to import modules, we use the following syntax:

```
import moduleName              #imports a module

from moduleName import name    #imports part of a module

from moduleName import *       #imports all of a module
```

Mathematical algorithms

Your knowledge of mathematical algorithms is vital, as many computing algorithms follow the same processes but not all are the same. Let's look at some examples and how these differ:

> **KEY POINT** ❗
>
> In computer science, signs such as = mean different things and different syntactical rules apply.

Mathematics	Computer science
The following instructions are the same in mathematics. A=B B=A In mathematics both these instructions would express that A and B are equal, so they have the same purpose.	In computer science = is used for assignment, so A=B copies the value of B into A whereas B=A copies the value of A into B.
In mathematics we work with relations. A relation B=A+1 means that it is true all the time	In computer science we work with assignments. We can have: A=5 B=A+1 A=3 The relation B=A+1 is true only after the second instruction and before the third one. After the third one A=3, but B is still 6

Mathematics	Computer science
The instruction A=A+3 is false in mathematics. It cannot exist.	In computer science A=A+3 means: the new value of A is equal to the old one plus three.
The instruction A+6=3 is allowed in mathematics (it is an equation).	A+6=3 has no meaning in computer science where the = is used for assignment as then the left side must be a variable so we would have to say three = A+6. In some languages we could use the following to see if they are equal A+6==3

Understanding what can be effectively programmed and executed by computers, therefore, relies on the understanding of computer algorithms and mathematics. Algorithms solve general problems, and not specific ones. Algorithms, therefore, are general **computational methods** used for solving particular problem instances.

Be careful with brackets:

(6 + 5) * 3

In this sum, brackets are used to do the addition first.

Output: 33

6 + (5 * 3)

Brackets here are used to do the multiplication first.

Output: 21

Computers can execute instructions very quickly and reliably without error, so algorithms and computers are a perfect match!

Translating a simple mathematical problem into pseudo-code

Let's look at a simple problem. Someone has given us a temperature of 82° Fahrenheit but we need a metric temperature. We will call Celsius and Fahrenheit variables, as they could be any number. In algebra we use letters to represent a value that we haven't decided on yet. In computer science we call these variables. We will examine variables in much more detail in chapter 6. For now we will follow the algebra example and call the Fahrenheit temperature 'F' and the Celsius temperature 'C'. The mathematical expression is:

C = 5(F − 32)/9

> **KEY POINT** ❗
>
> **Computational methods** are a way of approaching a problem by generating algorithms for various parts of the problem.

If we wanted to write this in English we could say:

```
Input F

subtract 32 from F to get Q

multiply Q by five to get X

divide X by nine to get C

Print C

Stop
```

Or we could write it using mathematical statements to assign values to each variable.

```
Input F

Q = F - 32

X = Q × 5

C = X/9

Print C

Stop
```

Any number entered as F will be converted to degrees C.

Using mathematical phrases and symbols

To symbolise the arithmetic operators (sometimes called relation operators in computer science, as they make a comparison) in programming, we use these symbols:

Command	Name	Example	Output
+	Addition	4+5	9
–	Subtraction	8–5	3
*	Multiplication	4*5	20
//	Integer division	19//3	6
%	Remainder	19%3	1
** or ^	Exponent	2**4	16
()	Grouping ()	(isFour == 4)	0 or 1/true or false

```
In AQA pseudo-code you use the following
syntax for standard arithmetic operations:
+, -, *, /.
```

```
In AQA pseudo-code you use the following
syntax for relational operators:
Less than <
Equal to =
Greater than >
Not equal to ≠
Less than or equal to ≤
Greater than or equal to ≥
```

In Python we have the following mathematical operators:

Add, subtract	+, −
Multiply, divide, mod	*, /, %
Comparison	>, <, <=, >=, !=, ==
Boolean operators	NOT, AND, OR
Exponentiation	**

But operators also have an important order of execution. If we look at some of the popular operators from above this is the order of execution:

1 () expressions in parenthesis
2 ** exponentiation
3 / and * (division and multiplication)
4 + and − (addition and subtraction)

In mathematics we use what are called real numbers. Nearly any number you can think of is a real number. In a computing sense a real number is just any positive or negative number which may or may not be a whole number.

Real whole numbers are called integers. Whole numbers greater than zero are called positive integers. Whole numbers less than zero are called negative integers. The integer zero is neither positive nor negative, and has no sign. We have a process that is called integer division. When you divide two numbers, you have a quotient and a remainder.

10 DIV 3 = 3 (quotient)

10 MOD 3 = 1 (remainder)

3 * 3 + 1 = 10

Integer division, including remainders, is usually a two-stage process and uses modular arithmetic.

For example, the calculation 11/2 would generate the following values:

Integer division: the integer quotient of 11 divided by 2
(11 DIV 2) = 5

Remainder: the remainder when 11 is divided by 2
(11 MOD 2) = 1

In AQA pseudo-code you use the following syntax for integer division. The red brackets < > are only to show where you add something; you don't need to put them in your code. IntExp, means any expression which can be evaluated to an integer.

<IntExp> **DIV** <IntExp>

Example:

9 DIV 5 evaluates to 1

5 DIV 2 evaluates to 2

8 DIV 4 evaluates to 2

In AQA pseudo-code you use the following syntax for modulus operator assignments. The red brackets < > are only to show where you add something; you don't need to put them in your code. IntExp, means any expression which can be evaluated to an integer.

<IntExp> **MOD** <IntExp>

Example:

9 MOD 5 evaluates to 4

5 MOD 2 evaluates to 1

8 MOD 4 evaluates to 0

The other term you will come across often in programming is floating-point number. The term floating point is derived from the fact that there is no fixed number of digits before and after the decimal point; that is, so the decimal point can 'float'.

Data type	Description	Example
str	A string of characters, which can include letters, numbers, spaces and symbols.	'some text'
int	An integer whole number, which *does not* have a decimal point.	10
float	A floating-point number, which *can* have a decimal point.	10.6
bool	A Boolean logical truth value, which is either True or False.	1

In computing we also have to make choices and these are often based upon mathematical decisions. We can use mathematical phrases like 'is less than' or 'is more than'.

There is a universally accepted set of symbols used to represent these phrases:

Command	Name
>	Greater than
<	Less than
>= or ≥	Greater than or equal to
<= or ≤	Less than or equal to
=	Equal to
<>	Less than or more than (can also be not equal to)
!= or ≠	Not equal to

In assessment material, AQA use the following symbols as relational operators:

=, ≠, <, >, ≤, ≥

Note how these can be paired up.

QUESTION

What are relational operators?

Logical operators: AND, OR, NOT

AND: if any of the conditions are False, the whole expression is False.

```
IF day = 'Saturday' AND noHomework = True THEN     #both must be true
   OUTPUT 'Let's go to the park!'
ENDIF
```

OR: if any of the conditions are True, the whole expression is True.

```
    IF month = 'EndJuly' OR month = 'August' THEN
       OUTPUT 'Great no school!'
    ENDIF
```

NOT: if the condition is NOT True, the expression will be True, so NOT Sunday will mean no church.

```
    IF NOT day = 'Sunday' THEN
       OUTPUT 'No church today'
    ENDIF
```

Comparing values

The IF command means that if a condition is True then the program runs a block of commands. If the condition isn't True, the block is skipped. In Python the block after the IF command is always indented.

```
ans = input('Is it November 5th? (y/n)')

if ans == 'y':

    print('It is bonfire night!')
```

We can modify this a little by adding an alternative by using ELSE:

```
ans = input('Is it November 5th? (y/n)')

if ans == 'y':

    print('It is bonfire night!')

    print('Time for fireworks.')

else:

    print('No fireworks yet!')
```

Examples of pseudo-code mathematical algorithms

We looked at a simple sequential algorithm earlier in this chapter to add two numbers together. So let us say that we wanted to write a **sequential** pseudo-code algorithm that reads two numbers, multiplies them together and prints out the result. We could write:

```
num1 ← USERINPUT          # read input 1

num2 ← USERINPUT          # read input 2

multi ← num1 * num2       # process

OUTPUT multi              # output
```

(For AQA we would use, input var ← USERINPUT (← is used as an assignment) and the pseudo-code does not support multiple inputs at once.)

Notice how we have named the two numbers as num1 and num2 and created a variable called multi to store the result of the calculation. This is because these are variable as they can be any number. They are not fixed. Notice also the use of # for comments.

> **KEY POINT** !
>
> A **sequence** is where a set of instructions or actions is ordered, meaning that each action follows the previous action.

If we explore mathematical operations to find the sum of five entered numbers, in simple English the algorithm may look like this:

1 Initialize sum = 0 and count = 0 (PROCESS)

2 Enter n (I/O)

3 Find sum + n and assign it to sum and then increment count by 1 (PROCESS)

4 Is count < 5 (DECISION)

   if YES go to step 2

   else

   Print sum (I/O)

and as a flowchart it may look like Figure 4.1.

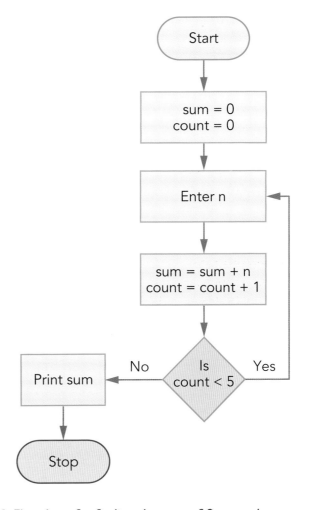

Figure 4.1 *Flowchart for finding the sum of five numbers*

Mathematics and Python

Let's explore other mathematical tasks in Python:

```
a = 12                                              #set variable 'a'
b = 7                                               #set variable 'b'
print('Addition: \t',a,'+',b,'=',a+b)              #output addition to screen
print('Subtraction: \t',a,'-',b,'=',a-b)           #output subtraction to screen
print('Multiplication: \t',a,'x',b,'=',a*b)        #output multiplication to
                                                    #screen
print('Division: \t',a,'÷',b,'=',a/b)              #output division to screen
print('Integer division: \t',a,'÷',b,'=',a//b)    #output floor division to
                                                    #screen
print('Remainder: \t',a,'%',b,'=',a%b)             #output remainder to screen
print('Exponent: \t',a,'squared=',a**b,sep='')     #output exponent to screen
```

Output:

Addition:	12 + 7 = 19
Subtraction:	12 − 7 = 5
Multiplication:	12 × 7 = 84
Division:	12 ÷ 7 = 1.7142857142857142
Integer division:	12 ÷ 7 = 1
Remainder:	12 % 7 = 5
Exponent:	12 squared = 35831808

Notice how we have used a string to show the conventional mathematics symbols such as '×'.

Probability and randomisation

An important mathematical concept that is used extensively in computer programming is that of **randomisation**. Probability theory is an important aspect of randomisation.

KEY POINT

Randomisation is a function in a computer program that allows random outcomes from a defined list or number sequence. It is often used in computer games.

EXAMPLE

Imagine tossing a coin: there are two possible outcomes, heads (H) or tails (T). If we were, however, to toss three coins, the possible outcomes are: HHH, HHT, HTH, THH, THT, HTT, TTH and TTT. So the probability of any of these is one in eight.

```
In AQA pseudo-code we can use the following
syntax for randomisation where we want a
Random integer generation any between two
integers.
RANDOM _ INT(IntExp, IntExp)
therefore:
RANDOM _ INT(2, 5)

# will randomly generate 2, 3, 4 or 5
```

Random numbers are important in programming. In Python there is a random module built specifically for this purpose. Using it is quite simple. The chance of heads or tails is random between two options. If we wanted to code this we would need to randomise the output to be either 0 or 1.

To generate a random integer you would use:

```
import random              #import the module
num = random.randint(a, b) #this chooses a random integer in the range
                           #(a, b) and assigns it to a variable.
                           #The notation (a, b) is used to indicate an
                           #interval from a to b that is inclusive of a and
                           #of b. That is, (1, 10) would be
                           #the set of integer numbers between 1 and 10,
                           #including 1 and including 10. The range
                           #would be inclusive of the integer used for a
                           #and b.
```

You can also use this module to generate a floating-point number and assign it to a variable called num:

```
import random           #import the module
num=random.random()     #select a random number and assign to the variable
print(num)              #print the variable random number
```

This will select a random floating-point number in the range (0, 1). This means the random number will be between 0 and 1, including 0.0

If we want a larger random number we can multiply it.

For example, a random number between 0 and 100, we could use randint or we could use multiplication:

```
import random

num=random.random() * 100

print(num)
```

In Python you can also generate a random choice. To generate a random value from a sequence we would use:

```
random.choice(['red', 'black', 'green'])
```

The choice function can be used for choosing a random element from a list.

```
import random

myList = [2, 109, False, 10, "yesterday", 82, "today"]

random.choice(myList)

chosen = random.choice(myList)

print(chosen)
```

We will explore here a few other ways to generate different random numbers in Python using the random function and another function in that module called sample. Remember that the first part of each algorithm will need to import the functions from the module.

To generate a floating-point number:

```
from random import random          #importing two functions from the
                                    #'random' module

num = random()                      #assign a random floating-point
                                    #number to a variable called num

print('Random float 0.0-1.0 : ' , num)   #output the value of the random
                                          #floating-point number
```

Possible output (remember each time a different set of random numbers will be shown):

Random float 0.0–1.0 : 0.8444218515250481

To generate an integer:

```
from random import random          #importing two functions from the
                                    #'random' module

num = random()                      #assign a random floating-point
                                    #number to a variable called num
```

```
num = int(num * 10)                     #multiply the floating-point number
                                        #and cast it to become an integer

print('Random integer 0-9 : ' , num)    #output the value of the integer
```

Possible output (remember each time only one random number will be shown):

Random integer 0–9 : 8

The example code below generates a random list of integers in different ways, first using a list and then using a loop:

```
from random import random, sample      #importing two functions from the
                                       #'random' module

numsList = [ ] ; a = 0                 #now we will create a list of random
                                       #numbers

while a < 6:                           #Add a loop to assign multiple random
                                       #integers to our list

    numsList.append(int(random() * 10) + 1)
                                       #assign multiple unique random
                                       #integers to the list

    a += 1

print('Random multiple integers 1-10: ', numsList)
                                       #output the list of random numbers

numsList = sample(range(1, 99) , 6)

print('Random integer sample 1-99 : ', numsList)
```

Possible output (remember each time a different set of random numbers will be shown):

Random multiple integers 1–10: [8, 5, 3, 6, 5, 8]

Random integer sample 1–99 : [39, 62, 46, 75, 28, 65]

Now let's explore a simple game using these concepts.

```
import random                          #import the random module

num = random.randint(1, 10)            #set the random range and define
                                       #as integer

guess = 0                              #set guess variable to 0

guesses = 0                            #set guesses variable to 0

while guesses < int(5):                #while loop to allow five guesses
                                       #then end loop
```

```
print('Guess my number 1-10 :')     #output string to screen

guess = input()                     #set variable guess to user input

guesses = guesses + 1               #add 1 to guesses variable

if int(guess) < num:                #see if guess is higher than number

  print('Too low')                  #to output message to screen

elif int(guess) > num:              #see if guess is lower than the
                                    #number

  print('Too high')                 #to send message to screen

else:                               #number must be the same as it is
                                    #not higher or lower

  print('Correct... My number is ' + guess)

                                    #to output message to screen

  break                             #stop the while loop
```

What if someone types a string, for example 'Two' rather than 2? We could add a line of code to solve this issue. We will also add a new variable to stop the loop if a correct answer is given:

```
import random

num = random.randint(1, 10)

flag = True                         #we are adding a new variable

guesses = 0                         #set guesses variable to 0

print('Guess my number 1-10: ' , end = ' ')

while flag == True:                 #If True run loop if not stop

  guess = input()

  guesses = guesses + 1             #add 1 to guesses variable

  if not guess.isdigit():           #checks it is not a string

    print('Invalid! Enter only digits 1-10')   #output string to screen

    break                           #stop the while loop

  elif int(guess) < num:

    print('Too low, try again : ' , end= ' ')
```

```
elif int(guess) > num:

    print('Too high, try again: ' , end = ' ')

else:

    print('Correct... My number is ' + guess)

    flag = False                                    #makes flag False to stop the
                                                    #while loop
```

CHAPTER REVIEW

Building upon the last two chapters, in this chapter we have explored computational mathematics.

We looked at the differences between mathematics and computational mathematics. We also added to your knowledge of both flowcharts and pseudo-code.

Building upon the use of selection in decision making, we explored logical operators.

Remember, before tackling any computer science task or question on this topic, you must:

- understand mathematical operations
- understand the term modules
- understand the differences between mathematics and computational mathematics
- think about the correct syntax needed in coding
- be familiar with and be able to use:
  - addition
  - subtraction
  - multiplication
  - real division
  - integer division, including remainders
- be familiar with and be able to use:
  - equal to
  - not equal to
  - less than
  - greater than
  - less than or equal to
  - greater than or equal to
- be able to use random number generation.

5 Boolean and Logic Gates

In computer science, the **Boolean** data type is a **logical** data type that has one of two values (usually called True or False, 0 or 1). It represents the **truth values** of logic and Boolean algebra. Boolean is very important in computer science.

Boolean: AND

The **AND** operator requires that both of its inputs are true for it to output true. In searches, you use **AND** to retrieve records or pages that contain both terms.

Boolean: OR

The **OR** operator requires at least one of the specified conditions to be True. In searches, you use OR to retrieve records or pages that contains *either* of two or more terms. The OR operator is generally used to assess similar, equivalent or synonymous conditions.

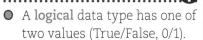

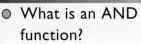

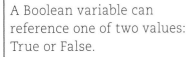

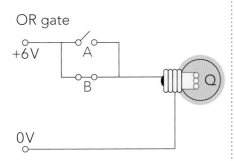

Figure 5.1 *A parallel circuit representing an OR gate*

Boolean: NOT

The **NOT** operator inverts the value of a Boolean expression. Thus if b is True x is False. If b is False x is True.

```
In AQA pseudo-code you use the following
syntax for Boolean Operations. The red
brackets < > are only to show where you add
something; you don't need to put them in your
code. BoolExp, means any expression which can
be evaluated to a Boolean, data type.
Logical AND    <BoolExp> AND <BoolExp>
Example:
(3 = 3) AND (3 ≤ 4)
Logical OR     <BoolExp> OR <BoolExp>
Example:
(x < 1) OR (x > 9)
Logical NOT    NOT <BoolExp>
Example:
NOT (another_go = False)
```

Understanding the concept of logic gates

Logic gates can be understood better if you think of simple **switches**. Logic functions depend on **binary** bits of information. You should know from Key Stage 3 that a bit can take on only two values, as it can be in one of two states. We will explore this in more detail later in the book. A simple switch is either open or closed.

The bits could be represented by a yes or a no or can be ON (conducting) or OFF (not conducting).

Whatever the two states might be, we will call one of the states a '1' and the other a '0'. It doesn't matter which we call 1 and which we call 0 if we are consistent but we will call the closed or conducting state of a switch a 1 and the open or non-conducting state a 0.

OR circuit

A parallel system of switches (see Figure 5.1) would make an OR circuit. That is, if any one or more of the switches, A or B, is in state 1, the system is in state 1 (conducting).

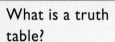
For a 2-input OR gate, the output Q is true if *either* input A 'OR' input B is True, giving the Boolean expression of: (Q = A OR B).

We show this in the form of what is called a truth table. The truth table specifies the state of the system for each state of the switches:

Inputs		Output
A	B	Q
0	0	0
0	1	1
1	0	1
1	1	1

This is also shown using the electrical diagrams in Figure 5.2. To help you understand the concept the diagram also shows the possible states.

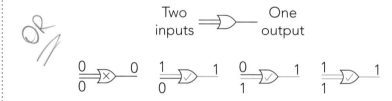

Figure 5.2 *Electrical diagrams showing inputs and states of an OR gate*

AND circuit

We can also look at how a series of switches makes an AND circuit. That is, all switches must be in the 1 state for the system to be in the 1 state (conducting).

For a 2-input AND gate, the output Q is true if *both* input A 'AND' input B are both True, giving the Boolean expression of: (Q = A AND B). The truth table for the system would look like this:

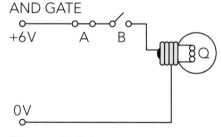

Figure 5.3 *A series circuit representing an AND gate*

Inputs		Output
A	B	Q
0	0	0
0	1	0
1	0	0
1	1	1

Figure 5.4 uses a circuit symbol to illustrate an AND gate, with possible states indicated.

Two inputs — One output

Figure 5.4 *Electrical diagrams showing inputs and states of an AND gate*

Turning problems into binary logic

Suppose we have a set of race starting lights with two coloured lights, amber and green. If both the amber and green lights are on, the race starts. First the amber light is on to warn the drivers that the race is about to start, next the green light comes on and the race starts. We could have a bit which is True if the light is on and False if the light is not on. We could now give the green bit a name, such as G and the amber bit a name A. Finally, we could have a bit named S which is true if the race can start. We know that the value for S is determined by the values of G and A, as the race can only start when both are on. We can therefore define S as follows:

S is True if A is True and if G is True

In Boolean notation, we would write

S = A AND G

You know from earlier chapters that the letters A, G, and S are called variables because we don't know their values when we look at the expression. We do know that they can take on the values of False and True. We also know that S's value will be determined once we know the values for A and G.

NOT circuits  *opposite (vice versa output)*

Unlike AND and OR gates, NOT gates have only one input and one output. The output is exactly the opposite of the input, so if the input is a 0, the output is a 1 and vice versa. Figure 5.5 shows how a NOT is represented in electronics.

The truth table would look like this:

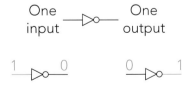

One input — One output

Figure 5.5 *Electrical diagrams showing input and states of a NOT gate*

Input	Output
0	1
1	0

5 Boolean and Logic Gates

How to read a truth table

You will now know that a truth table is simply a chart of the different possible truth values of a statement given the truth value of the simpler statements.

For example, the truth value shown below of a, b, c is True when a is True or b is True:

Input a	Input b	Output c
1	1	1
1	0	1
0	1	1
0	0	0

This makes sense, since it's an 'or' statement, like 'It is raining or it is sunny' and thus is True when either part of the statement a: 'It is raining' or b: 'it is sunny' is True.

Constructing truth tables with more inputs

A truth table is always a chart of 1s and 0s arranged to indicate the results (or outputs) of all possible inputs. All possible inputs are arranged in columns on the left and the resulting outputs are listed in columns on the right. The table gives the output of the circuit for all possible combinations of inputs. We can then write the result at each gate's output. There are 2 to the power n possible states (or combinations of inputs), where n is the number of inputs. For example, with three inputs there are $2^3 =$ 8 possible combinations of inputs.

Inputs			Output
A	B	C	
0	0	0	0
0	0	1	0
0	1	0	0
0	1	1	1
1	0	0	1
1	0	1	0
1	1	0	0
1	1	1	1

KEY POINT

A truth table is a diagram used to show the value of a Boolean expression for all possible variable combinations.

Constructing a circuit from logic

We can easily create a circuit diagram from the description of the logic using these symbols. Let's say we want a system where we have four inputs A, B, C and D. We want a circuit that outputs true if either A AND B or C AND D is true.

Part of the truth table would look like this:

Inputs				Output
A	B	C	D	
1	1	1	0	1
1	1	0	1	1
0	1	0	1	0
1	0	1	0	0
1	1	1	1	1
1	0	1	1	1
0	1	1	1	1

RESEARCH TASK

Use this book and other sources such as the internet to research how to construct truth tables for simple logic circuits.

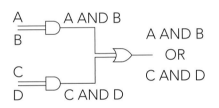

Figure 5.6 *Electrical diagram showing connected AND and OR gates*

We could create a circuit using two AND gates connected to an OR gate as shown in Figure 5.6.

Controlling a calculator display with logic gates

Calculator displays work using combinations of logic gates, indeed the whole calculator works using them. Each segment of a calculator's display is switched on and off by a series of logic gates that are connected together. If we look at a small section (Figure 5.7) of the display for a single number we can see how this would work.

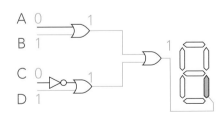

Figure 5.7 *Combination of logic gates to control section of calculator display*

5 Boolean and Logic Gates

We will explore the bottom segment coloured in the image (Figure 5.7) further.

We would need to use binary to turn this small segment on to display a number. You will learn about binary in chapter 13, but may remember it from Key Stage 3. The numbers needing this segment with their binary representation are: 0 (binary 0000), 1 (0001), 3 (0011), 4 (0100), 5 (0101), 6 (0110), 7 (0111), 8 (1000), and 9 (1001) – but this segment would not be on if we're showing the number 2 (0010).

We can make the segment switch on and off correctly for the numbers 0–9 by using a circuit of three OR gates and one NOT gate.

If we feed the patterns of binary numbers for these numbers into the four inputs, the segment will turn on and off correctly for each one.

For example, if we feed in the number 7 as the four inputs (0111) the gates will correctly switch on the segment.

The other six segments of each digit are controlled by other combinations of logic gates.

The truth table for this segment on the calculator display for the numbers would be:

Displayed decimal	Binary number	Inputs				Output
		A	B	C	D	
0	0000	0	0	0	0	1
1	0001	0	0	0	1	1
2	0010	0	0	1	0	0
3	0011	0	0	1	1	1
4	0100	0	1	0	0	1
5	0101	0	1	0	1	1
6	0110	0	1	1	0	1
7	0111	0	1	1	1	1
8	1000	1	0	0	0	1
9	1001	1	0	0	1	1

Boolean in Python

Python **Boolean operators** are spelled out as the words 'and', 'or', 'not'.

If we want to see if a number (a) is bigger than number (b) by more than two we could write:

```python
def a_bigger(a, b):
    if a > b and (a - b) > 2:
        return True
    else:
        return False
```

Notice that the if-test does not need to be in parenthesis in Boolean.

CHAPTER REVIEW

In this chapter we have explored Boolean and logic gates. We have also explored truth tables.

Remember, before tackling any computer science task or question on this topic you must:

- understand mathematical operations
- understand Boolean operators
- understand the differences between mathematics and computational mathematics
- think about the correct syntax needed in coding
- be familiar with and be able to use:
    - NOT
    - AND
    - OR
- be able to construct truth tables for a given logic statement (AND, OR, NOT)
- interpret the results of simple truth tables.

6 Variables and Constants

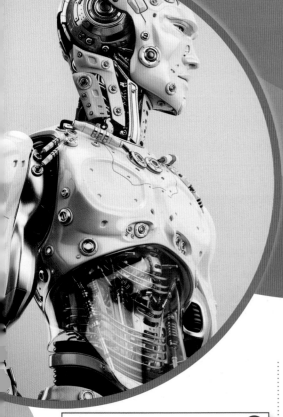

Variables

At the core of any program are **variables**. Variables are where all the dynamic information is stored.

When you use a keyboard to add your name to a running program, your name would almost certainly be stored as the value of a variable. Not all variables are the same though. In fact, there are many different types. We have used the term variables before for letters (as used in algebra) for the temperatures in the first section of the book. We used F (for Fahrenheit) and C (for Celsius).

In this section we need to explore variables in more detail. The ability to operate on different values each time a program is executed is invaluable in coded solutions. This is provided by variables. If you want a user to input something to the system, like a number that will change due to a calculation, this will need to be stored as a variable. Imagine variables as boxes. On the outside of the box is the variable name. Inside the box is the value of the variable. You can change and add to what is in the box but you can't change the box name.

What are variables?

So we have our variables as labelled boxes that store different types of **data**. We will be exploring variables throughout the book, but the types we will look at here are numbers, strings and Booleans.

- Strings: A string variable is a sequence of **alphanumeric** characters and allowed symbols that are contained within quotation marks. 'Hello world' is an example of a string. Strings can also be contained within double quotes. Strings are basically boxes used for storing text.

- Numbers: A number variable only stores numbers. You don't store them within quotes like strings.

- Booleans: We explored Booleans a little in the last two chapters. A Boolean variable is always one of two things: True or False. It is a bit like an on and off switch where you can ask questions. For example, you might ask, 'Is the TV on?' If you did, the response you'd get would be a Boolean value. True would mean the TV is on and False would mean it is not on. We will explore Booleans more in later chapters but you need to understand the concept in order to understand selection. We may want to say IF the TV is off, switch it on. IF statements are probably the easiest type of logic statement to understand. An IF statement is basically a statement that says IF the specified condition is true, then run this block of code. It can also be used to say, if the first condition isn't met, do this instead.

A variable can be assigned different values during a program's execution – hence, the name 'variable'. Wherever a variable appears in a program it is the value associated with the variable that is used, and not the variable's name.

But be careful as you cannot mix the data types in your box. It is not possible to add a number to a string. We will explore this more in chapter 17, but as this is a very common error in coding it is worth mentioning here as well.

KEY POINTS

- **Data** is information, such as text, symbols and numerical values.

- **Alphanumeric** refers to alphabetic and numeric characters, and is used to describe the collection of Latin letters and Arabic numeric digits.

RESEARCH TASK

Use this book and other sources such as the internet to research how to use variables and constants.

KEY POINT

In pseudo-code a computer can assign a value to a variable using ← to assign **VALUE** to **VARIABLE** (memory location).

As a human, you know the difference between a number and a string so if asked to add:

'one' plus 2

you will mentally convert the string 'one' into the number 1. A computer cannot do this, so you will get an **error** if you code it this way.

Variable values

Variables are assigned values by use of what is called an assignment operator, which is usually = or ←

In AQA pseudo-code they use the ← symbol to assign a variable.

```
num ← 11
```

The variable num now equals 11. But what if the program states:

```
num ← num + 1    #the variable num will be increased by 1
```

```
In AQA pseudo-code, you use the following
syntax to assign a value to a variable. The
red brackets < > are only to show where you
add something; you don't need to put them in
your code.
Syntax:
Variable ← <add value here>
Example:
counter ← 0
and:
myString ← 'Hello world'
```

Assignment and equality

So far we have looked at assignment. There is a big difference between assigning and testing for **equality**. Consider the following:

```
myVariable = 6;          #using Python

myVariable == 6;
```

Can you tell the difference?

The first is known as assignment. It means assign the value of myVariable to 6.

You are 'setting' a variable value. In AQA pseudo-code you use the ← to do this but many languages use the = sign.

The second statement is one of equality. It's a test that means 'Is myVariable equal to 6?' The answer you would get would be true or false. Notice the difference, == is used as the syntax.

Constants

Sometimes you use a **constant** in your code rather than a variable. You would use a constant instead of a variable if you know that a value should not be changed when the program is running.

Using a constant eliminates the risk that the value will be changed somewhere in the program code.

You should always use constants instead of typing values in your program code as this makes the code easier to understand and easier to update in the future.

```
In AQA pseudo-code you use the following
syntax for constant assignments. The red
brackets < > are only to show where you add
something; you don't need to put them in your
code. Exp means any expression.
<IDENTIFIER> ← <Exp>
Example:
constant PI ← 3.141
constant MY_CLASS ← 31
```

In many languages both variables and constants have to be declared. Declaring a variable or constant simply means defining its type and initialising it by setting an initial value (called initialising the variable). The type allows the compiler to interpret statements correctly.

```
                        #not in Python
extern int a = 3, b = 5;   #declaration of a and b
int a = 3, b = 5;          #definition and initialising a and b
byte a = 22;               #definition and initialises a
char b = 'x';              #the variable b has the value 'x'
```

6 Variables and Constants

Variables do not have to be initialised (assigned a value) when they are declared, but it is often useful to do this.

In Python you do not need to declare variables before using them, or declare their type. Every variable in Python is an object. But it is always good coding practice to check that a variable has valid data in it, before it is accessed for some other purpose.

A constant declaration specifies the name, data type and value of the constant. A constant holds a value that does not change. You cannot declare a constant in Python. Some Python programmers use names for the variables that are all-uppercase to show that the variable is intended to be a constant.

Inputs to variables

The variable may get its value within the program, for example:

```
num ← 11    #assign 11 to variable num
```

And, as we have seen, this can change as the program runs:

```
num ← num + 1  #adds 1 to variable num
```

But there are other ways a variable can be assigned and changed, not least through **user input**. When a user inputs data into the system it is usually stored in a variable.

```
num1 ← USERINPUT   #the user has to input a variable called num1
```

Creating a string variable in Python

As you now know, a string might include letters, numbers, symbols or spaces. Strings can be placed in variables.

```
a = 'Smile!'         #define variable 'a' with a string
b = 'The sun is out.' #define variable 'b' with a string
c = a + b            #define variable 'c'
print(c)             #output to screen
```

   Output: Smile! The sun is out.

```
c = b + 'It is Saturday.' + a   #adding an additional string to 'c'
print(c)
```

   Output: The sun is out. It is Saturday. Smile!

But what if we wanted to show the string 'It is Saturday.' as 'It's Saturday.' The apostrophe in 'It's' would cause us a problem as the string will have an extra apostrophe. We overcome this problem by using a '\' before it. This is called 'escaping'.

```
c = b + 'It\'s Saturday. ' + a
print(c)
```

Output: The sun is out. It's Saturday. Smile!

The input() function is used to accept input from the keyboard into a program. It waits until the user finishes typing and presses the 'return' or 'Enter' key.

```
name = input('Enter your name:')
print('Hello', name)
```

You will know from earlier sections in the book that two variables can be compared using the == operator or the != operator. Strings have to match exactly to get a True output. If we look at an example in Python:

```
subject = 'Computer Science is Wonderful'
#define the variable subject with a string
subject == 'Computer Science is Wonderful'
#compare our variable with a string
```

Output: TRUE   #they match

String manipulation

As you now know, a string is simply a list of characters in order, where a character can be anything a user can type on the keyboard in a single keystroke.

An empty string is a string that has 0 characters.

Python recognises as strings everything that is delimited by quotation marks (either " " or ' ').

We can also manipulate strings using some of Python's built-in methods. For example, we can change upper- and lowercase strings:

```
string = "Hello World"
print(string.upper())
```

Output: HELLO WORLD

```
string = "Hello World"
print(string.lower())
```

RESEARCH TASK

Use this book and other sources such as the internet to research how to use global and local variables.

Output: hello world

```
string = "Hello World"
print(string.capitalize())
```

Output: Hello world

```
string = "Hello World"
print(string.swapcase())
```

Output: hELLO wORLD

We can even reverse a string:

```
string = "Hello World"
print(' '.join(reversed(string)))
```

Output: d l r o W   o l l e H

We will explore strings further in later chapters.

We can also convert data to a string, for example:

```
myVariable = 5
myString = str(myVariable) #will convert the integer
                           #5 to the string '5'

print(myString)
```

Output: 5

Discovering the data type used

In Python we can also discover the data type within a variable by specifying the variable's name within the parentheses of the built-in type() function.

```
kilo=10
print(kilo , ' is ' , type(kilo))
temp=66.3
print(temp , ' is ' , type(temp))
flag=True
print(flag , ' is ' , type(flag))
target = 4 > 8
print(target , ' is ' , type(target))
```

Output:

10 is <class 'int'>

66.3 is <class 'float'>

True is <class 'bool'>

False is <class 'bool'>

Getting inputs

Inputs can come from a number of sources including the keyboard, touch screens, games controllers, barcode readers etc.

Often a program will have data for variables from both within the code and user input. In the example below the user input is for the route and the computer setting of a variable for the count.

Think back to our map in the first chapter (Figure 1.5) but now imagine it as a computer game screen with the user having to input the movement from C10 to the finish at L15 (Figure 6.1). User input will determine the route. But at H11 there is a banana that is worth points.

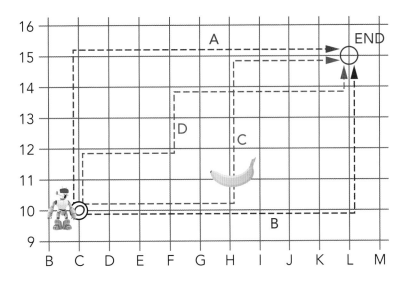

Figure 6.1 *Computer game screen*

The user navigates the man from C10 to L15 using pathway C. On the way the count variable will increase by 1.

```
banana ← banana + 1
```

Choosing names for variables and constants

The name should be as descriptive as possible.

Don't use generic names for variables and constants. Adding descriptive names improves the overall quality of the code, it makes it much easier to modify and read the code. It is good practice to give names that describe their purpose.

The computer stores variables and constants in an assigned memory location but the programmer does not need to know which memory location will be used to store it. The programming language software and operating system takes care of this.

If you find yourself writing names as soon as you need them in your code without even thinking on their name for a second, you are probably picking bad names for them. Similarly, if you revisit your code and can't understand what the purpose of a variable is from its name – it's a bad name. Normally variables have names written like this 'myVariable'. Notice the use of lower- and uppercase letters. This naming convention is often called camelCase naming because of the hump in the middle. Whilst camel case is often used, many coders prefer capitalised camel case, while others prefer underscores. Consistency is the important factor. Different languages also have different rules and conventions.

Should data be stored in a variable as character or numeric?

Sometimes an inexperienced programmer will write code with all of the variables defined as strings. The variables may contain numeric values, but if they are defined as a type string there will be very few things you can do later to analyse the data.

If a variable contains non-numeric information (e.g. names) then it clearly should be saved as a character string. But if the variable contains real numeric data which will be used in numeric calculations, such as weight or height, then it should be stored as a numeric variable.

QUESTION

What is a constant?

KEY POINT

Often programmers get errors because they use slang variable names, for example, 'paws' instead of 'pause', and then use the wrong name later in the code.

KEY POINT

Golden rule: spend a few minutes thinking about your variable names before you use them in your code.

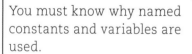

QUESTION

Describe the main reasons why it is important to choose descriptive names for variables.

KEY POINT

You must know why named constants and variables are used.

CHAPTER REVIEW

In this chapter we have explored variables and assignment. We have also explored the importance of correctly naming your variables.

Remember, before tackling any computer science task or question on this topic you must:

- understand the importance of variables and constants
- understand how to assign variables
- understand the difference between assignments and equality
- understand how to name variables and constants
- understanding strings and string operations
- think about the correct syntax needed in coding
- be able to use, understand and know how the following statement types can be combined in programs:
  - variable declaration
  - constant declaration
  - assignment (More on this topic in chapters 7, 8, 11, 12, 24.)
- be able to use meaningful identifier names and know why it is important to use them (More on this topic in chapter 24.)
- be able to obtain user input from the keyboard
- be able to output data and information from a program to the computer display.

7 Programming in Code

In this section we will look at programming in code, focusing primarily upon Python. Everything in Python is implemented as an **object**. A very simple view of an object would be a box that contains a piece of data. Students who go on to cover Object Oriented Programming will see that, in OOP, objects can contain other things as well as data. We used the idea of boxes in the last chapter when we looked at variables. The box also has a type, such as Boolean or integer. This determines what can be done with the data in the box.

The type of box also determines if the data value contained by the box can be changed, which is called mutable in programming or if it is the opposite and can't be changed which is called **immutable**.

In an immutable object box you can see the value but you can't change it. In a mutable object box, whilst you can't change its type you can see the value inside and can also change it.

Start up your Python editor and type the following into a file and save your file as HelloWorld.

```
print("Hello World!")
```

You have just produced your first piece of working code.

Strings in Python

Now we understand how to develop code and use variables we need to explore aspects of code that can change as a program runs.

Let's say we want a user to input a **string**. You will know from the last chapter that a string is simply a sequence of letters and numbers. This sentence is a string.

In Python, the input function is used for this purpose:

```
name = input('What is your name?')  #'What is your name?' is a string
```

Strings are always within quotes. This particular use of a string, for requesting input from the user, is called a prompt. Not only is the bit between quotes a string, so is the variable it is stored into, name, which has no quotes.

The input function displays the string on the screen to prompt the user to put in an input of their name.

To create a string in Python we can use:

```
s = "Hello World!"
```

or

```
s = 'Hello World!'
```

In most cases strings must be contained all on one line.

A string may contain zero or more characters, including letters, digits, special characters and blanks. A string consisting of only a pair of matching quotes (with nothing in between) is called the **empty** string.

KEY POINT ❗

We create a string by putting quotes around text so that the programming languages can tell it is a string, not a number or something else.

KEY POINT ❗

All the letters, numbers and symbols in this book could be a string. Think of a string as a collection of letters and/or numbers which are stored as text not numbers.

KEY POINT ❗

A **string** is a data type used to store a sequence of alphabetic characters and/or numeric characters.

RESEARCH TASK

Use this book and other sources such as the internet to research how to manipulate strings.

TASK

Write a short piece of code in your chosen language that will store a user input as a string.

Numbers can also be stored as strings, but be careful because when they are stored as strings they are not numbers.

> **EXAMPLE**
>
> Can you spot the difference between these two rows of values:
>
> | 22 | 45 | 98 | 3 |
> |----|----|----|---|
> | 22 | 45 | 98 | 3 |
>
> It is actually a trick question, because (visually) there is no difference. The difference is how the values in the bottom row are stored; they are stored as a text string, not a number. This is a very common mistake in programming and leads to problems if you want to carry out mathematical operations later in the code.

> **KEY POINT**
>
> A string may contain zero or more characters, including letters, digits, special characters and blanks.

> **KEY POINT**
>
> Numbers can be stored as strings but then they are no longer numbers.

> **KEY POINT**
>
> User input comes into Python as a string, which means that when you type the number 10 on your keyboard, Python saves the number 10 into a variable as a string, not a number.

String manipulation in Python

So, we now know that a string is a list of characters in order. We also know that a character is anything you can type on the keyboard in one keystroke, like a letter, a number, a space or a backslash. An empty string is a string that has 0 characters.

Python recognises as strings everything that is delimited by quotation marks (" " or ' ').

You can manipulate strings in Python, with Python's built-in methods.

Examine this bit of Python code in more detail:

```
myString = "Hello World"   #set the string
print(myString)            #show string on screen
```

Output: Hello World

If you want to access just part of the string you can use [ ] to access characters in a string:

```
myString = "Hello World"
letter = myString[0]
print(letter)
```

Output: H

Python has an index starting at 0 unlike pseudo-code index 1. We will explore this further in later chapters.

In Python, to access the fifth character in a string we would use:

```
myString = "Hello World"
letter = myString[4]
print(letter)
```

Output: o

In Python, to concatenate, which is to join two strings (string s1 and string s2):

```
s1 + s2
```

In Python, length (len) always returns the number of characters in string (s):

```
n = len(s)
```

Example:

```
myString = "Hello World"
print(len(myString))
```

Output: 11

You can also find letters in a string:

```
print(myString.count('l'))   #count how many times
                             #'l' is in the string
                             #myString
```

Output: 3

In Python, to split string (s) you would use:

```
s = 'Hello World'
s.split(' ')
s.split('r')
```

Strings often store many pieces of data. These are often stored in a comma-separated format, which simply means that each part is divided with commas. A space is another common delimiter, so in 'Hello World' the two words in our string are delimited by a space.

```
#Input string
myString = "London, Bristol, Birmingham, Liverpool"
#Delimited using commas
cityNames = myString.split(",")
for city in cityNames:          #Loop and print each city name
        print(city)
```

Output:

    London

    Bristol

    Birmingham

    Liverpool

Often lines must be split. This is done with split(). The split() method with a string argument separates strings based on the specified delimiter; with no arguments, split() separates strings using one or more spaces as the delimiter.

Variables

As you will know from the previous chapter, a variable is a **memory location** that is used to store a value that can be changed. Variables are identified by names.

In Python, variables are storage **placeholders** for text and numbers. Variables in Python are assigned with the equals sign, followed by the value of the variable. But be careful as there are some reserved words for Python that cannot be used as variable names.

Variable names are case sensitive but you can use any letter, the characters, '_' and numbers provided you do not start with them.

The value of a variable can be changed later on.

To store the value 10 in a variable named myVariable we would use:

```
myVariable = 10
```

To store the value of myVariable + 10 in a variable named myExtended:

```
myExtended = myVariable + 10
```

There are many different variable types in Python, including ones you should now understand:

```
myVariable = "hello"        #string

myVariable = 123            #integer
```

and new ones we will explore in later chapters:

```
myVariable = 3.14                    #double float
myVariable = [0,1,2]                 #list
myVariable = (0,1,2)                 #tuple
myVariable = open('hello.py', 'r')   #file
```

You can even assign a single value to several variables at the same time using multiple assignments:

```
a = b = c = 1   #Variables a, b and c are
                #assigned to the same memory
                #location, with the value of 1
```

Example code using variables:

```
myLength = 2
myWidth = 4
myArea  = myLength * myWidth
print("The area is: ", myArea)
```

Output: The area is: 8

Size of variables

We have looked at variables as being boxes that can hold something. The variable name is the label on the box. Not all variables take up the same amount of **memory**. These can vary according to the programming language used.

Indentation

Indenting is adding spaces/tabs in front of 'blocks' of code (such as IF), so that it is easier for you and other people to see how the code flows. It shows which parts of the code will run under certain situations.

KEY POINT

It is possible to use a word processor to create a Python program, but you must be sure to save the program as a plain text file.

KEY POINT

Just like humans, computers rely a lot on **memory**. They need to process and store data, just like we do. However, computers store data in digital format in a reserved location and of a set location size.

KEY POINT

Python expects the number of spaces in a block to be consistent. It doesn't matter how many spaces you insert, as long as you use the same number for every new line.

KEY POINT

White space is any section that is unused, for example, the space around an item in the code. White space is a useful tool in any coded solution as it helps to separate the blocks of code.

Why should you indent your code?

There are several benefits to indenting your code including:

- A user can see at a glance where the end of a code block is rather than having to read each line until they find it.
- A user can immediately ignore chunks of the code that aren't relevant to what they are currently doing.
- It is much easier to notice if a line of code is in the wrong place.

In Python, you are forced to indent parts of the code but it is good practice to do this in any coded solution, even when writing in pseudo-code.

Is white space more significant in Python source code?

Only the indentation level of your statements is significant (i.e. the white space at the very left of your statements). Everywhere else, white space is not significant and can be used as you like, just like in any other language.

You can also insert empty lines that contain nothing (or only arbitrary white space) anywhere.

The exact amount of indentation doesn't matter either, only the relative indentations of nested blocks (relative to each other) are important.

Adding comments to Python code

There are a number of ways to add comments to Python code.

As with the pseudo-code used throughout this book, single-line comments begin with the hash character (#) and are terminated by the end of line. Python just ignores all text that comes after the # until it gets to the end of the line.

Let's show this by using an example:

```
print("Hello World")            #this is a comment in Python

text = "#This is not a comment because it's inside quotes."

                                #this is also a comment in Python
```

Decisions in programming

The other thing you looked at in the last chapter was decisions. One of the most important aspects in programming is setting up conditions. Asking the question if …? Before moving on to the next chapter, we will explore this in a little more detail here.

The IF statement

Python provides the IF statement as the sole selection statement.

Consider the following example of a simple IF statement in Python:

```
if value < 0:
    print("The value is negative.")
```

Python does not use parentheses to enclose the condition but as the IF statement is a compound statement, it requires a colon (:) following the condition, even though there is only a single statement to be executed.

The format of the simple IF statement is shown below:

```
if <condition>:
    <statement-block>
```

ELSE structure

The IF statement can also contain an ELSE part to be executed when the logical condition is False. It too is a compound statement which is indicated by the required colon following the ELSE statement:

```
if <condition>:
    <statement-block-1>
else:
    <statement-block-2>
```

KEY POINTS

- To **compare** is to examine (two or more strings, etc.) in order to note similarities and differences.
- **Equivalency** is to look for equality in value, etc.

Comparison of two strings

Often a programmer needs to **compare** two strings. In Python, this can be achieved using ordinary operators.

The normal **equivalency** operator is also used in Python to evaluate strings. An example could be:

```python
myStr1 = 'A String'          #define string 1
myStr2 = 'A String'          #define string 2
if myStr1 == myStr2:         #check if they are the same
  print("They Are The Same") #if they are output this string
else :                       #if they are not the same output
                             #the next string

  print("They Are Not The Same")
```

Output: They Are The Same

CHAPTER REVIEW

In this chapter we have built upon the last few chapters of the book and explored the use of programming languages, focusing on Python.

We looked at indentation, strings and decisions in programming.

Remember, before tackling any computer science task or question on this topic you must:

- think about the correct syntax needed in coding
- understand decisions in programming
- be able to use, understand and know how the following statement types can be combined in programs:
  - variable declaration
  - constant declaration
  - assignment
  - iteration
  - selection
  - subroutine (procedure/function) (More on this topic in chapters 6, 8, 11, 12, 24.)
- be able to obtain user input from the keyboard (More on this topic in chapters 2, 3, 5.)
- be able to output data and information from a program to the computer display. (More on this topic in chapters 2, 3, 5.)

8 Looping and Selection

In the first section of this book we learnt that computer programming is all about creating a set of instructions to complete a specific task. You do this in your everyday life, you just don't think of what you do in a programming way. In the first section of the book we also explored selection and the use of IF statements and how these can be represented in flowcharts and code.

Let's look at an example of a simple sequence. You get home from school and want to make yourself a jam sandwich, you know that you will first need to get two slices of bread, butter each piece, spread the jam and finally put the two pieces of bread together. You can't put the jam on the bread first, or put the slices of bread together before you spread the butter and jam, everything has a correct sequence. To create any food, you have to follow a recipe. A recipe, like a correctly sequenced program, is useful for replicating an action.

KEY POINT !

Functions and procedures are quite similar as they are bits of code that can be recalled at any point in your program and used again and again but functions can return a value.

KEY POINTS !

There are three fundamental control structures:

- sequence
- selection
- looping.

These are basic to all imperative programming languages. You must be able to write and understand programs using these statement types.

KEY POINTS !

- A **loop** is part of a program that repeats itself (to prevent the need for the same piece of code to be typed out multiple times).

- Iteration is the process of repeating a particular action. In an **indefinite loop**, the number of iterations is not known when we start to execute the body of the loop, as it depends on when a certain condition becomes true.

- In **definite loops**, the number of iterations is known before we start the execution of the body of the loop.

KEY POINT !

In pseudo-code, **FOR** is a 'counting' loop.

In the context of computing, programming means creating a set of instructions not for a human to perform but for a computer to perform. These actions are performed in order to accomplish a specific task.

In practice even a simple task contains a number of actions, many of which are repeated. We explored this when we looked at cleaning your teeth. You had a procedure to do, cleaning your teeth each day, and a function to do, brushing x number of times. But remember that a computer can only do exactly what we tell it to do. So we need to explore each action in much more detail.

You have already learnt, in the last chapter, about selection.

Remember:

- A sequence control structure is simply a series of procedures that follow one another.

- A selection (IF-THEN-ELSE) control structure involves a choice.

Understanding detail and loops

The last of the three basic steps in coding is the use of **loops**. We will explore loops in more detail in later chapters. You may think that writing a set of instructions with a loop for a computer to repeat will be simple, but computer programming must be exact. The simplest loop construct is called **indefinite iteration**. This is where the loop controls no variables and simply executes its body repeatedly until a condition is not True. Loops can also control variables and this type of loop is referred to as **definite iteration**. So the terms definite and indefinite come from the number of iterations which is, for example, definite in a **FOR** loop, as it is controlled by the loop counter, but indefinite in a WHILE loop, because this is condition controlled and it is not known how many times the loop will iterate until the condition is no longer True.

EXAMPLE

The following instructions are taken from a shampoo bottle:

- `wet hair`
- `apply shampoo`
- `work to a rich lather`
- `rinse`
- `repeat application.`

For us to use the shampoo, these instructions are fairly simple and easy to follow. But for a computer they are useless. You know enough about the **process** not to put the whole bottle of shampoo onto your hair at one time. You also know that you only need to repeat the application one time, if this was a computer program it would *repeat forever*. Using these instructions without additional information would not always achieve the same result.

Forever loops in Python

Some indefinite iteration loops run forever. If you set the condition in a WHILE loop to be True, it can never be False and the loop will never end. This can be useful. Let's look at an example of this:

```python
while True:
    answer = input('Type a word and press return:')
    print('Please do not type \'' + answer + '\' again ')
```

Output:

Type a word and press return: Saturday

Please do not type 'Saturday' again

Type a word and press return:

This loop will repeat forever.

Adding conditions

Remember that whenever you write any algorithm, it must:

- be detailed enough to describe what needs to be done to solve the problem
- be unambiguous enough so that anyone could perform the actions
- always give the same results with the same input
- give the correct results.

Let's now consider the same problem using a flowchart (Figure 8.1), but add some extra conditions to meet these requirements.

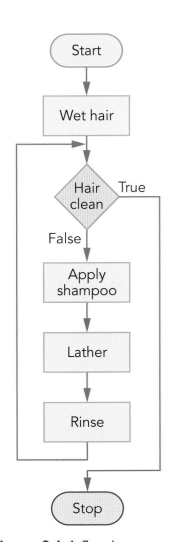

Figure 8.1 *A flowchart*

KEY POINT

A condition-controlled loop causes a statement or set of statements to repeat as long as a condition is true. In Python you use the WHILE statement to write a condition-controlled loop.

KEY POINT

A repetition structure causes a statement or set of statements to execute repeatedly.

KEY POINT

In pseudo-code, the command WHILE is a loop (repetition) with a simple conditional test at its beginning.

We can also use structured English:

```
Wet hair
Loop While only when hair is not clean
   Apply shampoo
   Lather
   Rinse
End Loop
```

With these refinements, we are starting to get an algorithm that could work. Notice how we have added a 'loop while' or 'while loop' statement with a testable condition to see their hair is clean.

The test is at the start/top of the loop. The body of the loop is indented to show clearly what is happening within the loop. We have also added an **end** statement to denote the end of the block of the code that is within the loop.

You need to understand that looping must always specify a number of steps or until a condition is true.

So we could write in English:

```
INPUT a number
WHILE number is not >9 repeat the following two instructions
   ADD number to total
   INPUT next number
PRINT total
```

If we wanted to write the pseudo-code to output the numbers 1 to 50 inclusive using a while loop, we would write:

```
n ← 1
WHILE n ≤ 50
   OUTPUT n
   n ← n + 1
ENDWHILE
```

We now have created a repeating loop which is also called an **iteration**. A WHILE loop does not always execute – if the loop condition is False (number is greater than 9) then the loop won't do anything.

Exploring different types of loops

- A WHILE is a loop (repetition) with a simple conditional test at its beginning. This is what we used for shampooing hair.
- A REPEAT-UNTIL is a loop with a simple condition test at the bottom.
- A FOR is a 'counting' loop.

```
In AQA pseudo-code you use the following
syntax for a WHILE iteration (while the
Boolean expression is True, repeat the
statements). The red brackets < > are only
to show where you add something; you don't
need to put them in your code. BoolExp, means
any expression which can be evaluated to a
Boolean, data type.
WHILE <BoolExp>
    <statements here>
ENDWHILE
Example:
a ← 1
WHILE a < 5
    OUTPUT a
    a ← a + 1
ENDWHILE       # will output 1, 2, 3, 4
```

Sometimes we know how many times a loop will need to run. For example, print the odd numbers from 1 to 101. The opposite of this is when we do not know how many times the loop will need to run, for example if we want to ask the user to guess a pre-determined number between 1 and 101. You will not know how many guesses it will take.

In AQA pseudo-code you use the following syntax to create a FOR iteration. The red brackets < > are only to show where you add something; you don't need to put them in your code. IntExp, means any expression which can be evaluated to an integer.

FOR <Identifier> ← <IntExp> **TO** <IntExp>

    <statements here>

ENDFOR

Example:

FOR a ← 1 TO 4

    OUTPUT a

ENDFOR   # will output 1, 2, 3, 4

In the example of brushing our teeth we do know the number of times we need the loop to run, so we could have what is called a FOR counting loop to brush x times. If we did not want to use a FOR loop but wanted a condition that continued until the teeth were clean we could use a REPEAT-UNTIL teeth are clean loop. Unlike a WHILE loop, a REPEAT-UNTIL loop will always execute. It should be noted that a REPEAT-UNTIL loop doesn't exist in some languages, including Python.

In AQA pseudo-code you use the following syntax for a REPEAT-UNTIL iteration (repeat the statements until the Boolean expression is True). The red brackets < > are only to show where you add something; you don't need to put them in your code. BoolExp, means any expression which can be evaluated to a Boolean, data type.

REPEAT

    <statements here>

UNTIL <BoolExp>

Example:

a ← 1

REPEAT

    OUTPUT a

    a ← a + 1

UNTIL a = 5   # will output 1, 2, 3, 4

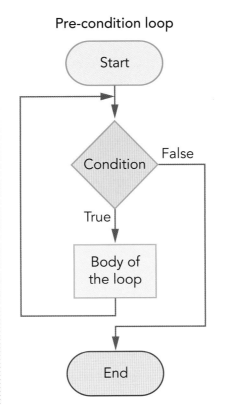
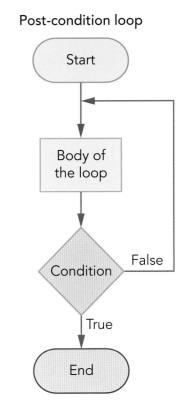

Pre-condition loop   Post-condition loop

Figure 8.2 *Pre- and post-condition flowchart examples*

WHILE statements

WHILE statements will continue to loop until the condition is False.

```
WHILE condition
    sequence
ENDWHILE
```

KEY POINT

WHILE statements are efficient loops that will continue to loop until the condition is false.

KEY POINT

In pseudo-code, REPEAT-UNTIL is a loop with a simple conditional test at the bottom.

REPEAT-UNTIL statements

REPEAT-UNTIL statements will continue to loop until the condition is true.

The difference between a WHILE loop and a REPEAT-UNTIL loop is therefore that in a WHILE loop the condition is checked before the first iteration of the loop.

Here is a quick example, obviously 5 does not equal 8 so the condition is False:

```
WHILE 5 = 8          #the code in the loop will
                     #never run
REPEAT UNTIL 5 = 8   #the code in the loop
                     #will run forever as 5
                     #will never be 8
```

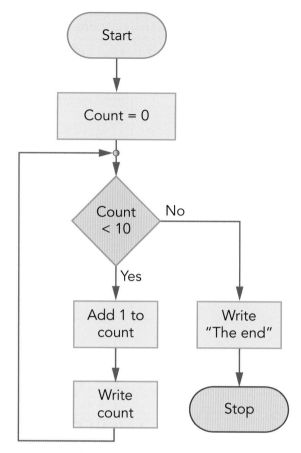

Figure 8.3 *A WHILE loop*

Look at a looping structure with a REPEAT-UNTIL loop in a flowchart (Figure 8.3).

This will have the following pseudo-code:

```
count ← 0
WHILE count < 10
    count  ← count + 1
    OUTPUT count
ENDWHILE
OUTPUT 'The end'
```

In AQA pseudo-code, an example of a WHILE loop, referred to as an indefinite iteration with the condition at the start, would be as follows. The red brackets < > are only to show where you add something; you don't need to put them in your code.

```
WHILE NotSolved
    <instructions here>
ENDWHILE
```

FOR statements

In AQA pseudo-code, an example of a definite iteration would be as follows. The red brackets < > are only to show where you add something you don't need to put them in your code.

```
FOR i ← 1 TO 10
    <instructions here>
ENDFOR
```

Selection

KEY POINT

Sequences are often not a simple line, with the next action depending upon the last decision. This is called selection.

We now know that in practice sequences are not a simple line, usually the next action depends upon the last decision. We also know that this is called selection. In selection one statement or a block of statements within a set of statements is executed depending on the state of the processing of the program at that instance.

We started to explore selection when we looked at IF statements in the last chapter.

In AQA pseudo-code, you use the following syntax for a selection where IF <expression> is true then first <command> is executed, otherwise second <command> is executed. The red brackets < > are only to show where you add something you don't need to put them in your code.

Syntax:

```
IF <add expression here> THEN
    <add command here>
ELSE
    <add command here>
ENDIF
```

Example:

```
IF Answer = 'correct' THEN
    OUTPUT 'Well done'
ELSE
    OUTPUT 'Have another go'
ENDIF
```

KEY POINT

Selection is when a path through the program is selected based on a condition.

An example of selection in both pseudo-code and flowcharts (Figure 8.4) would be:

```
IF condition is true THEN

    PROCESS step(s) 1

ELSE

    PROCESS step(s) 2

ENDIF
```

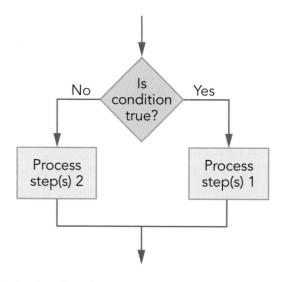

Figure 8.4 *Selection flowchart*

In AQA pseudo-code, you use the following syntax for a selection where IF <expression> is true then you want the command to be executed. The red brackets < > are only to show where you add something: you don't need to put them in your code.

Syntax:

```
IF <add expression here> THEN

    <add command here>

ENDIF
```

Example:

```
IF Answer = 20 THEN

    Score ← Score + 1

ENDIF
```

Conditional sequences

To explore programming in terms of what is called a condition sequence and loops in more detail, we will look at the rock, paper scissors game (see Figure 8.5).

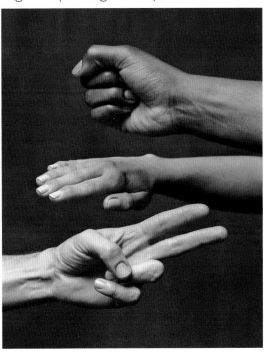

Figure 8.5 *Rock, paper, scissors*

If the first player is a rock and the second scissors the first player wins but if the second player is paper then they win.

This game led to one outcome or sequence of events to be executed if a statement was true, and another outcome or sequence of events to be triggered if the statement was False.

In most programming languages these structures take the form IF-THEN-ELSE. Our game also contains repetitions, when the game was over it started again. Another name for this is a looping structure (a list of instructions to do more than once). You write this type of program to make the computer repeat a certain command or sequence of commands. The loop may run for a predetermined number of times, until a certain condition becomes true, or as long as a certain condition remains True.

TASK

Produce a looping sequence to show the scoring system for the game rock, paper, scissors, where the winner of each game scores 1 point and the overall winner is the best of 21.

TASK

Design a simple rock, paper, scissors game in Python or your chosen language.

8 Looping and Selection

In AQA pseudo-code you use the following syntax to create an IF-ELSE selection. The red brackets < > are only to show where you add something; you don't need to put them in your code. BoolExp, means any expression which can be evaluated to a Boolean data type.

IF <BoolExp> **THEN**

    <statements here>

ELSE

    <statements here>

ENDIF

Example:

a ← 1

IF (a MOD 2) = 0 THEN

    OUTPUT 'even'

ELSE

    OUTPUT 'odd'

ENDIF

You could tell the computer to:

- do the following 20 times
- do the following once for each word in the list
- repeat the following until the user carries out a particular action.

In AQA pseudo-code, you use the following syntax where you want a WHILE loop. The red brackets < > are only to show where you add something; you don't need to put them in your code.

Syntax:

WHILE <add condition here>

    <add command here>

ENDWHILE

Example:

WHILE Flag = 0

    OUTPUT 'All fine'

ENDWHILE

Selections are usually expressed as 'decision' key words such as IF...THEN...ELSE...ENDIF, SWITCH or CASE. They are at the heart of all programming.

Let's see what this might look like using pseudo-code:

```
IF condition is true THEN
    perform instructions in Action1
ELSE
    perform instructions in Action2
ENDIF
```

or

```
IF condition THEN
    sequence 1
ELSE
    sequence 2
ENDIF
```

Or we could have an example which says:

```
IF student's mark in this exam is greater
than or equal to 60 THEN
    OUTPUT 'passed'
ELSE
    OUTPUT 'failed'
ENDIF
```

```
In AQA pseudo-code you use the following
syntax to create an ELSE-IF selection. The
red brackets < > are only to show where you
add something; you don't need to put them
in your code. BoolExp, means any expression
which can be evaluated to a Boolean, data
type.
```

IF <BoolExp> **THEN**

```
    <statements here>
```

ELSE IF BoolExp **THEN**

```
    <statements here>
    <possibly more ELSE IFs>
```

```
ELSE

    <statements here>

ENDIF

Example:

a ← 1

IF (a MOD 4) = 0 THEN

    OUTPUT 'multiple of 4'

ELSE IF (a MOD 4) = 1 THEN

    OUTPUT 'leaves a remainder of 1'

ELSE IF (a MOD 4) = 2 THEN

    OUTPUT 'leaves a remainder of 2'

ELSE

    OUTPUT 'leaves a remainder of 3'

ENDIF
```

ELIF statements

In Python, we have the following ELIF statement:

```
if test:       #do this if test is true

elif test 2:  #do this if test2 is true

else:          #do this if both tests are false
```

Sometimes you will have a function with multiple conditional statements. In these instances you need to be careful how you use IF statements.

For example, if you use the IF statement here in Python:

```
a = 2

if a > 1: a = a+1

if a > 2: a = a+1

    a     #this code sets the value of a

    4     #this is the value of a after running the
          #code
```

It will not be the same as using an ELIF statement:

```
a = 2

if a > 1: a = a+1

elif a > 2: a = a+1

    a    #this code sets the value of a

    3    #this is the value of a after running the
         #code
```

An ELSE statement can be combined with an IF statement but there can only be one ELSE statement following IF. The ELIF statement allows you to check multiple conditions to see if they are True and execute a block of code as soon as one of the conditions evaluates to True. Unlike ELSE, for which there can be at most one statement, there can be a number of ELIF statements following an IF.

```
if <expression1>:

    <statement-block-1>

elif <expression2>:

    <statement-block-2>

elif <expression3>:

    <statement-block-3>

else:

    <statement-block-4>
```

In Python we have the following FOR iteration syntax:

```
for                     #keep doing this until a
                        #condition is met
                        #test is false

for x in aSequence:     #do this for each member
                        #of a Sequence
                        #e.g. each character in
                        #a string, each item in a
                        #list, etc.

for x in range(10):     #do this 10 times
                        #(0 through 9)

for x in range(5,10):   #do this 5 times
                        #(5 through 9)
```

KEY POINT

A WHILE loop is a control flow statement that allows code to be executed repeatedly based on a given Boolean condition. The WHILE loop can be thought of as a repeating IF statement. It will be executed continuously until the condition is met.

KEY POINT

The statements in the FOR loop repeat continuously for a specific number of times that are previously set by the programmer or the user.

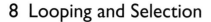

CHAPTER REVIEW

In this chapter we have explored loops in more detail.

Remember before tackling any computer science task or question on this topic you must:

- understand the importance of loops
- think about the correct syntax needed in coding
- be able to use definite and indefinite iteration, including indefinite iteration with the condition(s) at the start or the end of the iterative structure. (More on this topic in chapter 24.)

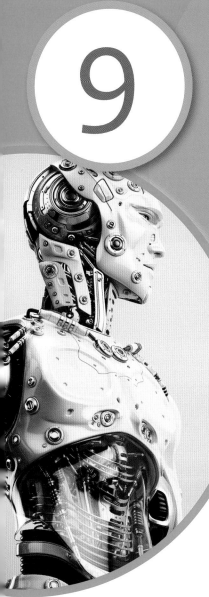

9 Comparing Pseudo-code, Flowcharts and Python

To recap on what you have now learnt in earlier chapters, and to reinforce this learning, it will help if we look at some examples that use pseudo-code, flowcharts and Python for the same action.

First, we need to explore the inputs and outputs from a variable x.

Flowchart	Pseudo-code	Python 3
x ←USERINPUT	x ← USERINPUT	x = input()

We now compare how we show output of a variable using flowcharts, AQA pseudo-code and Python forms:

9 Comparing Pseudo-code, Flowcharts and Python

Flowchart	Pseudo-code	Python 3
OUTPUT x	OUTPUT x	print(x)

To fully understand selection, we now need to compare how we would show the IF...THEN condition in flowchart, AQA pseudo-code and Python form.

Flowchart	Pseudo-code	Python 3

x < 5? — Yes → OUTPUT 'Yes' / No	IF x < 5 THEN
	    OUTPUT 'Yes'
	ENDIF
		if x < 5:
		    print("Yes")

In most instances we want this decision to lead to different outcomes and we will use the ELSE statement. For example, a decision flowchart adding interest at different rates according to the amount you have in a bank account could look like Figure 9.1:

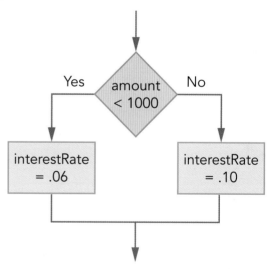

Figure 9.1 *Flowchart demonstrating ELSE*

The pseudo-code for this same action would be:

```
IF amount < 1000 THEN
    interestRate ← .06   #the "yes" or "true" action
ELSE
    interestRate ← .10   #the "no" or "false" action
ENDIF
```

Now let's look at a coded example of this same decision concept in Python, but using a text string:

```
if name == 'Steve':    #you will notice the use of == in this coded example
                       #this is the equality operator used in Python
    print('You have such a cool name!')
else:
    print('Not a bad name, but I think the coolest name is Steve.')
```

So in the code we have two options. If the name entered is Steve the program prints one string, if it is anything else it prints a second string.

Let's look at a further example comparing the IF...THEN...ELSE condition in flowchart, AQA pseudo-code and Python form:

Flowchart	Pseudo-code	Python 3
	```IF x < 5 THEN OUTPUT 'Yes' ELSE OUTPUT 'No' ENDIF```	```if x < 5: print("Yes") else: print("No")```

TASK

Produce a simple coded solution in your chosen programming language for a user to input their name and for a simple message to be printed using the data entered.

Loop statements

Let's say you wanted something printed 100 times. By using a loop statement, you don't have to code the print statement a hundred times; you simply tell the computer to display a string that number of times.

In Python a WHILE loop statement can be written as follows:

```
count = 0
while count < 100:
    print("Computer Science is great fun!")
    count = count + 1
```

KEY POINT !

Iteration is the name given to the repetition of a sequence of computer instructions a specified number of times or until a condition is met.

KEY POINT !

Indefinite iteration is the name given to the repetition of a sequence where the number of repetitions is unknown.

Figure 9.2 *A counting loop*

KEY POINT !

A common programming error involves infinite loops (i.e. the loop runs forever). If your program takes an unusually long time to run and does not stop, it may have an infinite loop. If you run the program from the command window, press CTRL+C to stop it.

So what is happening here? Let's look at a simple flowchart (Figure 9.2) for the same concept.

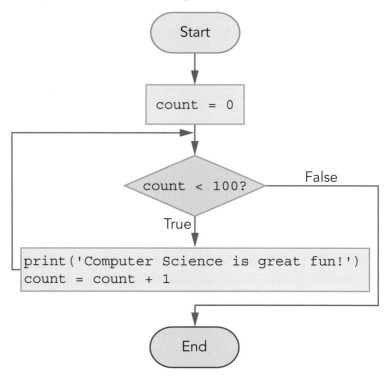

While the count is less than 100, the program will continue to print and add 1 to the variable called count. Once it reaches 100 it will stop. It is worth noting here that we can have a pre-conditioned loop where the code checks the condition first and only runs the loop if the condition passes. The loop will not run if the condition is False to begin with. We also have a post-conditioned loop where the condition is checked at the end of the loop each time it runs. A post-conditioned loop will always be executed once, and if the condition is False at the end of the loop it will be repeated again.

So comparing the WHILE loop condition in flowchart, AQA pseudo-code and Python form will look something like this:

Flowchart	Pseudo-code	Python 3

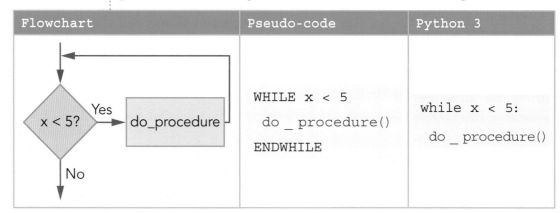	WHILE x < 5
	  do _ procedure()
	ENDWHILE
		while x < 5:
		  do _ procedure()

We can also loop with user input.

In AQA pseudo-code:

```
REPEAT
    OUTPUT 'Enter a number from 1 to 4'#asks user to enter a number
    num ← USERINPUT              #the number entered is stored in the
                                 #variable num
    OUTPUT num                   #prints the number entered on screen
UNTIL num = 4                    #this will keep repeating the question
                                 #until the number 4 is entered
```

QUESTION

What is an infinite loop?

The following Python code creates a simple 'guess the number' game.

```
import random          #import module
guessesTaken = 0       #setting our counter to 0
print('Hello! What is your name?')
myName = input()       #user to input their name
number = random.randint(1, 20) #selecting the number from 1–20
print('Well, ' + myName + ', I am thinking of a number between 1 and 20.')
while guessesTaken < 6:        #we have a count called guessesTaken
    print('Take a guess.')    #there are four spaces in front of print
    guess = input()
    guess = int(guess)
    guessesTaken = guessesTaken + 1
    if guess < number:
        print('Your guess is too low.')    #there are eight spaces in front
                                           #of print
    if guess > number:
        print('Your guess is too high.')
    if guess == number:
        break                  #a break here to exit the loop. A better
                               #way to exit the loop is to change
                               #the loop condition so that the loop is
                               #exited because the condition is met when a
                               #correct guess is made.
```

```
if guess == number:

    print('Good job!')

if guess != number:

    print('Nope. The number I was thinking of was:')

    print(number)
```

KEY POINT !

A count-controlled loop iterates a specific number of times. In Python you use the FOR statement to write a count-controlled loop.

As you can see WHILE loops and IF statements are an essential part of programming. You will also see that there is more than one way to exit a loop, and we can convert the data held in a variable to an alternative data type.

In AQA pseudo-code:

```
WHILE myVar <= 60          #if value of myVar is less or equal to 60
    OUTPUT myVar           #prints the value of myVar on screen
    myVar ← myVar + 1      #adds 1 to the value of myVar
ENDWHILE
```

TASK

Re-write the code shown on this page in your chosen language using a conditional statement instead of the break command to exit the loop.

A WHILE statement is also often called an iterative/looping control statement as it repeatedly executes a set of statements that are based on a Boolean expression or condition.

As long as the condition of a WHILE statement is True, the statements within the loop are (re)executed. Once the condition becomes False, the iteration terminates and control continues with the first statement after the WHILE loop.

```
In AQA pseudo-code, you use the following syntax for a count-controlled
loop. Executes <command> a fixed number of times. The red brackets < >
are only to show where you add something; you don't need to put them in
your code.
Syntax:
FOR <id> ← <expression here> TO <expression here>
    <add command here>
ENDFOR
```

Example:

```
FOR Index ← 1 TO 10
   OUTPUT ArrayNumbers[Index]
ENDFOR
```

Even number count

Say we want to write pseudo-code that will count all the even numbers up to five numbers.

The given criteria are:

- The user wants to see the first five even numbers starting from 0.
- We know from our knowledge of mathematics that even numbers are 0, 2, 4, etc. and that the first five even numbers are 0, 2, 4, 6, 8.

So, if we want to write code to find a set number of even numbers we could use a condition-controlled loop as shown below, where the user first enters the number of even numbers (count) required:

```
count ← USERINPUT
even ← 0
x ← 0
WHILE x < count:
    even ← even + 2
    x ← x + 1
    OUTPUT even
ENDWHILE
```

In AQA pseudo-code, you use the following syntax for a count-controlled loop using a step. The red brackets < > are only to show where you add something; you don't need to put them in your code.

Syntax:

```
FOR <id> ← <add expression here> TO <expression here> STEP <expression here>
   <add command here>
ENDFOR
```

Example:

```
FOR Index ← 1 TO 500 STEP 25
   OUTPUT Index
ENDFOR
```

Averages, highest and lowest number algorithm

Say we want to work out an average of five numbers and to search through the data to find the smallest (minimum) and largest (maximum) of the five user-entered numbers. We then want to write the results found with a message describing what they are. We could write:

KEY POINT

An algorithm is a sequence of steps to solve a problem.

```
OUTPUT 'please enter 5 numbers'   #string asking the user to enter
                                  #numbers
n1 ← USERINPUT                    #the variables being defined by the user
n2 ← USERINPUT
n3 ← USERINPUT
n4 ← USERINPUT
n5 ← USERINPUT
OUTPUT 'The average is'           #string being printed to screen
avg ← (n1+n2+n3+n4+n5)/5          #process for working out the average
OUTPUT avg                        #output the variable (avg) value to screen
IF n1 < n2 THEN                   #decision/process to find highest number
  max ← n2
ELSE
  max ← n1
ENDIF
IF n3 > max THEN
  max ← n3
ENDIF
IF n4 > max THEN
  max ← n4
ENDIF
IF n5 > max THEN
  max ← n5
ENDIF
OUTPUT 'The maximum is'
OUTPUT  max                       #output the value of the variable (max)
                                  #showing maximum number
IF n1 > n2 THEN                   #process to find lowest number
  min ← n2
ELSE
  min ← n1
ENDIF
IF n3 < min THEN
  min ← n3
ENDIF
IF n4 < min THEN
  min ← n4
ENDIF
IF n5 < min THEN
  min ← n5
ENDIF
OUTPUT 'The minimum is'
OUTPUT min                        #output the variable value (min) to show minimum
```

Nested loops

Sometimes we have a number of loops. It is time to explore what are called **nested loops**. They consist of an outer loop and one or more inner loops (Figure 9.3). Each time the outer loop is repeated, the inner loops are re-entered and started again as if new.

> **KEY POINT**
>
> **Nested loops** consist of an outer loop and one or more inner loops. Each time the outer loop is repeated, the inner loops are re-entered and started again as if new.

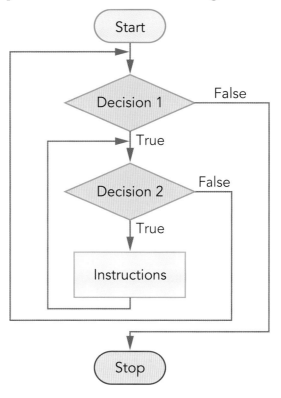

Figure 9.3 *Nested loop*

In AQA pseudo-code, an example of a nested loop, referred to as a nested iteration, would be as follows. The red brackets < > are only to show where you add something; you don't need to put them in your code.

```
WHILE NotSolved
    <instructions here>
    FOR i ← 1 TO 10        #this is the nested iteration
        <instructions here>
    ENDFOR
    <instructions here>
ENDWHILE
```

Let's look at another example of a nested loop, this time using Python. We will explore these concepts in further detail later in the book, for now we just want to explore the concept behind the code and its use. First, we need a few students in an imaginary school all taking different subjects for their GCSEs:

9 Comparing Pseudo-code, Flowcharts and Python

```
students = [("Sally", ["CompSci", "Physics"]),
            ("Robert", ["Art", "CompSci", "Stats"]),
            ("Charlotte", ["CompSci", "French", "Economics"]),
            ("Steve", ["CompSci", "French", "Economics", "CommLaw"]),
            ("Carole", ["Sociology", "French", "Law", "Stats", "Music"])]
```

So, we have assigned a list of five students, called **elements** in programming, to a variable called students.

If we print out each student name, and the number of subjects they are enrolled for:

```
#print all students with a count of their courses
for (name, subjects) in students:
    print(name, "takes ", len(subjects), "GCSEs")
```

Python would give us the following output:

Sally takes 2 GCSEs

Robert takes 3 GCSEs

Charlotte takes 3 GCSEs

Steve takes 4 GCSEs

Carole takes 5 GCSEs

Let's say we want to ask how many students are taking Computer Science, 'CompSci'.

This needs a **counter**, and for each student we need a second embedded loop that tests each of the subjects in turn:

```
#Count how many students are taking CompSci
counter = 0
for (name, subjects) in students:
    for s in subjects:                          #a nested loop!
        if s == "CompSci":
            counter = counter + 1
print("The number of students taking Computer Science is", counter)
```

The output will be:

The number of students taking Computer Science is 4

The next nested selection example is for a game. What if we wanted to design a game with a **menu** on the screen where a user can select to drive one of three types of car:

1 Porsche
2 Mercedes
3 Ford

We must pay particular attention to where the IFs end. The nested IF must be completely contained in either the IF or the ELSE part of the containing IF. Watch for and line up the matching ENDIF.

```
gameNumber ← USERINPUT
IF gameNumber = 1 THEN
   Car = "Porsche"
ELSE
   IF gameNumber = 2 THEN
     Car = "Mercedes"
   ELSE
     Car = "Ford"
   ENDIF
ENDIF
```

Figure 9.4 shows this as a flowchart:

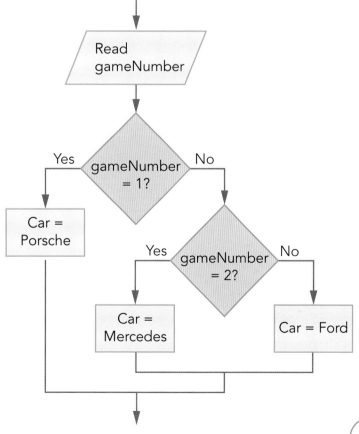

Figure 9.4 *Nested selection*

9 Comparing Pseudo-code, Flowcharts and Python

As the code gets more complex you will be realising how important it is to work out what you need before starting to program. Flowchart symbols and pseudo-code are the building blocks needed to express any desired logic in the form of a computer program.

In AQA pseudo-code, an example of a nested selection would be as follows. The red brackets < > are only to show where you add something; you don't need to put them in your code.

```
IF GameEnded THEN

    <instructions here>

    IF Score > HighestScore THEN   #this is the nested selection

        <instructions here>

    ENDIF

    <instructions here>

ENDIF
```

KEY POINT !

Using flowcharts or pseudo-code we can easily describe the purpose of a given algorithm and explain how a simple algorithm works.

QUESTION

Write in pseudo-code an algorithm to take four input values and to output:
● the total value
● the highest value
● the lowest value
● the average.

TASK

Produce a REPEAT–UNTIL flowchart to show how to make a breakfast of tea and toast.

Derived structures

As we have already seen, flowcharts and pseudo-code code can be represented by basic structures. However, on occasions it is useful to use some additional structures, each of which can themselves be constructed from the above structures. These are sometimes called **derived structures** which are simply structures created by combining other pre-existing structures. Derived structures allow a programmer to group different kinds of data or parts of a code that belong to a single entity.

Choosing the best structure is based upon a few rules:

● Are you repeating or copying/pasting code you have already used?

● Which way uses the least lines of code? Normally less is better.

● There are times when using more lines of code is more efficient but you should never repeat yourself when coding.

CHAPTER REVIEW

In this chapter we have explored loops in more detail and also compared flowcharts, pseudo-code and Python to see how similar loops would be shown using the correct syntax.

Remember, before tackling any computer science task or question on this topic you must:

- understand the importance of loops
- understand derived structures
- think about the correct syntax needed in coding
- be able to use, understand and know how the following statement types can be combined in programs:
  - iteration
  - selection (More on this topic in chapters 6, 8, 11, 12, 24.)
- be able to use definite and indefinite iteration, including indefinite iteration with the condition(s) at the start or the end of the iterative structure
- be able to use nested selection and nested iteration structures. (More on this topic in chapters 10, 14.)

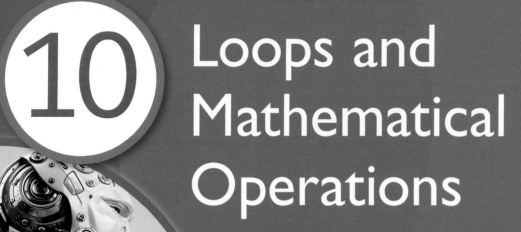

10 Loops and Mathematical Operations

Loops

We often use loops with procedures for mathematical operations.

If we now compare a WHILE loop with a procedure in flowchart, AQA pseudo-code and Python form they would look like this:

Flowchart	Pseudo-code	Python 3

	WHILE x < 5
	   do_ procedure()
	ENDWHILE
		while x < 5:
		   do_ procedure()

A REPEAT loop with a procedure in flowchart, AQA pseudo-code and Python form would look like this:

Flowchart	Pseudo-code	Python 3

	REPEAT
	  do_procedure()
	UNTIL x < 5
		```while True:```
		 ``` do_procedure()```
		 ``` if x < 5:```
		 ``` break```
		
		 Python has no REPEAT LOOP so a similar effect can be achieved by using a WHILE loop. We could also recode this code to avoid the use of a break by adding a condition that is met to exit the loop. Using 'break' in code frequently makes code hard to follow, so often structured programmers (re)write programs without 'break' statements. Care needs to be taken, however, as sometimes replacing them with the introduction of additional variables and/or code duplication can also make the program harder to understand.

A FOR loop in flowchart, AQA pseudo-code and Python form looks like this:

Flowchart	Pseudo-code	Python 3

	FOR count ← 1 TO 4
	  do_procedure()
	ENDFOR
		```for count in range```
		 ```(1,5):```
		 ``` do_procedure()```

Minimum and maximum

Sometimes a user wants to find the maximum and minimum. We looked at this in chapter 9 when we wanted to find the highest and lowest number.

We will now explore a small program that will allow a user to type in a list of numbers and from this list calculate the minimum and maximum. To make the algorithm a little simpler, we will ask the user to enter a count of the numbers in the list before entering the actual numbers.

The algorithm for this might be:

```
Get count of numbers.
Enter numbers and find maximum and minimum.
Output results.
```

Of course, the user may enter any number of numbers, even no numbers. Entering no numbers may seem a bit strange but it is not uncommon, when writing a general-purpose function, to allow for the possibility of no inputs (referred to as 'null input'). We will explore functions in more detail in chapter 11 but, basically, a function is a subprogram not a program and all functions return a value. For now let's modify our algorithm to accept this.

```
count ← USERINPUT
IF count > 0 THEN
   OUTPUT maximum
   OUTPUT minimum
ENDIF
```

KEY POINT

To **execute** is to carry out an instruction on a computer.

KEY POINT

Looping is repeating parts of a sequence that repeat over and over again. Like eating breakfast every day at 7.30 am.

In our new algorithm, once the count of the numbers is known a loop is **executed** that number of times, each time reading in a number and somehow using that number to find the maximum and minimum. Repeated execution of a set of statements is called iterations.

In this loop the number of times the loop is executed is known, that is equal to the count of numbers.

```
FOR i ← 1 TO n
   Do body of loop
ENDFOR
```

Algorithms often repeat a set of instructions a set number of times. Note that the body of the loop is a compound statement.

So we have the following new version of the algorithm:

```
count ← USERINPUT
IF count > 0 THEN
   FOR i ← 1 TO count
     number ← USERINPUT
     #process number
   ENDFOR
ENDIF
```

We now need to compute the maximum and minimum values. If you wanted to do this manually one way of doing it would be to start at the beginning of the list and work through the list systematically always remembering the smallest number seen so far. Whenever a number is found smaller than the memorised number, the memorised number would be replaced by the new, smaller number. At the start of the list the smallest number yet seen is, of course, the first number and when the end of the list is reached the memorised number is the smallest. We could do a similar thing for the largest number.

As a result of the way that the search part of the algorithm has been written, it will only work if at least two numbers have been entered, so the algorithm starts with an IF statement to display an error message if fewer numbers are entered.

```
count ← USERINPUT
IF count < 2 THEN
   OUTPUT 'Please enter a valid number'
ELSE
   number ← USERINPUT
   small ← number
   large ← number
   FOR i ← 1 TO count-1
     number ← USERINPUT
     IF number < small THEN
         small ← number
     ENDIF
     IF number > large THEN
         large ← number
     ENDIF
   ENDFOR
   OUTPUT small
   OUTPUT large
ENDIF
```

Mathematical arrays

When we want to use loops to work out mathematics we often store the numbers in an **array**. We will explore these again in more detail in chapter 18, but for now we will explore the concept in mathematics.

You may have used arrays as a child when you learnt your multiplication tables. By progressively adding another column of three objects, you can visualise basic number facts graphically.

1 × 3	2 × 3	3 × 3	4 × 3
or	or	or	or
3 × 1	3 × 2	3 × 3	3 × 4

Figure 10.1 *Arrays of dots*

In Figure 10.1 we have an array of dots. Each column has three dots. So two columns would be six dots, five columns 15 dots.

This is quite a difficult array as it actually has two dimensions with rows and columns. But we also have what are called one-dimensional arrays. You can think of arrays as boxes that hold a number: you are allowed to look at what's in the box or replace its contents with something else.

If myArray is an array of length n, you can imagine it has n boxes lined up in a row.

> In AQA pseudo-code you use the following syntax for the assignment of an array. The red brackets < > are only to show where you add something; you don't need to put them in your code. Exp means any expression.
>
> <Identifier> ← [<Exp>, <Exp>, …, <Exp>]
>
> Example:
>
> myArray ← [1, 3, 6, 7, 14, 18]

It should be noted that array indexing can start at 0 or 1 depending upon the programming language. Python, by default, uses lists instead of arrays with indexing starting at zero.

You can use arrays in the same way you use variables:

```
x ← myArray[2]     #sets x to the third value
                   #in the array (here, 6)

myArray[3] ← 2     #sets the fourth value in the
                   #array to the value 2
                   #(replacing 7)
```

Sometimes you will use a variable to specify which element of the array you mean:

```
y ← myArray[i]     #sets y to the i'th array value
```

> In AQA pseudo-code you use the following syntax to update an element of an array. The red brackets < > are only to show where you add something; you don't need to put them in your code. IntExp, means any expression which can be evaluated to an integer.
>
> ```
> <Identifier>[<IntExp>] ← <Exp>
> ```
>
> Example:
>
> ```
> primes[5] ← 17
> # array is now [1, 3, 6, 7, 14, 17]
> ```

Consider the following array:

```
myArray = [2,4,6,8]
```

The array shows the two times table. If we go to the third indexed number we will have 2×3, the fourth indexed number will be 2×4.

```
myArray = [3,6,9,12,15]
```

would represent the three times table.

> In AQA pseudo-code you use the following syntax to access an element of an array. The red brackets < > are only to show where you add something; you don't need to put them in your code. IntExp, means any expression which can be evaluated to an integer.
>
> ```
> <Identifier>[<IntExp>]
> ```
>
> For example, if we first define an array:
>
> ```
> array1 ← [2, 3, 5, 7, 11, 13]
> ```

10 Loops and Mathematical Operations

And now want to write the pseudo-code to
change the number 13 in the array to 17, we
first refer to the position in the array and
then add the integer that we want to replace
the existing number with, so:

```
array1[5] ← 17
# array1 is now [2, 3, 5, 7, 11, 17]
Example:
primes[0]

# evaluates to 1 (questions on exam papers will
always state whether indexing begins at 0 or 1,

#here 0 has been assumed)
```

Finding the mathematical mean

EXAMPLE

If we have n numbers and want to find
their arithmetic mean, the simplest
method is to put the numbers into an
array then sum all of the values and divide
by the number of values:

```
SUBROUTINE simple_mean(array, n)
    sum ← 0
    FOR i ← 1 TO n
      sum ← sum + array[i]
    ENDFOR
    RETURN sum / n
ENDSUBROUTINE
```

CHAPTER REVIEW

In this chapter we have built upon your extended knowledge of loops from the last few
chapters and also integrated knowledge of computational mathematics.

Remember, before tackling any computer science task or question on this topic you must:

- understand the importance of loops
- apply computational mathematical knowledge
- understand derived structures
- think about the correct syntax needed in coding
- be familiar with and be able to use:
  - addition
  - subtraction
  - multiplication
  - division
- be able to use definite and indefinite iteration, including indefinite iteration with the condition(s)
  at the start or the end of the iterative structure (More on this topic in chapters 8, 24.)

11 Subroutines

A **subroutine** is a computer program contained within another program. It operates semi-independently of the main program.

There are two basic forms of subroutines:

- named code that does a particular task; often called procedure
- code that does a task but also returns a value; often called function.

The basic idea of a subroutine is to group a collection of statements into a named piece of code that can be invoked by simply calling the subroutine by its name.

In AQA pseudo-code you use the following syntax for a subroutine definition. The red brackets < > are only to show where you add something; you don't need to put them in your code.

KEY POINT !

A **subroutine** is a computer program contained within another program. It operates semi-independently of the main program.

11 Subroutines

```
SUBROUTINE <Identifier>(<parameters>)
    <statements>
ENDSUBROUTINE
Examples:
SUBROUTINE show_add(a, b)
    result ← a + b
    OUTPUT result
ENDSUBROUTINE
SUBROUTINE say_hi()
    OUTPUT 'hi'
ENDSUBROUTINE
```

In effect, we can give a section of code a name and use that name as a statement in another part of the program. When the name is reached in the code, the processing in the other part of the program stops while the named code is executed. When the named code finishes executing, processing resumes with the statement just below the named code.

The place where the named code appears is called the **calling** unit.

These two types of subroutines have many names:

- C++ calls the first a **void** function and the second a **value-returning** function.
- Java calls both of them methods.

Whatever the subroutines are called in your chosen language, they are powerful tools for abstraction and decomposition.

Many subroutines come as part of the **library** that comes with the language. For example, mathematical problems often need to calculate trigonometric functions.

The **import** function in a programming system imports new predefined functions.

```
In AQA pseudo-code you use the following syntax
for calling a subroutine. The red brackets < >
are only to show where you add something; you
don't need to put them in your code.
<Identifier>(<parameters>)
Example:
OUTPUT add(2, 3)
answer ← add(2, 3)
```

Procedures and functions in subroutines

Using subroutines

Subroutines are the one of the most important concepts in any programming language design.

Subroutines usually have the following characteristics:
- Each subroutine has a single entry point.
- Each subroutine has a name.

There are two ways that a subroutine can gain access to the data that it is to process and these are through variables or through **parameter** passing. Parameter passing is more flexible than through variables.

Subroutines call statements must include the name of the subprogram and a list of parameters to be bound to the formal parameters of the subroutine. These parameters are called actual parameters.

Procedures

Procedures are collections of code that perform a specific task. They often also use parameters.

EXAMPLE

Let's imagine that you are washing a cup. Your process of washing a cup could be:
- Take cup 'a' # 'a' is a variable parameter as it can be assigned to more than one cup.
- Dip cup 'a' into soapy water.
- Cover every inch of cup 'a' with soap.
- Rinse cup 'a' with clean water to remove the soap.
- Dry cup 'a'.

So every time you need to wash a cup, you do the same procedure. Dip, soap, rinse, dry. You will use the same sequence, repeated over and over again each time you wash a cup. This is a procedure. When you call a procedure in programming it will do the jobs that the procedure is programmed to do. By replacing instructions with one single procedure statement, if makes code easier to read and debug.

Functions

Functions are structurally the same as procedures but are based on the idea of mathematical functions. Functions are called by their names in expressions, along with the required actual parameters. A function can be included in a command (for example print(max(3,4,6)).

So a function is just like a procedure except that it returns a value. In Python a function can even return more than one value. For example, a function could be used if somebody asks you to count the number of cars in a car park. You would go to the car park, count, and then report the number of cars to the person who first asked you. That is a function. A function simply returns another value back into the program, such as complex calculation results, the position of the mouse cursor or the number of cars that entered the car park.

In Python a function definition *must* come *before* it is called.

Functions can return almost anything: numbers, strings, characters, anything. You can even use functions to replace procedures completely.

This is the case in some languages where there are no special implementations of procedures.

The concept of a function is vital in mathematics.

Functions are often used in computer languages to implement mathematical functions. The function computes one or more results, which are determined by the parameters passed to it. When the function is called, the calling unit lists the subprogram name followed by a list of identifiers in parentheses.

There are two types of function:

- built-in functions
- programmer-defined functions.

We looked at built-in functions in chapter 4. Built-in functions are predefined functions built into the language to perform a wide range of operations. Built-in functions are functions that are always available for your code to call.

Functions serve two primary development roles:

1. Functions reduce the amount of code needed as they are the simplest way to use similar actions in your code in more than one place and more than one time. Functions allow a

programmer to group and generalise code to be used many times later. They allow us to code an operation in a single place and use it in many places.

2. Functions also provide a tool for splitting systems into pieces that have well-defined roles. For instance, to make a pizza at home, you would start by mixing the dough, then roll it out, then add cheese and other toppings, then put it in the oven.

If you are programming a pizza-making robot, functions and procedures would help you divide the overall 'makepizza' task into small parts with one function and procedure for each subtask in the process. It's easier to implement the smaller tasks in isolation than it is to implement the entire process at once.

The difference between a function and a procedure is that a function returns a value and a procedure just executes commands.

A function in Python is first defined by a def statement. Unlike functions in compiled languages such as C, def in Python is an executable statement. The function does not exist until Python reaches and runs the def.

Functions are subroutines and often they have what is called a parameter interface. This is where the parameters for the subroutine are defined. If a subroutine has a parameter interface, you supply values to all of the parameters in its interface when you call it.

The syntax for Python looks like this:

```
def function-name(Parameter):

    statements, i.e. the function body
```

The parameter can consist of none or more parameters.

Parameters in functions can be called arguments.

Define a function in Python

The definition of a function will always have the keyword def and the function's name at the beginning of the code.

```
def greeting():   #a colon marks the end of the function's
                  #name and the start of the code it contains

    print('Hello!')  #this is the code within the function
```

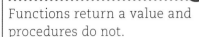

KEY POINT

Functions return a value and procedures do not.

QUESTION

What are the two main roles of a function?

Call a function in Python

Typing the function name followed by parentheses into the shell window calls the function and shows the output.

```
greeting()      #parentheses show that this is a
                #function call, not a variable
```

Output: Hello!

The function body always consists of indented statements. It gets executed every time the function is called.

Parameters can be mandatory or optional, depending on the function. The optional parameters (zero or more) must follow any mandatory parameters.

A return statement ends the execution of the function call and 'returns' the result, that is the value of the expression following the return keyword, to the caller. If the return statement is without an expression, the special value 'None' is returned.

By default, all names assigned in a function are local to that function and exist only while the function runs. To assign a name in the enclosing module, functions need to list it in a global statement. This is important as in chapter 12 we will explore something called **scope**.

You will need to understand scope in order to effectively use subroutines, as local variables usually:

- only exist while the subroutine is executing
- are only accessible within the subroutine.

KEY POINT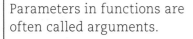

Parameters in functions are often called arguments.

Optional parameters

Functions can sometimes have optional parameters. In effect these are default parameters. Not all languages do this, but where they do default parameters are still parameters, but they don't have to be given as they are predefined in the programming language used. In this case, the default values are used.

EXAMPLE

This little script greets a person. If no name is given, it will greet everybody:

```
def Hello(name="everybody"):

    #Greets a person

    print("Hello " + name + "!")

  Hello("Steve")

  Hello()
```

The output looks like this:

    Hello Steve!

    Hello everybody!

For this small programming task this function is of no real value, but functions can be very useful when writing code.

Return values in subprograms

So we now know that functions return values. These are called **return values**. The problem is return values have what is called scope.

We will look at scope in chapter 12, but for now you need to understand that every time you call a procedure or a function, when the procedure or function finishes, it is removed together with everything declared by it.

```
In AQA pseudo-code you use the following
syntax for a subroutine return value. The red
brackets < > are only to show where you add
something; you don't need to put them in your
code. Exp means any expression.
RETURN <Exp>
Example:
SUBROUTINE add(a, b)
    result ← a + b
    RETURN result
ENDSUBROUTINE
```

That means that a variable used in a procedure, can't be used after the procedure finishes as it no longer exists.

Abstraction and generalisation in subprograms

Abstraction and **generalisation** are often used together. You will remember the term abstraction from chapter 1.

Generalisation widens the applicability of a procedure within a given domain. For example, changing a procedure that adds up two numbers into one that could add up any number of numbers or one that could do more than one operation on a pair of numbers would be generalisation.

Abstraction reduces complexity by hiding irrelevant detail, generalisation reduces complexity by replacing multiple tasks which perform similar functions with a single construct. Programming languages provide programmers with the tools for generalisation through variables and parameters. Generalisation places the emphasis on the similarities between objects and actions.

Programming languages provide abstraction through procedures, functions and modules, which permit the programmer to distinguish between what a program does and how it is implemented.

Say we wish to create and use a subprogram called 'rectangle' that will calculate areas, we will then need to add parameters to its variables. Because of our subprogram's generalisation, we can make the subprogram calculate the areas of a square or rectangle by simply changing these variables. When you use a name as a parameter it binds the parameter to what is called an **argument**.

The terms parameter and argument are often used for the same thing, indeed in many Python tutorials parameters are called arguments. But in many languages they are very different. A parameter refers to the variable found in the function when it is defined. A parameter is always a variable, it can change.

```
function(x) = x+x     #x is a parameter
```

An argument is the actual value passed.

```
function(2)   #2 is the argument of the function
```

CHAPTER REVIEW

In this chapter we have explored subroutines.

Remember, before tackling any computer science task or question on this topic you must:

- understand procedures
- understand functions
- understand the concept of subroutines
- be able to explain the advantages of using subroutines in programs
- describe the use of parameters to pass data within programs
- use subroutines that return values to the calling routine
- know that subroutines may declare their own variables, called local variables,
  and that local variables usually:
  - only exist while the subroutine is executing
  - are only accessible within the subroutine (More on this topic in chapter 12.)
- understand parameters in procedures and functions
- be able to use, understand and know how the following statement types can be combined in programs:
  - subroutine (procedure/function). (More on this topic in chapters 6, 7, 8, 12, 24.)

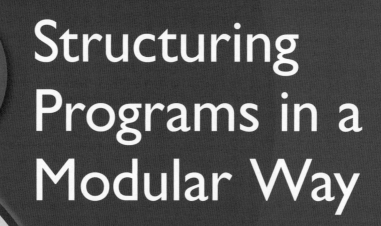

12 Structuring Programs in a Modular Way

You will now understand how programs are made up of subroutines that consist of sequences, selection and repetitions. A single program could include all of these, with some elements nested within others. It is possible to divide any problem into tasks and each task into subtasks. It is important to do this until each subtask is simple enough to be easily constructed in code.

Structured programming

Structured programming is sometimes also called modular programming. It is important that structured programming uses clear, well-documented interfaces such as local variables and parameters alongside clearly defined return values. Defined functions are coded in a separate module. This means that modules can be reused in other programs. After a module has been tested individually, it is then integrated with other modules into the overall program structure. Structured programs use looping constructs such as "for", "until", and "while".

Each basic subroutine of a program should perform a simple task. So far, we have been thinking about these tasks in terms of individual actions or subtasks. A subtask could require a single unit, or a combination of units. Generally speaking, a function returns a value and can be included within an expression, a procedure doesn't.

```
In AQA pseudo-code, you use the following
syntax to define a procedure. The red brackets
< > are only to show where you add something;
you don't need to put them in your code.
Syntax:
SUBROUTINE <pname> (<p1>,<p2> ,…)
    <add command here>
ENDSUBROUTINE
Example:
SUBROUTINE find_smallest(a, b, c)
    IF a < b AND a < c THEN
        small ← a
    ELSEIF b < c THEN
        small ← b
    ELSE
        small ← c
    ENDIF
    OUTPUT small
ENDSUBROUTINE
```

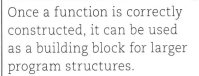

KEY POINT

Once a function is correctly constructed, it can be used as a building block for larger program structures.

A modular approach to programming has many benefits. First it makes the coding so much easier. Once written, modules can be checked individually and then be placed in the correct order within the program. Some tasks are quite generic, for example you may need to perform a particular mathematical operation within your code. It would seem pointless to make every programmer have to write their own code for something so common.

To avoid unnecessary work all programming languages have predefined modules that can be called. It is possible to 'call' any module. When a module is called, the name for this is a subroutine or procedure. A procedure is a special kind of module that performs a task or set of tasks that can be added to another program as a subtask of that particular program.

EXAMPLE

Define an example procedure in English for playing Monopoly:

```
SUBROUTINE Monopoly_Move()

    Throw dice.

    Move the number of spaces on the board
    shown on dice.

    IF on "Go to Jail" THEN

        Go to Jail

    ELSEIF on "Chance" OR "Community Chest" THEN

        Draw a card and follow its instructions

    ELSE

        Follow the usual rules for the square
        (buying property, paying rent, collecting
        £200 for passing "Go")

    ENDIF

ENDSUBROUTINE
```

We can now call this procedure for each player in turn until game ends. We could also define the procedure with parameters for each player:

```
SUBROUTINE Monopoly_Move(<p1>,<p2>,…) #parameters
added for the number of players

    <player_x>

ENDSUBROUTINE
```

```
In pseudo-code, you use the following syntax
to call a procedure or a function. The red
brackets < > are only to show where you add
something; you don't need to put them in your
code.
Syntax:
<id>(<add parameters here>, ...)
Example:
result ← add(firstNumber, secondNumber)
```

Understanding scope

You now understand the terms procedure and function but you will not be able to read or write large computer programs without understanding the concept of **scope**.

The scope of something (function, variable, etc.) in a program is the range of code that it applies to.

Let's look at an analogy in everyday life. You have people you know on a social networking site. What you write on a public group or wall is global scope, but if you have a group between just your friends, it's local scope – only people in the group can see what you put here. You may even have a special language that you use with your friends that no one outside this group would understand. This is a bit like defining a function called friends with things no one outside the group can access or use.

This would then be called local scope (local to a particular function, so the variable can only be used inside the function of friends). On the wall anyone can access what you post, it is global in real terms and in programming terms (useable from anywhere) so would be called global scope.

Now imagine your program as a virtual social media site with each module separate. Parts of it will be restricted to local use and can only be accessed within the module where they exist (Figure 12.1).

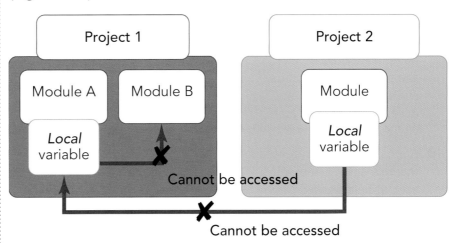

Figure 12.1 *Local variables*

Other parts are global, these are accessible from anywhere (Figure 12.2).

KEY POINT

Scope is often either global or local. Global scope is where a variable is declared in the main body of the source code, outside all subroutine, while local scope is a variable declared within the body of a subroutine.

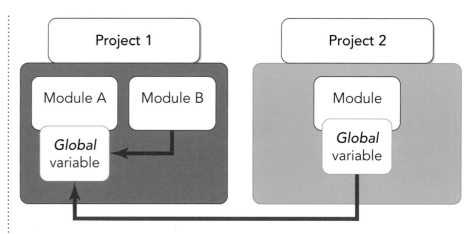

Figure 12.2 *Global variables*

In some programming languages, special things happen when variables go in and out of scope. Memory may be allocated to hold data, or memory may be freed when variables go out of scope. Scope is also useful for **error-checking**.

The scope of a variable in a program is the lines of code in the program where the variable can be accessed. So the concept of scope applies not only to variables and variable names but also to the names of procedures.

There is another term that is used to describe scope and that is **visibility**. You should be aware that the two terms are the same in terms of programming.

Local scope

Unlike global scoped variables, local variables have their scope limited to the block where they are declared. A block is the body of a control structure, the body of a subroutine, or a place such as the file with the code where the variable is declared. So the term local scope refers to when a variable can be read and modified *only* from within the subroutine or place in which it is declared.

Local scope has the highest **priority** with regard to the other scope levels. So, in addition to these variables, if you have variables with the same names declared at a global scope level (see below), the code within a subroutine utilises the variables declared within the subroutine, not the variables with the same name declared at the project level.

KEY POINT ⓘ

Visibility is another name for the scope of a variable in a program. It is the lines of code in the program where the variable can be accessed.

KEY POINTS ⓘ

● Different subroutines can have local variables with the same names because the subroutines cannot access each other's local variables.

● A local variable is created inside a subroutine and cannot be accessed by statements that are outside the subroutine. It has local scope.

● The term local scope refers to when a variable can be read and modified *only* from within the subroutine in which it is declared.

Global scope

Global scope variables are those which can be accessed from anywhere within the project that contains their declaration, as well as from other projects that refer to that initial project.

Python and scope

Consider some Python code:

```
x = 1          #by default in Python this creates what is called a global
               #variable. We will explore this later in the book. A global
               #variable can be modified outside of where it is defined.

def a():
    global x   #Whenever you want to access a global variable in a function,
               #you must declare that you are using it as a global or you
               #will just create a local variable x that shadows the global
    x = 4      #because we have stated that x is global it will
               #change this variable from 1 to 4, if we had not set to global
               #it would have remained as 1 outside of the local function of a

def b():
    print(x)

a()            #calls the function a, which sets the global variable x to 4
b()            #calls the function b, which outputs the new global variable
```

The output will be:

```
    4
```

We can also return the local variable and assign it to the global:

```
    def a():
        x = 4
        return x
    x = a()
```

Why is it better to use local scope?

It is good programming style to use local variables whenever possible. This helps to avoid cluttering the global environment with unnecessary names.

Other benefits of using local scope include:

● the source code is easier to understand when the scope of individual elements are limited

● subroutines can be more easily reused if their variables are all local

- global variables can be read or modified by any part of the program. A global variable can be accessed or set by any part of the program, and any rules regarding its use can easily be broken or forgotten.
- global variables are available everywhere; you may unknowingly end up using a global variable when you think you are using a local variable
- testing your code is harder if you use global variables.

CHAPTER REVIEW

In this chapter we have explored modules and how to structure programs in a modular way.

We have also explored local and global scope.

Remember, before tackling any computer science task or question on this topic you must:

- understand the importance of scope
- know that subroutines may declare their own variables, called local variables, and that local variables usually:
  - only exist while the subroutine is executing
  - are only accessible within the subroutine (More on this topic in chapter 11.)
- use local variables and explain why it is good practice to do so.

13 Binary and Hexadecimal Numbers

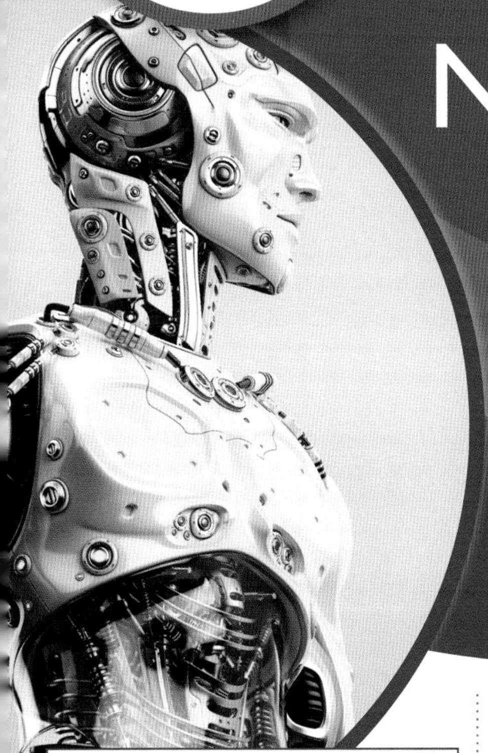

KEY POINTS

- The **central processing unit** (CPU) is the electronic circuitry within a computer that carries out the instructions of a computer program.
- **Machine code** is a set of instructions that a computer can execute directly. Machine code is written in a binary code, and each statement corresponds to one machine action.
- **Compiling** refers to converting (a program) into machine code or lower-level form in which the program can be executed.

Ones and zeros

KEY POINT

All data that is stored in a computer is converted to sequences of 0s and 1s.

Every **central processing unit** (CPU) has its own unique language (called **machine code**). Programs must be rewritten or **compiled** to work on different types of computers. We will explore machine code in a little more detail in the next chapter but first we will look at how the system functions.

Have you ever wondered why switches have a 1 for on and a 0 for off (see Figure 13.1)? It is based on binary computer code. 1 means 'on' and 0 means 'off'. Everything a computer does is based on ones and zeros.

Imagine the computer is made up switches and each switch controls a light which can either be On or Off, One or Zero.

Each sequence of On-and-Off lights could represent a different number. Let's imagine that we have two lights each with their own switch. They could be:

both Off

first Off, second On

Figure 13.1 *On/off symbols*

KEY POINTS

- A single binary digit (like '0' or '1') is called a 'bit'. For example, 11010 is five bits long.
- The word bit is made up from the words 'binary digit'.

KEY POINT

The number of different bit patterns that can be formed using 2 bits is four.

first On, second Off

both On

Binary code takes each of those combinations and assigns a number to it, like this:

both Off = 0

first Off, second On = 1

first On, second Off = 2

both On = 3

Maybe you are thinking that it would take rather a lot of switches and lights to make a computer work like this, but consider if we had six lights, as in Figure 13.2, that were On On Off On Off Off.

On   On   Off   On   Off   Off

Figure 13.2 *Bulbs On or Off*

Rather than giving a light just one score let's give the different lights in the sequence different scores. The first light is 32, the second 16, then 8, 4, 2, 1.

The value of those six bulbs (called a point value) would be:

32 + 16 + 0 + 4 + 0 + 0 (remember – we only give points if they're turned On!)

And that adds up to 52. So, we would say the sequence of lights is worth 52. But we would write it as: 110100

Humans also use a different number system to computers as they use what are called decimal (or denary) numbers. Don't worry about the name, it just means that our numbers have a base of 10. Many people believe that we have a base-10 system because we originally learnt to count using our ten fingers. Base 10 just means that it has 10 units. Humans use the numerals 0, 1, 2, 3, 4, 5, 6, 7, 8, 9 but computers do not count this way.

Unlike humans, computers do not have ten fingers. Computer memory is based on transistors which have only two states, on or off (based upon base voltage low or base voltage high). Each transistor is an on/off switch. But where we have only two hands, computers have millions of transistors. Maybe humans use the decimal system because we have two hands and ten fingers to count on; the computer may only have one finger but it does have the equivalent of lots and lots of hands (the transistors).

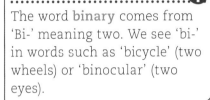

Binary numbers

Even though computers are based on a **binary** system, they have to convert the numbers into our 10-unit decimal system so that we can understand them.

'Hello World' in binary is:

01001000011001010110110001101100011011110010000001010111 011011110 1110010011011000110010

How it is represented in machine code is shown below.

c7 28 2a 2a 3c 5c 2b 00 00 00 00 00 00 6f 00 00
3c 5c 2b 5c 28 2a 2a 00 00 00 00 00 00 72 00 00
2a 2a 2a 3c 5c 2b 00 00 00 00 00 00 6c 00 00
3c 2b 5c 28 2a 2a 00 00 00 00 00 00 64 00 00
2a 2a 3c 5c 2b 5c 01 00 00 00 00 00 00 21 00 00
2b 5c 28 2a 2a 3c 00 00 00 00 00 00 00 00 00
2a 3c 5c 2b 5c 28 00 00 00 00 00 00 00 00 00
5c 28 2a 2a 3c 5c 00 00 00 00 00 00 64 00 00 00
3c 5c 2b 5c 28 2a 00 00 00 00 00 00 48 00 00 00
28 2a 2a 3c 5c 2b 00 00 00 00 00 00 65 00 00 00
5c 2b 5c 28 2a 2a 00 00 00 00 00 00 6c 00 00 00
2a 2a 3c 5c 2b 5c 00 00 00 00 00 00 6c 00 00 00
2b 5c 28 2a 2a 3c 00 00 00 00 00 00 6f 00 00 00
2a 3c 5c 2b 5c 28 00 00 00 00 00 00 2c 00 00 00
5c 28 2a 2a 3c 5c 00 00 00 00 00 00 20 00 00 00
3c 5c 2b 5c 28 2a 00 00 00 00 00 00 57 00 00 00

Converting to binary numbers

Converting decimal numbers to binary numbers is relatively simple. First we will explore counting in binary and decimal to see how binary numbers compare.

Decimal number	How we convert	Binary number
0	We start at 0 for the number of bits required. Here we have 7 bits.	0000000
1	Then we add a 1 on the right.	0000001
2	As we already have a 1 at the right it changes back to 0 again, but we carry a 1 one place in.	0000010
3	Now we add a 1 on the right again as it is a 0.	0000011
4	We add 1 to the number on the right but that digit is already at 1 so it goes back to 0 and 1 is added to the *next position* on the left, but it is also a 1 so it becomes a zero and we carry the 1 one place to the left.	0000100
5	Now we add a 1 on the right again as it is a 0.	0000101
6	As we want to add a 1 to the right and it is already a 1 we make it an 0 and put the 1 up one place to the left.	0000110
7	Now we add a 1 on the right again as it is a 0.	0000111
8	Start back at 0 again (for all three digits), and a 1 is carried to the left.	0001000
9	And so on...	0001001

So if we look at binary numbers we can see that, counting from the right, the first digit has a weight of 1 (2^0), the second digit has a weight of 2 (2^1), the third a weight of 4 (2^2), the fourth a weight of 8 (2^3) and so on up to 128 (2^7).

We can easily construct a table to show this:

Binary digit table							
2^7	2^6	2^5	2^4	2^3	2^2	2^1	2^0
128	64	32	16	8	4	2	1

Therefore, if we have an 8-bit binary number 01100110 and place this in our table it would look like this:

Decimal digit value	128	64	32	16	8	4	2	1
Binary digit value	0	1	1	0	0	1	1	0

We can now easily convert it to a decimal number:

64 + 32 + 4 + 2 = 102

To convert from decimal numbers to binary we divide the number successively by 2 and print the remainder in reverse order. So, if we have a decimal number of 51 we can work out its binary number as follows:

Number divided by 2	Result	Remainder
51/2	25	1
25/2	12	1
12/2	6	0
6/2	3	0
3/2	1	1
1/2	0	1

Answer: 110011

Using our knowledge of Python, we could even write a simple function to convert a decimal number into a binary number using a loop:

```
def binary(number):    #define a function so we can use again
   if number > 1:
      binary(number//2) #note how the function calls itself
   print(number % 2,end = ") #the % (modulo) operator gives the
                                remainder from the division
dec = int(input("Please enter an integer: "))
                          #user to input a decimal number
binary(dec)               #call our function
```

Output:

    Please enter an integer: 51

    110011

Adding binary numbers

Adding binary numbers is also relatively simple.

You first align the numbers you wish to add as you would if you were adding decimal numbers.

    0   1   1   1
    1   1   1   0

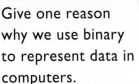

QUESTION

Give one reason why we use binary to represent data in computers.

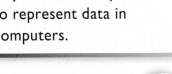

QUESTION

Write the binary code for the decimal number 67. Use eight binary digits.

13 Binary and Hexadecimal Numbers

You then add the two numbers in the far right column, again as you would decimal numbers.

```
0  1  1  1
1  1  1  0
──────────
         1
```

Add the numbers following the rules of binary addition (1 + 0 = 1, 0 + 0 = 0) unless both numbers are a 1.

If they are both 1, write 0 below and carry a 1 to the next column. (Remember it is not 'ten' but 'one zero'.)

```
0  1  1  1
1  1  1  0
──────────
      0  1
```

Move on to the next column to the left. We use the rule 1 + 1 + 1 = 1 carry 1.

```
0  1  1  1
1  1  1  0
──────────
   1  0  1
```

We start on the right and move across the columns to the left. If there are no more columns, we add a new one.

```
   0  1  1  1
   1  1  1  0
─────────────
1  0  1  0  1
```

Remember that 1 + 1 = 10 and 1 + 1 + 1 = 11. Always remember to carry the 1.

If we want to add three binary numbers this is achieved in exactly the same way. When we add three numbers the rule is that 1 + 1 + 1 + carry 1 = 1 0 0.

```
   1101
   1011
   1101
─────────
100101
```

Add rightmost column = 1 + 1 + 1 so we have 1 and need to also carry 1 to the next column

Add next column = 0 + 1 + 0 but we also have the 1 carried so 0 and we carry 1 again to the next column

Add next column 1 + 0 + 1 + the 1 that was carried so the answer is 1 with the carry of 1

In the fourth column we have 1 + 1 + 1 with a carry of 1 as well. Adding four 1s results in a 0 in this column with a 1 carried two columns to the left

Two new columns need to be created for the 1 to be carried across by two columns

The answer: 100101

Binary shift

If we shift the decimal point in a decimal number to the right it multiplies the number by 10.

So 1.2 would become 12. If we move the point two places it would become 120. This is because we use a 10-unit numbering system. Binary uses a 2-unit system and therefore a left shift one place to the left in a binary number is the same as multiplying by 2.

Shift left 1 place.

Decimal	128	64	32	16	8	4	2	1
Input	0	0	1	0	0	1	0	1
Result	0	1	0	0	1	0	1	0

A left shift of 2 places is the same as multiplying by 4.

Decimal	128	64	32	16	8	4	2	1
Input	0	0	1	0	0	1	0	1
Result	1	0	0	1	0	1	0	0

A left shift of 3 places is the same as multiplying by 8.

Decimal	256	128	64	32	16	8	4	2	1
Input	0	0	0	1	0	0	1	0	1
Result	1	0	0	1	0	1	0	0	0

In general shifting N places left is the same as multiplying by 2 to the power N (written as 2^N).

If we shift to the right 1 place this is the same as dividing by 2.

Decimal	256	128	64	32	16	8	4	2	1
Input	0	0	1	0	0	1	0	1	0
Result	0	0	0	1	0	0	1	0	1

It is worth noting that for odd numbers this will be an approximation for integer values. For example, 15 shifted would give 7. This is because we lose the last digit in the number.

KEY POINT

Binary shifts can be used to perform simple multiplication/division by powers of 2.

A right shift of 2 places is the same as dividing by 4.

Decimal	256	128	64	32	16	8	4	2	1
Input	0	0	1	0	0	1	0	0	0
Result	0	0	0	0	1	0	0	1	0

A right shift of 3 places is the same as dividing by 8.

Decimal	256	128	64	32	16	8	4	2	1
Input	0	0	1	0	0	1	0	0	0
Result	0	0	0	0	0	1	0	0	1

In general shifting N places right is the same as dividing by 2 to the power N (written as 2^N).

Hexadecimal numbers

Computers can also use what are called **hexadecimal** (hex) numbers. There are 16 hexadecimal digits. As computers are binary machines, working with 1s and 0s, you may be asking the question as to why hexadecimal is used. After all, everything in a computer consists of combinations of 1s and 0s. The answer is the number of bits used for each number. You need four bits to code decimal numbers between 0 and 15. The reason for using hex is that one hex digit corresponds to exactly four bits and converting between the two is very easy as it can be done on a digit-by-digit basis. Humans find hex representation easier to remember and understand than the equivalent binary representation that a computer uses.

Hexadecimal digits look exactly the same as the decimal digits up to 9 but then there are the letters (A, B, C, D, E, F) in place of the decimal numbers 10 to 15.

So, a single hexadecimal digit can show 16 different values instead of the normal 10 like this:

Decimal	0	1	2	3	4	5	6	7	8	9	10	11	12	13	14	15
Hexadecimal	0	1	2	3	4	5	6	7	8	9	A	B	C	D	E	F

KEY POINT

Hexadecimal is a number system based on 16, where the numbers 10 to 15 are represented by the letters A to F.

KEY POINT

The word 'hexadecimal' means 'based on 16' (from Greek *hexa*: 'six' and Latin *decima*: 'a tenth part').

QUESTION

Briefly describe the term hexadecimal.

Hexadecimal to binary

Converting from hexadecimal to binary and binary to hexadecimal is fairly simple. We simply look up each hexadecimal digit to obtain the equivalent group of four binary digits.

Hexadecimal	Binary
0	0
1	1
2	10
3	11
4	100
5	101
6	110
7	111
8	1000
9	1001
A	1010
B	1011
C	1100
D	1101
E	1110
F	1111

A hexadecimal number of A2DE would give the following 4 sets of binary digits:

1010   0010   1101   1110

Binary = 1010001011011110

Binary to hexadecimal

We convert from binary to hexadecimal in reverse, so to convert 01001110 to hexadecimal we can use the table to find the digits. Using the table, 0100 is converted to digit 4 and 1110 to digit E. The answer, therefore, is 4E.

Exponents

In mathematics, a base is a number that is raised to a power. Another name for power is exponent. An exponent tells you how many times the base number is used as a factor. A base of five raised to the second power is called 'five squared' and means 'five times five.' Five raised to the third power is called 'five cubed' and means 'five times five times five.' The base can be any sort of number including whole numbers or decimal numbers. For example, 3^4 can be written as 3 raised to the 4th power, which simply means you multiply 3 times itself 4 times ($3 \times 3 \times 3 \times 3$). Converting binary to decimal is really quite simple. All you do is apply the same technique, except this time using a 2 instead of a 10.

For example, if we want to know what a binary number 100011_2 (base 2) is in our decimal system (base 10) we can calculate this by the following:

100111 = 32 + 0 + 0 + 4 + 2 + 1 = 39

This is because each move to the left in a base 2 system multiplies by a factor of two:

32   16   8   4   2   1

Hexadecimal uses a base of 16 so $4B7F_{16}$ (base 16) is:

4B7F = 16,384 + 2816 + 112 + 15 = 19,327

This is because each move to the left in a base 16 system also adds another multiplication to our equation hence each move to the left is raised by the power of 16 so relative to its position we have:

4	B	7	F
16^3	16^2	16^1	16^0
4096	256	16	1

When we then add the values at each position:

F = 15 × 1 = 15

7 = 17 × 16 = 112

B = 11 × 256 = 2816

4 = 4 × 4096 = 16,384

When we add these together we get the answer.

Decimals to hexadecimal

Converting decimal number to hexadecimal numbers is much harder than converting decimals to binary numbers.

We always work *backwards* to convert these numbers.

QUESTION

How many possible values are in a single-digit base-16 number system?

So a decimal number of 1128 is converted to hexadecimal as follows:

What to do	Division	Integer	Remainder (in hexadecimal)
Start by dividing the number by 16, that is 1128/16. 1128 divided by 16 is 70.5. So the integer division result is 70, record this in the Integer column. The remainder is (70.5 – 70) is 0.5. This is then multiplied by 16, giving a result of 8. Record this in the Remainder column.	1128/16	70	8
Now divide the result number by 16: 70/16. 70/16 = 4.375. So the integer division result is 4. The remainder, 0.375, is multiplied by 16, which is 6.	70/16	4	6
The next stage is 4/16 = 0.25. The integer division result is 0. The remainder, 0.25, is multiplied by 16, which is 4.	4/16	0	4
Stop because the result is already 0 (0 divided by 16 will always be 0).			
We now have the hexadecimal equivalent of the decimal number by working up from the bottom of our remainder column: 468			

Hexadecimal to decimal

So what if the number 1128 was a hexadecimal number and not a decimal number, and we wanted to find its decimal equivalent? This would be calculated as follows:

The last number is 8. It represents $8 \times (16^0) = 8$

The next number is 2. This represents $2 \times (16^1) = 32$

The next number is 1. This will be $1 \times (16^2) = 256$

And lastly $1 \times (16^3) = 4096$

If we add the totals together, 1128 in hexadecimal = 4392 in decimal.

You may want to remember some of the powers of 16.

Power of 16	Result
16^0	1
16^1 = 16	16
16^2 = 16 × 16	256
16^3 = 16 × 16 × 16	4096
16^4 = 16 × 16 × 16 ×16	65536

You may be wondering about the letters. They work the same way, so FA8 working backwards would be:

$8 \times 1 = 8$

$10 \times 16 = 160$ (remember A = 10 and this has to be multiplied by 16^1)

$15 \times 256 = 3840$ (remember F = 15 and this has to be multiplied by 16^2)

The total in decimal would be 4008.

QUESTION

True or False: 51 is hex for 'q'.

QUESTION

What is a base-2 number system also known as?

QUESTION

What is a base-16 number system also known as?

QUESTION

Convert the decimal number 188 to hexadecimal (remember to write down the remainder in hexadecimal, not decimal).

QUESTION

Work out the decimal representation of the hexadecimal number D48.

13 Binary and Hexadecimal Numbers

Python has a set of built-in functions bin() and hex() to convert decimal numbers into other number systems. These functions take an integer (in decimal) and return a string.

```
dec = int(input("Please enter an integer: "))

print("The decimal value of",dec,"is:")

print(bin(dec),"converted to binary.")

print(hex(dec),"converted to hexadecimal.")
```

Output:

Please enter an integer: 51

The decimal value of 51 is:

00110011 converted to binary.

0033 converted to hexadecimal.

CHAPTER REVIEW

In this chapter we have explored binary and hexadecimal numbers.

Remember, before tackling any computer science task or question on this topic you must:

- understand the binary number system
- understand the hexadecimal number system
- understand how binary can be used to represent whole numbers
- understand how hexadecimal can be used to represent whole numbers
- understand the following number bases:
  - decimal (base 10)
  - binary (base 2)
  - hexadecimal (base 16)
- be able to convert in both directions between:
  - binary and decimal
  - binary and hexadecimal
  - decimal and hexadecimal
- understand that computers use binary to represent all data and instructions
- explain why hexadecimal is often used in computer science
- be able to add together up to three binary numbers
- be able to apply a binary shift to a binary number
- describe situations where binary shifts can be used.

14 The Language Computers Actually Use

Now we know some basics about computational thinking, algorithms and the number system computers use, we need to understand how computers work and how they handle **data**. Raw data is unprocessed data and refers to a collection of numbers and characters. Data can be something simple and can seem random. When data is processed, organised, structured or presented in a given context which makes it useful, it is called **information**.

Machine code

Although you are learning a programming language, using numbers and characters that are used in common English, computers only understand **machine code**. Computers do not understand our language, which uses words and letters. But machine code, while easily understood by computers, is almost

KEY POINT !

Data are the facts or details from which **information** is derived. Data itself has no meaning, but becomes information when it is interpreted.

KEY POINT !

Machine code is the language made up of binary coded instructions that is used directly by a computer.

impossible for humans to use because it consists entirely of numbers.

The code to add two numbers might look something like this:

49 00 FE 49 00 FF 91 00 22 F1 00 FA D1 00 FE 91 00 22 71 00 FA A1 00 20 F1 00 1F 51 00 1F 00

High- and low-level languages

You may be wondering how a computer will understand your programming if it can only read machine code made up of 1s and 0s and you are using words and numbers. It is similar to you speaking English but the person you are giving instructions to only speaking a foreign language. To enable the computer to understand us we use another form of abstraction, and a **compiler** or **interpreter**. First, we write our code in a format we can understand. We say that this is a **high-level language**. Our language is removed from the computer language by abstraction. In computer science, a **low-level language** is a programming language that provides little or no abstraction from a computer's instruction set, whereas a high-level language is one a human can more easily understand.

You may be a little confused here as we used the same term 'abstraction' when we identified the problem when we were looking at computational thinking in the first chapter. We did this by removing unnecessary information and data. Abstraction here is similar in that it is the process of extracting the underlying essence of a concept, removing any dependence on the low-level code needed by the computer. It refers to the distinction between the properties of an entity and its internal needs. It is abstraction that allows us to ignore the internal details of a complex device such as a computer, car or microwave oven, and just use it. To drive a car, you don't need to know how the steering wheel turns the wheels, you just need to know that it does. This is also an abstraction.

Assembly language

Assembly language is at the level of telling the processor what to do.

> **KEY POINT** ❗
>
> A computer's CPU can only understand instructions that are written in machine code.

> **KEY POINTS** ❗
>
> ● A **compiler** is a computer program that translates C, C++, BASIC, Pascal and similar high-level programming languages into machine language.
>
> ● An **interpreter** is a program that executes a source program by reading it one line at a time and doing the specified operations immediately.
>
> ● A **high-level language** is a programming language designed to allow people to write programs without having to understand the inner workings of the computer.
>
> ● A **low-level language** is a programming language that provides little or no abstraction from a computer's instruction set.

> **KEY POINT** ❗
>
> **Assembly language** has a 1:1 correspondence with machine code.

As we know, the word 'low' refers to the small or non-existent amount of abstraction between the language used and machine code. Because of this, low-level languages are often described as being 'close to the hardware'. This code is what the hardware uses.

If we look at an example of assembly language you will see how it differs from a high-level language.

```
model small
data
opr1 dw 1234h
opr2 dw 0002h
result dw 01 dup(?),'$'
code
   mov ax,@data
   mov ds,ax
   mov ax,opr1
   mov bx,opr2
   clc
   add ax,bx
   mov di,offset result
   mov [di], ax
   mov ah,09h
   mov dx,offset result
   int 21h
   mov ah,4ch
   int 21h
   end
```

KEY POINT

Machine code and assembly code are low-level. Everything else is high-level.

QUESTION

What is the purpose of an interpreter?

KEY POINT

Assembly language is a low-level programming language. It uses mnemonic codes and labels to represent machine-level code. Each instruction corresponds to just one machine operation.

QUESTION

What are the advantages of writing in high-level code compared to machine code?

Assemblers, compilers and interpreters

As you will know by now, computers can only understand machine-level language (binary, 0 and 1).

You also know that it is difficult to write and maintain programs in low-level machine code. Programs written in the code of high-level language and some low-level language need to be converted into machine code using **translators**.

Translators are just computer programs which accept a program written in high-level or low-level language and produce an equivalent machine-level program as output.

These translators are of one of three types:

- assembler
- compiler
- interpreter.

Machine code and assembly language

Machine code is the only form of program instructions that the computer hardware can understand and execute directly. Machine code is represented by using binary and is the basic language that all the computer's instructions will be in. All other forms of code must be translated into machine code in order to be executed by the computer's hardware. We say 'binary' because machine language is a base-2 numbering system (made up of 0s and 1s), and 'bi' means two.

Machine code is different for each type of computer. A program in machine code for a PC will not run on another system using a different processor.

Assembly language is the next step up, using specific keywords and terms. Assembly language is a low-level language that is specific to the architecture of the CPU. Assembly language is therefore a representation of machine code using symbols, not the machine code itself. Because machine code is specific to each type of computer hardware, assembly languages are also specific to each type of computer. However, all machine languages and assembly languages look very similar, even though they are not interchangeable.

KEY POINT

Binary is a system of numbers using only two digits 0 and 1 (also called the base-2 system), unlike the decimal (or denary) system in everyday use that uses 0 to 9 (base-10).

KEY POINT

A **translator** is a program to convert high-level or assembly level commands into machine code.

KEY POINT

The internal, logical structure and organisation of the computer hardware is called the computer architecture.

The use of easy-to-understand representations, rather than binary, helps programmers to write programs in assembly language without having to deal with very long binary strings. The machine code for an instruction to add two numbers could be 01101110, but in assembly language this can be represented by the symbol ADD.

A high-level language is a language that is convenient for human beings to understand. High-level programming languages must be translated into machine code for execution. This process is called compilation if a compiler is used.

An **assembler** is used to assemble the code of some low-level language into machine-level language. An assembler translates each instruction in the source program into a single machine code instruction.

KEY POINT

An **assembler** is a program that translates assembly language into machine code.

Compilers and interpreters

Compilers and interpreters are used to convert the code of high-level languages into machine code.

KEY POINT

Assembler directives are instructions to the translating program.

Although both compilers and interpreters perform essentially the same task, there is a difference in the way they work.

Interpreter	Compiler
It converts the program into machine code one statement at a time or calls a routine in its own code to execute the command.	It converts all the code of the program into machine code at the same time.
It takes less time to analyse the source code, but the overall program execution time is slower.	The first time the program is run it takes a large amount of time to analyse the source code, but once the compilation has taken place there is no need for any translation on subsequent runs of the program.
A client buying the software would need the translator software.	A client buying the software would not need the translator software.
It continues translating the program until the first error is met, in which case it stops.	It generates error messages after searching all the errors of a program and then lists them.

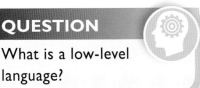

QUESTION

What is a low-level language?

An interpreter checks a program statement by statement. After checking one statement, it converts that statement into machine code or calls a routine in its own code to execute the command and then executes that statement. The process continues to the last statement of the program. Rather than producing a machine code copy of a program that will be executed later, an interpreter actually executes a program from its high-level form. Compiled languages are normally faster and

more efficient than interpreted languages during execution. Systems that require high performance are therefore often created in a compiled language. A compiler would usually be used for software distribution, whereas an interpreter might be used when developing software or where the software might have to run on a range of hardware platforms.

TASK

Do some research into how assembly languages are used now, what they are used for and why.

RESEARCH TASK

Use this book and other sources such as the internet to research how to identify and correct errors in algorithms.

Why use low-level languages?

Because there are fewer steps involved for the machine, assembly language, instructions tend to be processed faster than high-level languages even though there are many more lines of code that need to be written by the programmer.

High-level languages were created so that programmers didn't have to write large numbers of assembly or binary instructions to do simple tasks. They are referred to as high-level because there are more steps that need to be taken to translate them into machine language. They first need to be converted to assembly language and then the assembly language needs to be converted into machine code.

Writing in low-level and high-level languages

There are both advantages and disadvantages of writing in low-level languages. Low-level languages allow you to directly interact with the hardware and memory. Since you are writing at machine level you control the level of performance of the code, whereas when writing in a high-level language you have to rely on the compiler to optimise your code. By using pointers, you can directly access and set the value of addresses in memory. However, low-level languages are procedural and almost always require more lines of code. There is also less support than high-level languages, in both development and debug environments, making low-level languages very hard to read or learn. Assembly language is also often used in embedded systems.

When writing things like device drivers it is easier to talk with hardware devices and input/output (I/O) ports in a low-level language, as not all high-level languages support low-level I/O.

Higher level languages have a major advantage over machine and assembly languages as they are similar to the language we use every day of our lives. This makes higher level languages easier to learn and use. Software can be developed more quickly (and hence more cheaply) in a high-level language as the commands are more powerful so fewer are required.

Hardware and software integration

But understanding machine code on its own is not enough, you need to explore the interaction between code (programming language) and databases/text-files, prototyping, software development, computer models and websites. It is also important to understand the interactions between the code and the developments in hardware.

CHAPTER REVIEW

In this chapter we looked at machine code and high- and low-level programming.

Remember, before tackling any computer science task or question on this topic you must:

- understand programming in a high-level language
- understand how instructions within a computer must be in a low-level language
- understand the terms compiled and assembled languages
- know that there are different levels of programming language:
  - low-level language
  - high-level language
- explain the main differences between low-level and high-level languages
- understand the advantages and disadvantages of low-level and high-level languages
- know that machine code and assembly language are considered to be low-level languages and explain the differences between them
- understand the advantages and disadvantages of low-level language programming compared with high-level language programming.

15 Computing and Data Representation

Translating the data

Let's consider what happens when we put data/information into a computer. When you add data to your computer you enter it in a format that you understand, using characters and numbers that you are able to read. But this has to be translated into a computer-readable, low-level format. As this is done through an input device, we call it **input**. Of course, once the computer has processed the data for us to understand it, it needs to be converted back into a format that we understand using an output device, so this is referred to as **output**. Together these are referred to as I/O.

In pseudo-code you will often see the words: GET, USERINPUT, INPUT or READ used for inputting data. For outputting data you will see the words: OUTPUT, RETURN, PRINT, DISPLAY, WRITE and PUT.

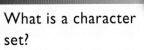
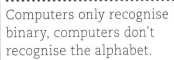
Character sets

You may be wondering, if computers can only work in 1s and 0s how can things like text be represented? Text is represented by character sets. A character set is simply a list of characters such as a, b, c, d and the numerical codes used to represent each letter or character. By agreeing to use a particular character set, computer manufacturers have made the processing of text data easier.

We will explore two character sets: ASCII and Unicode.

Representing text using ASCII

ASCII stands for American Standard Code for Information Interchange. As we have seen, computers can only understand numbers, so an ASCII code is the numerical representation of characters such as 'a' to 'z', '@' or even an action of some sort.

The original ASCII only uses 7-bit numbers to represent the letters, numerals and common punctuation used in the English language. As there are two possibilities per bit, we have $2^7 = 128$ possible values it can represent, from 0 to 127 inclusive. Remember, 0 is also a reference so we have 128 possible values to store our characters.

Each of those 128 values is assigned to a character (Figure 15.1). For example, in ASCII the number 65 (01000001) represents an upper-case letter A and 61 (00111101) represents an equals sign. So if the output sent to a display receives an ASCII value of 65, it displays an upper-case letter A on the screen. There is no real reason that A has to be character number 65, that's just the number the developers working on telegraph systems chose when ASCII was first developed.

If we wanted to translate 'Hello' from 'Hello World' into ASCII it would look like this:

ASCII	01001000	01100101	01101100	01101100	1101111
Text	H	E	l	l	o

	0000	0001	0010	0011	0100	0101	0110	0111
0000	NULL	DLE		0	@	P	`	p
0001	SOH	DC1	!	1	A	Q	a	q
0010	STX	DC2	"	2	B	R	b	r
0011	ETX	DC3	#	3	C	S	c	s
0100	EDT	DC4	$	4	D	T	d	t
0101	ENQ	NAK	%	5	E	U	e	u
0110	ACK	SYN	&	6	F	V	f	v
0111	BEL	ETB	'	7	G	W	g	w
1000	BS	CAN	(	8	H	X	h	x
1001	HT	EM	)	9	I	Y	i	y
1010	LF	SUB	*	:	J	Z	j	z
1011	VT	ESC	+	;	K	[	k	{
1100	FF	FS	,	<	L	\	l	|
1101	CR	GS	-	=	M	]	m	}
1110	SO	RS	.	>	N	^	n	~
1111	SI	US	/	?	O	_	o	DEL

Figure 15.1 *ASCII codes*

Extended ASCII

ASCII works fine for English strings such as 'Hello World!', but what if we want to store a German string such as: 'Es gefällt mir nicht' (translates as: I do not like it)? Basically we can't use ASCII for this as it doesn't have a code for ä.

So it was decided that as ASCII had an extra bit which was not used, if ASCII was made into a 8-bit code rather than 7, it could store another 128 values. This system is called extended ASCII.

The problem was that different groups used the same initial ASCII characters, but came up with different extended ASCII character set numbers. For example, in the Western Europe extended ASCII character set, number 224 represents a lower-case letter A with a grave accent. But in Eastern Europe the same number represents a lower-case letter R with an acute accent. Added to this a 256-character set is no use in languages like Chinese and Japanese, where there are thousands of characters in common use.

For other languages including Chinese, Japanese, Hebrew, etc. there needed to be a different coding systems. The most common choice is Unicode.

QUESTION

Using ASCII, convert 46 6F 6F 74 62 61 6C 6C to text.

KEY POINT

Unicode is a system of up to 32 bits to code the character set of a computer (usually 16-bit or 32-bit versions).

The Unicode character set

Although originally designed for 16 bits, the latest version of Unicode stores each character with up to 32 bits. Unicode can also use 8 bits. It presently contains over 110,000 characters and has space for 1,114,111 different values that can be used for characters, so at present only around 10% are used.

Figure 15.2 shows just a few of the foreign language characters supported. The first 128 character are the same as ASCII.

Code (hex)	Character	Source
0041	A	English (Latin)
042F	Я	Russian (Cyrillic)
262F	☯	Symbols
03A3	Σ	Greek
211E	℞	Letterlike symbols
21CC	⇌	Arrows
28FF	⣿	Braille
2EDD	⻝	Chinese/Japanese/Korean (Common)

Figure 15.2 *Some foreign language character codes*

Using Python to convert from character to Unicode

In Python it is easy to get a Unicode value from a character using the function chr() and to convert the other way using ord().

For example, for the character a, we can use the following to find its Unicode code:

```
ord('a')
```

Output: 97

In reverse:

```
chr(97)
```

Output: a

Writing in hexadecimal

Using this knowledge, we can see how this would work if we wanted to explore the use of hexadecimal.

When we start to program, we normally start with 'Hello World'. This looks easy, but let's explore what is happening if we write 'Hello' in hexadecimal.

We type 'Hello'. This consists of separate letters 'H' 'e' 'l' 'l' 'o'.

We can use binary or hexadecimal (hex) for this. You learnt about these from other sections of the book, but for this we use hex. First, we revise the equivalents in each system:

Decimal	Binary	Hexadecimal
0	0000	0
1	0001	1
2	0010	2
3	0011	3
4	0100	4
5	0101	5
6	0110	6
7	0111	7
8	1000	8
9	1001	9
10	1010	A
11	1011	B
12	1100	C
13	1101	D
14	1110	E
15	1111	F

So, F3C2 in hex would look like this in binary: 1111 0011 1100 0010

So if we now convert each letter to ASCII we will have:

H = Write 48 (hex)

e = Write 65 (hex)

l = Write 6C (hex)

l = Write 6C (hex)

o = Write 6F (hex)

TASK

Write the word 'Computer' in binary using ASCII.

QUESTION

What is a universal encoding system that provides a unique number for every character, regardless of language, program or platform?

Data standards

Of course, computers need to show more than text. To help programmers, each data system is controlled by a set of **data standards**. This is needed so that different systems can still read the language we code in. Some of the most common file data standards are shown in the table below.

Type of data	Standards
Images	JPEG, GIF, TIFF, BMP, GIF, etc.
Sound	WAV, MP3, AU, etc.
Moving images	Quick Time, MPEG-2, MPEG-4
Alphanumeric	ASCII, Unicode
Outline graphics/fonts	True Type, PDF, PostScript

Difference between analogue and digital data

Many things in the natural word are continuous. A number line is continuous, with values growing infinitely large and small. You can always come up with a number larger or smaller than any given number. The numeric space between any two integers is infinite. For example, any number can be divided in half.

But the world is not just infinite in a mathematical sense. The spectrum of colours is a continuous rainbow of infinite shades.

Theoretically, you could always close the distance between you and your home by half, and you would never actually reach home.

Computers, on the other hand, are finite. Computer memory and other hardware devices have only so much room to store and manipulate data and sampled data. In computer science we can only work towards representing enough of the world to satisfy our computational needs and our senses of sight and sound.

There are two types of data:

● Analogue data is continuous, analogous to the actual information it represents. For example, a mercury thermometer is an analogue device. The mercury rises in

direct proportion to the temperature. Computers cannot work with analogue information.

- Digital data breaks the information up into separate steps. This is done by breaking the analogue information into pieces and representing those pieces using binary digits.

Computers need to convert analogue data to digital data as they are binary devices and cannot store continuous values.

Computing systems can only store a limited amount of information, even if the limit is very large. To be able to fully understand data representation, you need to first understand the differences between digital and analogue data. Analogue data is continuous, analogous to the actual information it represents.

For example, a mercury thermometer is an analogue device. The mercury rises in direct proportion to the temperature. Computers cannot work with analogue information. Digital data breaks the information up into separate steps.

Bits and bytes

Bit (b)   A bit has a value of 1 or 0.

Byte (B)   A byte is eight bits.

Bits are so small that we cannot use them for comparison from now on, so we use bytes instead.

Originally the following conventions set by standards bodies were used:

New name	Old name	Value
Kibibyte (KiB)	Kilobyte (kB)	1,024 bytes
Mebibyte (MiB)	Megabyte (MB)	1,048,576 bytes (or it is easier to remember as 1,024 kibibytes)
Gibibyte (GiB)	Gigabyte (GB)	1,024 mebibytes or 1,048,576 kibibytes
Tebibyte (TiB)	Terabyte (TB)	1,024 gibibytes or 1,048,576 mebibytes

KEY POINT ❗

The magic number to remember used to be 1024 but now it's 1000.

Now that base-10 definitions have been officially standardised, software is phasing out the base-2 usage and often refers to powers of 10. The only place you will often find the computer industry referring to powers of 1,024 is with regard to the size of RAM modules. The new base-10 definitions are shown below.

Name	New value
Kilobyte (kB)	1,000 bytes
Megabyte (MB)	1,000,000 bytes (or it is easier to remember as 1,000 kilobytes)
Gigabyte (GB)	1,000 megabytes or 1,000,000 kilobytes
Terabyte (TB)	1,000 gigabytes or 1,000,000 megabytes

Bitmaps and binary images

The quality of image you see as an output on a display is based upon the resolution. The first type of **resolution** you are likely to come across on any computer device is the number of pixels.

When we talk about **bitmap** images we are talking about a regular rectangular mesh of cells called **pixels**, each pixel containing a colour value (Figure 15.3). A pixel (short for picture element), is the smallest area of an image that can be individually altered; it is a single dot.

Bitmaps have two parameters, the first is the number of pixels and the second is the colour depth per pixel. There are other attributes that are applied to bitmaps but they come from these two fundamental parameters. The number of pixels is defined by the height and width.

 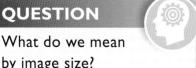
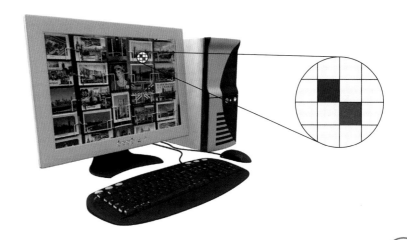

Figure 15.3 *Pixels on a computer screen*

Bitmaps are always orientated horizontally and vertically. Pixels are usually defined as being square although in practice they may be rectangular and have other aspect ratios.

In the majority of situations bitmaps are used to represent images on the computer.

There are a large number of pixels making up the computer's display. To give you some idea of what this means, a modern monitor is 1,920 × 1,080 which represents a grid of 1,920 pixels wide, by 1,080 pixels high.

If we change the display settings to 2,560 × 1,440 there will be many more pixels on the display. Because the monitor has not changed size, the pixels will become smaller, making each element on the screen smaller but giving better definition. The advantage of using higher resolutions is that smaller pixels let us display images with much more detail.

Black-and-white image using binary

Using what we now know, we can easily describe a black-and-white image using binary, as shown in Figure 15.4.

1	1	1	1	1	1	111111
1	0	1	1	0	1	101101
1	0	1	1	0	1	101101
1	1	1	1	1	1	111111
1	0	0	0	0	1	100001
1	1	1	1	1	1	111111

Figure 15.4 *Image in binary code*

Colour depth

Although **colour depth** affects the amount of memory a picture requires, it does not affect the size at which the image is displayed. It has a major effect on the quality of the image.

The resolution of an image is determined by the number of pixels. These are individually addressable points that make up the screen image. In a similar way it can be the number of dots that make up a printed image. The more pixels or dots that are used to create an image, the more detailed the image can be and the sharper it will appear when we look at it.

QUESTION

How does the resolution of an image affect the size of the file?

RESEARCH TASK

Use this book and other sources such as the internet to research how to convert binary data into a black-and-white image, and how to convert a black-and-white image into binary data.

KEY POINT

Colour depth (or bit depth) refers to the number of bits used for each pixel or dot. The more bits, the more colours that can be represented.

When using any bitmap image, whatever resolution we choose, the picture's data has to be stored for each pixel or printer dot. This means the higher the resolution, the more data there will be that needs to be stored. But as well as the pixel data we also have colour depth data. This data is used to describe the maximum number of colours that are used in the image. The higher the number of colours used, the more realistic the image will appear. As with the number of pixels, the chosen colour depth affects the file size of the image: the more colours that we want to record, the larger the data set will be for the given image.

Each pixel in a bitmap contains colour information. The information content is always the same for all the pixels in a particular bitmap. The amount of colour information can vary according to what the application requires but there are some standards. Typical colour depths include 1-bit (mono), 8-bit, 16-bit and 24-bit. To work out how many colours that is, simply calculate 2 to the power of the number of bits.

> ## KEY POINT ❗
>
> If you want to calculate the size of an image, you need to use colour depth and the number of pixels within your calculations.
>
> Size in pixels = W × H
> Size in bits = W × H × D
> Size in bytes = (W × H × D)/8
>
> where W = image width, H = image height and D = colour depth in bits.

Colour and RGB

1-bit (black-and-white)

This is the smallest possible information content that can be held for each pixel. Pixels with a 0 are referred to as black, and pixels with a 1 as white. Although only two states are possible they are often interpreted not as black and white but as any two colours: 0 is mapped to one colour, 1 is mapped to another colour.

8-bit greys

Each pixel takes 1 byte (8 bits) of storage, resulting in 256 different states. These states are mapped onto a range of greys from black to white. The bitmap produced is referred to as a greyscale image.

0 is normally black and 255 white (Figure 15.5). The grey levels are the numbers in between, for example in a linear scale 127 would be a 50% grey level.

Figure 15.5 *Grey levels*

0   255

24-bit RGB

Moving on from 8-bit grey we have 8 bits allocated to each primary colour red, green, and blue. In each colour the value of 0 refers to none of that colour and 255 refers to fully saturated colour. Each component has 256 different states so there are 16,777,216 possible colours.

8-bit indexed colour

Indexed colour is a much more economical way of storing colour bitmaps without using 3 bytes per pixel. Each pixel has one byte associated with it. But the value in that byte is not a colour value but an index into a table of colours, called a palette or colour table.

If there are fewer than 256 colours in the image the bitmap will be the same quality as a 24-bit bitmap but will be stored with one third the data. Colour and animation effects can be achieved by simply modifying the palette, which immediately changes the appearance of the bitmap.

32-bit RGB

This is the same as 24-bit colour but with an extra 8-bit bitmap known as an alpha channel. This channel can be used to create masked areas or represent transparency.

Calculating image sizes

Although file sizes will be slightly larger than the simple calculation will suggest, due to other data necessary to create the image, it is possible to calculate an approximate file size for an image.

In a black-and-white image, with a colour depth of one bit per pixel, file size is calculated using the number of pixels divided by 8 to convert it to bytes.

To calculate the number of pixels, we simple multiply the width in pixels by the height:

$100 \times 100 = 10,000$ pixels

Therefore, a 100 by 100 black-and-white image will be:

$(100 \times 100)/8 = 1,250$ bytes

We now need to divide by 1,000 to get kilobytes, so

1,250/1,000 = 1.25 kB

If we have a colour image, we need to multiply by the number of bits needed for the colours. This is what colour depth relates to. Therefore, for a 256-colour bitmap of the same size the equation will be:

((Number of pixels × bits needed for 256 colours)/8)/1,000

So first we need to work out the number of pixels which is:

100 × 100 = 10,000

Next we need the number of bits needed for our 256 colours. In an 8-bit colour graphic image file, each pixel is represented by one 8-bit byte, so a 256-colour image would require a colour depth of one byte (8 bits).

10,000 × 8 = 80,000

80,000/8 = 10,000

10,000/1,000 = 10 kB

Photographic images

Originally, cameras used film. They were based upon the first pinhole camera (Figure 15.6).

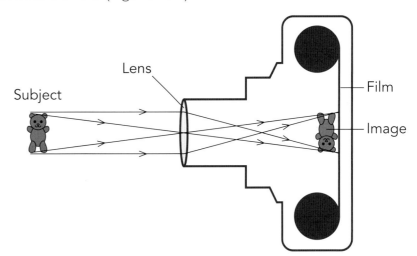

Figure 15.6 *Pinhole camera*

An image was projected onto a sheet of light sensitive paper (film) placed at the back of a box. The photographic paper was coated with light sensitive chemicals (called emulsion), which recorded an analogue image of the scene. Emulsion in the areas on the photographic paper which received light would undergo a chemical change based upon the light that hit it and those areas not receiving light would not.

In contrast, the process of taking a digital photograph is very different (Figure 15.7). A camera lens is used to focus the light from a scene not onto a film but onto a silicon detector (a sensor circuit). The sensor surface is divided into a two-dimensional pixel grid, sometimes called picture-elements.

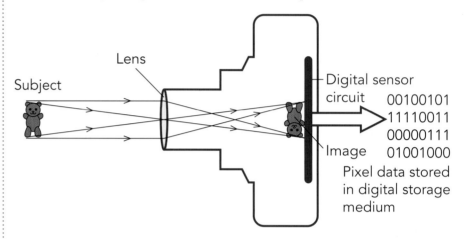

Figure 15.7 *Digital camera*

The light intensity at each pixel (an analogue quantity) is sensed and converted to a multi-bit binary number.

Sound systems

Original sound is analogue, it's how our ears work. But to turn this sound into something a computer can handle we need to create a digital sound wave (Figure 15.8).

Figure 15.8 *Conversion of analogue wave to digital*

To compare digital and analogue sound, you need to look at a variety of factors.

Sample rate

In analogue recordings, the machine is constantly recording any sound or noise that is coming through the microphones. In digital recording you don't have a constant recording, you have a series of **samples** or snapshots which are a measure of amplitude at a given point in time and are taken from the sound being recorded.

If you think about how animation works, a series of separate pictures that have a slight difference are shown one after another to make it look like something is moving. In this case, digital recording takes a series of 'snapshot pictures' of what the sound is like and turns it into a digital recording.

The vertical lines in the images indicate the times at which the samples were taken. As with images, the more snapshots you have the better the sound quality (Figure 15.9), but at a cost of memory use and storage space.

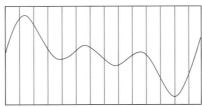

Lower sample rates take fewer snapshots of the waveform …

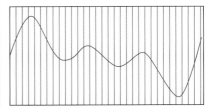

Faster sample rates take more snapshots …

resulting in a rough recreation of the waveform

resulting in a smoother and more detailed recreation of the waveform

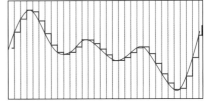

Figure 15.9 *Different sample rates*

Sample rates are measured in hertz (Hz) or thousands of hertz (kHz–kilohertz). For example, 44.1 kHz is equal to 44,100 samples of audio recorded every second.

The sample rate you choose depends on what the audio is going to be used for. If you wanted to record a song to put on to CD you would usually use 44.1 kHz.

Sample resolution

The other important factor in determining audio quality is the **sample resolution**. This refers to how many different values the samples can take on. The higher the sample resolution, the more accurate the representation of the level of each sample. But the higher the sample resolution the more memory is required to store each sample.

Digital audio is normally found in one of two resolutions:

- 8-bit: used for some lower-quality recording formats
- 16-bit: this is the standard for CD audio and sound cards. With 16-bit samples there are 65,536 different values, which is more than the human ear can distinguish between.

Calculating file sizes

We can calculate sound file sizes based on the sampling rate and the sample resolution using the following formula:

File size (bits) = rate × res × secs = sampling rate

where res = sample resolution and secs = number of seconds

EXAMPLE

If we want 30 seconds of mono sound, where the sample rate is 44,100 Hz and the sample resolution is 16 bits, we will have:

44,100 × 16 × 30 = 21168000 bits

(divided by 8 as we have 8 bits in a byte then divide by 1,000 to convert to kilobytes)

= 2,646 kB

(divided by 1,000 to get MB)

= 2.64 MB

The size of 30 seconds of stereo sound would be:

(44,100 × 16 × 2 × 30)/(8 × 1,000)

= 5,292 kB

≈ 5.3 MB

By increasing the number of bits (units of information), the amount of detail contained in each sample is increased. An example would be the sentence: 'The large black cloud opened up covering the ground with white snow.' This contains more information than 'It snowed.' The more data the more information you have.

Bitrate

Digital music files are measured by the amount of information they can play per second. It is usually measured in kbps, or kilobits per second. This is the amount of sound information presented to the listener every second. The bitrate is the number of bits per second.

Sound files played over internet radio are 56 or 64 kbps, to allow faster transport over networks. The standard for near-CD quality is 128 kbps, and some files go up to 320 kbps.

If we have a 30-second audio file sampled at a rate of 44.1 kHz and quantised using 8 bits we can calculate its size by:

bitrate = bitsPerSample × samplesPerSecond × number of channels

To get the file size we would simply multiply the bitrate by the duration (in seconds), and divide by 8 (to get from bits to bytes):

fileSize = (bitsPerSample × samplesPerSecond × channels × duration)/8

EXAMPLE

A stereo recording has two channels for recording with 8-bit bit depth so the bitrate is:

8 × 44,100 × 2 = 705,600 kbps

So in this case 30 seconds of stereo will take up:

(8 × 44,100 × 2 × 30)/8 = 2,646,000 bytes

QUESTION

What effect does a high bitrate have on the number of sound files that can be stored on a CD?

CHAPTER REVIEW

In this chapter we have explored how data is represented in a computer.

We looked at sample rates, bitmapped images, data size and the differences between analogue and digital data.

Remember, before tackling any computer science task or question on this topic you must:

- understand what a character set is and be able to describe the following character encoding methods:
  - 7-bit ASCII
  - Unicode
- describe the purpose of Unicode and the advantages of Unicode over ASCII
- know that Unicode uses the same codes as ASCII up to 127
- convert character to code and vice versa
- understand how data is stored digitally within the computer
- know that:
  - a bit is the fundamental unit of information
  - a byte is a group of 8 bits
- know that quantities of bytes can be described using prefixes; know the names, symbols and corresponding values for the decimal prefixes:
  - kilo, 1 kB is 1,000 bytes
  - mega, 1 MB is 1,000 kilobytes
  - giga, 1 GB is 1,000 megabytes
  - tera, 1 TB is 1,000 gigabytes
- understand sample rates and sample resolution
- be able to describe the following for bitmaps:
  - size in pixels
  - colour depth
- calculate bitmap image sizes
- be able to describe how a bitmap represents an image using pixels and colour depth
- convert binary data into a black-and-white image (and vice versa)
- be able to describe using examples how the number of pixels and colour depth can affect the file size of a bitmap image
- understand that sound is analogue and that it must be converted to a digital form for storage and processing in a computer
- understand that sound waves are sampled to create the digital version of sound
- be able to describe the digital representation of sound in terms of:
  - sample rate
  - sample resolution
- calculate sound file sizes based on the sample rate and the sample resolution.

16 Data Size, Storage and Compression

If we stored photos of 3 MB in size on a hard drive with the following memory volumes this would be the outcome:

Hard drive capacity	Number of 3 MB digital images that could be stored
1 kilobyte (kB)	None
1 megabyte (MB)	None
1 gigabyte (GB)	333
1 terabyte (TB)	333,333
1 petabyte (PB)	333,333,333
1 exabyte (EB)	333,333,333,333
1 zettabyte (ZB)	333,333,333,333,333
1 yottabyte (YB)	333,333,333,333,333,333

This assumes that our photos are only 3 MB in size. **RAW** photographs can be over 100 MB in size. To achieve a size of 3 MB the file must be compressed.

Data compression

Data **compression** is a set of steps for packing data into a smaller 'electronic space' (data bits), while still allowing for the original data to be accessed and used. This is often achieved by eliminating the repetition of identical sets of data bits (redundancy).

Compression results in much smaller storage space requirements and is often much faster for communications.

Run-length encoding

We know that compressed data works more effectively on our mobile phones and portable computers. Now we need to learn how this works. We will first look at a bitmap image (you learnt about bitmapped images in the last chapter).

Run-Length Encoding (RLE) is a data compression algorithm supported by most bitmap file formats, for example TIFF, BMP, and PCX.

RLE is suitable for compressing any type of data, but the content of the data affects the compression ratio achieved by RLE. So let's explore what it is best suited to by looking at how it works.

RLE works by reducing the size of a repeating string. A repeating string is called a run, and is typically encoded into two bytes:

● the first byte represents the number of characters in the run and is called the run count

● the second byte is the value of the character in the run, which is in the range of 0 to 255, and is called the run value.

EXAMPLE

Uncompressed, a string character run of 20 X characters:

XXXXXXXXXXXXXXXXXXXX

would require 20 bytes to store the string in its uncompressed form.

The same string after RLE encoding would require only two bytes:

20X

The 20X code generated to represent the character string is called an RLE packet.

In our example, the first byte, 20, is the run count and contains the number of repetitions.

The second byte, X, is the run value and contains the actual repeated value in the run.

It is like going to a restaurant with 20 of your friends. If there are four things on the menu, the waitress will not write down a long list of 20 orders, she will simply write the menu item and put alongside this how many people want each item, for example burger × 2.

Compressing images

The most straightforward way of storing a bitmap is simply to list the bitmap information, byte after byte, row by row. Files stored by this method are often called RAW files.

To store using RLE, a new packet must be generated each time the run character changes, or each time the number of characters in the run exceeds the maximum count.

EXAMPLE

Here is a description of RLE on a simple black-and-white image. This works best for bitmaps with only a few colours. Consider the small, 16 × 10 pixel image of the pi symbol in Figure 16.1.

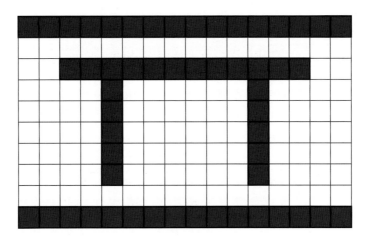

Figure 16.1 *Pixel image of pi symbol*

If we consider representing the pixels as letters, for example the blue pixels can be represented with the letter B, the first row would be BBBBBBBBBBBBBBBB, which could be compressed to 16 B.

In RAW format this would be:

```
B B B B B B B B B B B B B B B B
0 0 0 0 0 0 0 0 0 0 0 0 0 0 0 0
0 0 B B B B B B B B B B B B 0 0
0 0 0 0 B 0 0 0 0 0 0 B 0 0 0 0
0 0 0 0 B 0 0 0 0 0 0 B 0 0 0 0
0 0 0 0 B 0 0 0 0 0 0 B 0 0 0 0
0 0 0 0 B 0 0 0 0 0 0 B 0 0 0 0
0 0 0 0 B 0 0 0 0 0 0 B 0 0 0 0
0 0 0 0 0 0 0 0 0 0 0 0 0 0 0 0
B B B B B B B B B B B B B B B B
```

Using run-length encoding the first three rows would be:

```
16 B
16 0
2 0 12 B 2 0
```

While there are more details involved in actual implementations of RLE than described here, you can see how it would work.

Text

Long runs are rare in certain types of data. It is unlikely in text that the same character will occur in long runs as it did in our image. In a standard ASCII document only a few words would even have two characters the same. To encode a run in RLE requires a minimum of two characters worth of information as a run of single characters actually takes more space. Even data consisting entirely of two-character runs would remain the same size after RLE encoding. If only two of your friends go to the same restaurant, and each person orders a different item from the menu, there is no saving of time or space for the waitress to add how many people require each item.

But if we compare an ASCII document with a black-and-white image that is mostly white, such as a scanned page of a book, it will encode very well, due to the large amount of contiguous data that is all the same colour – white.

> **KEY POINT**
>
> ASCII (American Standard Code for Information Interchange) is a 7-bit system to code the character set on a computer.

Anything with relatively few runs of the same colour will not work as well as images with large areas of the same colour.

CHAPTER REVIEW

In this chapter we have explored data size, storage and compression.

Remember, before tackling any computer science task or question on this topic you must:

- understand the term compression
- explain how data can be compressed
- convert a black-and-white image into binary data.

17 Data Types

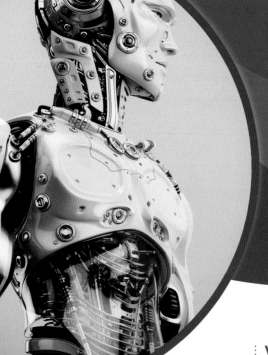

Why are data types important?

Most programming languages use statically typed variables. This means that when a variable is created the programmer must specify what type of data the variable will be using. The data type cannot be changed once it has been set.

Setting the type of a variable helps to prevent errors that might occur when a program is executed. Operations such as data sorting also rely on knowing what type of values are stored. Strings need to be sorted into alphabetical order whilst reals and integers need to be sorted into numeric order.

Data types

We need to explore how data is used in more detail. The most common types of data, and the ones you will be using, are called **primitive** data types.

Primitive data types are predefined types of data which are supported by the programming language.

Data can be stored in many different forms and the proper term for these forms is **data types**. In computing it is these forms that determine what actions, for instance, searching, sorting or calculating, can be performed on the data when it is held within a field of a database or a spreadsheet.

Figure 17.1 shows some of the common primitive data types that you will be using.

KEY POINT !

A **data type** is a classification of various types of data, such as real, integer or Boolean.

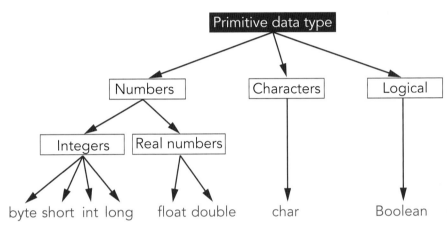

Figure 17.1 *Tree of data types*

In Python we have the following data types:

```
int        #32-bit integer
long       #Integer > 32 bits
float      #Floating point number
bool       #Boolean
str        #string
```

RESEARCH TASK

Use this book and other sources such as the internet to research data types.

Integer data types

Integer data types deal with whole numbers NOT decimal numbers.

An integer is a whole number (not a fractional number), but it can be positive, negative, or zero.

Examples of integers could be: −9, 3, 5, 8, 98 and 103.

KEY POINT !

An **integer** is a data type for representing whole numbers.

17 Data Types

QUESTION

In mathematics which of the following are integers?

6, −7, 2.6, 10, 4.5, 17, 17.0

Examples of numbers that are not integers could be: −1.33, 1 3/4, 3.14 and 1500.45

Different programming languages state the data types in different ways. Some versions of Python can be forced to use what is called a floating-point real number (described below).

```
int(17.0 / 8.0)

    #this will force Python to return an

    #integer rather than a float
```

but

```
float(16 / 8)

    #this will force Python to return a float value
```

Integers are usually sub-categorised in accordance with their capability of representing negative values, for example within C and C++ the data type unsigned short can deal with whole numbers from 0 to 65,535, whereas short can deal with whole numbers from −32,768 to +32,767.

You will need to research your chosen programming language to see how it deals with integers.

TASK

Explore how your chosen programming language deals with integers.

String data types

A string is a data type stored as a sequence of characters, often implemented as an array of bytes. As we have explored before, a string is usually stored as either a constant, or as some kind of variable.

Manipulating characters in a string

Often in coding you will want to change, explore or evaluate the contents of strings. You may wish to find characters or substrings within a string, change the case, and other tasks.

In AQA pseudo-code you use the following syntax for finding the length of a string. The red brackets < > are only to show where you add something; you don't need to put them in your code. StringExp means any expression which can be evaluated to string data type.

LEN(<StringExp>**)**

Example:

```
LEN('AQA computer science')
  # evaluates to 20 (including space)
```

In AQA pseudo-code you use the following syntax for a finding a character position in a string. The red brackets < > are only to show where you add something; you don't need to put them in your code. CharExp means any expression which can be evaluated to a character data type. StringExp means any expression which can be evaluated to string data type.

POSITION(<StringExp>, <CharExp>**)**

Example:

```
POSITION('AQA computer science', 'm')
  # evaluates to 6 (as with arrays, exam
  # papers will make it clear whether
  # indexing starts at 0 or
  # 1, here 0 has been assumed
```

In AQA pseudo-code you use the following syntax for a substring (the substring is created by the first parameter indicating the start position within the string, the second parameter indicating the final position within the string and the third parameter being the string itself). The red brackets < > are only to show where you add something; you don't need to put them in your code. StringExp means any expression which can be evaluated to string data type, IntExp and expression of an integer data type.

SUBSTRING(<IntExp>, <IntExp>, <StringExp>**)**

```
Example:
SUBSTRING(6, 14, 'AQA computer science')
  # evaluates to 'mputer sc'
```

In AQA pseudo-code you use the following syntax for concatenation. The red brackets < > are only to show where you add something; you don't need to put them in your code. StringExp means any expression which can be evaluated to string data type.

```
<StringExp> + <StringExp> + <StringExp>
```

Example:

```
'AQA' + 'computer' + 'science'
  # evaluates to 'AQAcomputerscience'
```

Real data types

A **real** data type contains numeric data in a decimal form. It is used in situations where more accurate information is required than an integer can provide, as an integer is a whole number.

A few examples of where a real data type may be used are:

distance in kilometres (km)	23.62, 3.51222, 109.33
speed in metres per second (m/s)	62.5, 10.2
weight in kilograms (kg)	20.666, 32.7

But real data types cannot store the measurement symbol (km, kg, etc.) or the units of measurement (for instance, kilometres or metres/second). If you want to use the real data type you must remember to add the measurement symbol separately and print the units after the field displaying the data type.

It is worth noting that in the case of money (currency) the data type can be real or integer. For small values it is most likely that decimal places will need to be included and, therefore, a real data type will be required. If the values being considered are large, such as the cost of houses, then it is doubtful that decimal places would be important, in which case only whole numbers would be considered and therefore the integer data type would be used.

RESEARCH TASK

Use this book and other sources such as the internet to research data types (integer, string, real, Boolean, char).

You may be asking yourself that if real data type can hold any number, why use the integer data type?

Well there are two reasons why the integer data type would be used.

- Processing speed: The speed it takes a computer to calculate using real numbers is a lot longer than whole numbers held as integer data types.
- Storage: Real data types take up more memory than integer data types, so if decimal points are not required it is better to use integers.

One of the common problems encountered by people learning programming is choosing the wrong data types. The use of unsuitable data types can lead to programs behaving unexpectedly, with lots of time wasted in trying to understand what is going wrong.

TASK

Explore how your chosen programming language deals with real data type.

KEY POINT

Char is an alphabetic character or symbol in the written form of a natural language. Python does not support characters.

Char data types

Another primitive data type we will explore here is **char**. This is simply a character, for example, 'a'.

> In AQA pseudo-code you use the following syntax for string and character conversion. The red brackets < > are only to show where you add something; you don't need to put them in your code StringExp means any expression which can be evaluated to string data type.
>
> Converting string to integer
>
> **STRING_TO_INT**(<StringExp>)
>
> Example:
>
> STRING_TO_INT('8')
>
>   # evaluates to the integer 8
>
> Converting string to real
>
> **STRING_TO_REAL**(<StringExp>)
>
> Example:
>
> STRING_TO_REAL('16.3')
>
>   # evaluates to the real 16.3

```
Converting integer to string
INT_TO_STRING(<IntExp>)
Example:
INT_TO_STRING(16)
   # evaluates to the string '16'
Converting real to string
REAL_TO_STRING(<RealExp>)
Example:
REAL_TO_STRING(16.3)
   # evaluates to the string '16.3'
Converting character to character code
CHAR_TO_CODE(<CharExp>)
Example:
CHAR_TO_CODE('a')
   # evaluates to 97 using ASCII/Unicode
Converting character code to character
CODE_TO_CHAR(<IntExp>)
Example:
CODE_TO_CHAR(97)
   # evaluates to 'a' using ASCII/Unicode
```

Python and data type conversion

Python provides several built-in functions that allow you to convert one data type to a different data type. Whilst in practice these functions do not actually convert the original value, they do return a converted representation of the original value. In programming this is referred to as a 'cast' operation.

Casting is when you convert a variable value from one type to another. In Python, this is done with functions such as int(), or float() or str().

QUESTION

What is the difference between 'integer' and 'real' data types?

Function	Description
int(x)	Converts x to an integer whole number
float(x)	Converts x to a decimal floating-point number
str(x)	Converts x to a string

Often you want to change a string into a proper number. For example, this code:

```
x = '80'

y = '-70'

print(x + y)
```

prints the following, as the numbers are strings:

80-70

If we use the int() function:

```
x = '80'

y = '-70'

print(int(x) + int(y))
```

we will get:

10

A float() does basically the same thing, but using real numbers:

```
x = '80'

y = '-70'

print(float(x) + float(y))
```

The output would be:

10.0

We will explore this further:

```
num1 = input('Please enter a number: ')
                              #asking user to enter a number
num2 = input('Please enter another number: ')
                              #asking user to enter a second number
print('Input is: ', type(num1), type(num2))
                              #outputs the input data types
totalNum = num1 + num2
print('Total: ', totalNum, type(totalNum))
                              #outputs the total and its data type
```

```
totalNum = int(num1) + int(num2)
                                      #converts data type to integer

print('Total: ', totalNum, type(totalNum))
                                      #outputs the total and its data type

totalNum = float(num1) + float(num2)
                                      #converts data type to float

print('Total: ', totalNum, type(totalNum))
                                      #outputs the total and its data type
```

Output:

Please enter a number: 4

Please enter another number: 4

Input is: <class 'str'> <class 'str'>   #each number is actually
                                        #stored as a string

Total: 44 <class 'str'>   #result also gets concatenated as a string
                          #data type

Total: 8 <class 'int'>   #we have now converted the data type
                          #to an integer

Total: 8.0 <class 'float'>   #we have now converted the data
                             #type to a float

KEY POINT ❗

A character is a data type that stores a single character.

KEY POINT ❗

Booleans are variables that store just two values, for example, True or False.

Review of data types

Basic primitive data types may include:

- character (character, char)
- string
- integer (integer, int, short, long, byte) with a variety of precisions
- floating-point number (float, double, real, double precision)
- Boolean, logical values True and False.

More sophisticated data types that you will come across and which can be built-in include:

- tuples in ML, Python
- linked lists in Lisp
- complex numbers in Fortran, C (C99), Lisp, Python, Perl 6, D
- rational numbers in Lisp, Perl 6
- hash tables in various guises, in Lisp, Perl, Python, Lua, D.

CHAPTER REVIEW

In this chapter we have explored data types. We have also explored conversion.

Remember, before tackling any computer science task or question on this topic you must:

- understand the concept of a data type. (More on this topic chapter 8.)
- understand and use the following data types:
  - integer
  - string
  - real
  - Boolean
  - character.

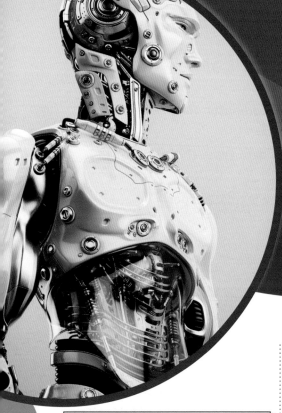

18 Data Structures

Data structures include numbers, lists, tuples, dictionaries, arrays and objects.

Data structures

The study of data structures is about organising data so that it is suitable for computer processing.

Computer hardware views storage devices, like **internal memory** and **disks**, as holders of elementary data units (bytes), each accessible through its **address** (usually an integer). The address is the **location** in memory, just like your physical address is where you live.

Most data structures can be viewed as simple containers that can be used to store a collection of objects of a given type. The container could be a sentence. The objects (actions within the sentence) are called the **elements** of the container.

You will have thought about data structures when you first learnt about using computers. The files and folders you use are part of a simple data structure. In the same way, programmers have to think about the data structure in the code. In your friend's address, the city has areas, the areas have roads, roads have houses and your friend is one of the people in a particular house.

Choosing the correct structures

As we explored in the last section, a data structure can be defined as a collection of different data elements which are stored together in a clear, structured form.

In programming, one of the most important design decisions involves which data structure to use. Arrays are among the most common data structures.

Arrays and linked lists are both designed to store multiple elements, most often of the same type. An array is an ordered arrangement of data elements that are accessed by referencing their location within the array. A linked list is a group of elements, each of which contains a pointer that points to the following element. (This information is useful for your overall knowledge of the subject but be aware that linked lists are not required for the specification.)

It is fair to say that data structures are used in almost all of today's program or software solutions as they provide a method of managing huge amounts of data efficiently. For example, this could be in a large database or an internet indexing service. In most programming situations, efficient data structures are a key to designing efficient algorithms. In fact some formal software design methods and programming languages emphasise data structures, rather than algorithms, because they are regarded as the key organising factor in software design.

How the data is stored

To explain data structures, we will first revisit some of the knowledge you gained in earlier chapters. In a computer, data is saved or stored in a place called memory. Whatever type of memory this may be, memory is always divided into units. Memory units can only contain one item at a time. The amount of

KEY POINT

A telephone directory is, essentially, a collection of pointers called telephone numbers which link to people.

RESEARCH TASK

Use this book and other sources such as the internet to research data structures (records, one-dimentional arrays, two-dimentional arrays).

data that will fit into a memory unit varies from computer to computer; understanding this is beyond the scope of this book. Each byte of memory is like a building with its own address called a memory address.

The address of a memory unit never changes, but obviously what is stored there will change frequently. The town has people living inside the buildings as bits of data. The small town inside your computer is a very neighbourly place. A program refers to buildings by name rather than by address, and puts Steve's data inside Steve's building. However, if you need to come up with hundreds of names for hundreds of buildings it would be very complex, unless you use what is called an array.

Useful data structures in Python

Lists

A list stores a group of items one after the other. It keeps them in order for you. You can add or remove items as you wish, sort your list or search to see if it contains a specific value.

Imagine a local DVD rental shop. When you want to check if a particular film is available you would conduct a search. If the film is available, but has been borrowed by a user, a delete from list option could be used to remove the film from the list of those available. When the film is returned it will be inserted back in the list.

In programming, we need to be able to do all of these operations. At a high level, these are often called comparison methods and direct access methods. You may come across the term hashing, which is an example of direct access methods.

Tuples

Tuples are very similar to lists in that they are used to store sequences of information. Unlike lists, they can't be altered after they have been created. Tuples are covered in more detail later in this chapter when we explore records.

Dictionaries

Dictionaries store values with keys, so you can look them up with the key. You can use them to build complex nested data-structures or just for storing values. Dictionaries also support operations like inserting, deleting and searching.

Arrays

An **array** is a way to reference a series of memory locations (buildings) using the same name. Each memory location is represented by an array element. An array element is similar to one variable except that it is identified by an index value not a name. An index value is a number used to identify an array element.

There are many situations during the writing of code when programmers need to hold related data as a single item and then use an index value to access it, for example a list of employee's names or makes of car.

One method of doing this would be to assign a variable to each item, such as:

name = "Jim"

girl = "Susan"

man = "Bill"

etc.

Now, although this method does work, what if you wanted to find out what the second name was? The answer is that with this system you have no way of knowing, as there is no positional information contained within the assigned variables. To be able to this we need what is called a one-dimensional array.

One-dimensional arrays

Look at the box of eggs in Figure 18.1. It is an example of a one-dimensional array. Each item has something in common, its 'egginess'. But each egg also has a difference. It will be different in weight, size, colour or even shape. But what is important, here, is that each of the eggs has a specific location in the box, an **index**. It has a position relative to the other eggs. If we say we want egg 2, we do not want egg 11, even though they look alike.

> **KEY POINT**
>
> An **array** is a data structure made up of a series of variables all of the same type, grouped under one identifier. Elements are accessed using an index.

> **KEY POINT**
>
> A variable is a name/location in memory/identifier. It is used to store a value which can change during execution of the code.

> **KEY POINT**
>
> A one-dimensional array is a single variable that can store a list of values. To create an array, you first must define an array variable of the desired type.

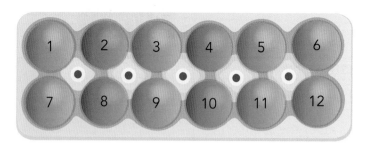

Figure 18.1 *Array of eggs*

> In AQA pseudo-code, you use the following syntax to assign a value to an element of a one-dimensional array. The red brackets < > are only to show where you add something you don't need to put them in your code.
>
> Syntax:
>
> Array[index] ← <add value here>
>
> Examples:
>
> arrayClass[1] ← 'Steve'
>
> arrayMarks[3] ← 66

One-dimensional arrays are a data structure that allows a list of items to be stored with the capability of accessing each item by pointing to its location within the array. In Python you would need either to use a module or create a list rather than use an array as Python does not support arrays without a module:

```
carMakers = ["Ford", "Land Rover", "Vauxhall",
             "Nissan", "Toyota"]
```

The first line of code defines a variable, carMakers, as a list rather than an array, which is storing a number of items. Now, let's say that you wish to access the fifth car make (Toyota), what you do is use a position number, for example:

```
car_name = carMakers[4]
```

This line of code will return the 5th car make in the array as the first item is at position 0. The process of using a position number is called indexing and the position number is called the index. The items within an array are called the array elements.

KEY POINT

An element is an item of an array. Each element can be accessed by referencing its location in the array.

KEY POINT

Python does not support arrays without use of a module, but lists are a suitable alternative.

Arrays are useful in programming when you want to use a list of values with a common link.

In AQA pseudo-code, if you wanted to use the alphabet in an array you would not use:

```
a ← "a"
b ← "b" etc.
```

you would code:

```
alphabet ← ["a","b","c","d","e"]
```

Then if you needed the letter e, for example, you would call it by saying:

```
alphabet[5]    #The number 5 refers to the position of e in the array.
               #When finding the position using AQA's pseudo-code we can
               #start at 1 or 0, you will be told which to use as an
               #index in the question
```

1	2	3	4	5
a	b	c	d	e

The reason why this type of array is referred to as a one-dimensional array is because it only uses a single number to point to the position of array elements.

In the 'carMakers' example above, the elements would be indexed as follows:

car_name = carMakers[0]	(would return Ford)
car_name = carMakers[1]	(would return Land Rover)
car_name = carMakers[2]	(would return Vauxhall)
car_name = carMakers[3]	(would return Nissan)
car_name = carMakers[4]	(would return Toyota)

```
In AQA pseudo-code, you use the following
syntax to initialise a one-dimensional array
with a set of values. The red brackets < >
are only to show where you add something; you
don't need to put them in your code.
Syntax:
Array ← [<add value here>, ...]
Example:
arrayValues ← [1, 2, 3, 4, 5]
```

QUESTION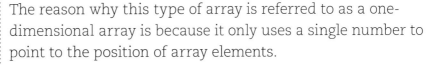

Explain the term one-dimensional array.

KEY POINT ❗

It is worth noting that it is common practice within programming for the first element within an array to be given an index of 0 rather than 1.

QUESTION

Explain the difference between one- and two-dimensional arrays.

KEY POINT

You can declare all elements of an array in one statement.

	0	1	2	3
0	A	B	C	D
1	E	F	G	H
2	I	J	K	L
3	M	N	O	P
4	Q	R	S	T

Figure 18.3 *Two-dimensional array*

Two-dimensional arrays

Two-dimensional arrays are a little more complex than one-dimensional arrays, but really they are nothing more than an array of arrays, in other words an array in one row and another in the next row. So now, our eggs have row A and row B, each with six eggs (Figure 18.2). We have egg A1 and egg B1 and they are both different eggs.

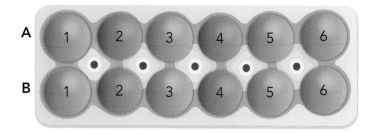

Figure 18.2 *Two-dimensional array of eggs*

The best way of understanding a two-dimensional array is to think of it as a way of holding and accessing information within a matrix or grid made up of rows and columns (Figure 18.3). You may have used this method to define a cell in a spreadsheet, where you give the location by row and column.

```
In AQA pseudo-code you use the following
syntax for updating an element in a two-
dimensional array. The red brackets < > are
only to show where you add something; you
don't need to put them in your code. IntExp,
means any expression which can be evaluated
to an integer.
<Identifier>[<IntExp>][<IntExp>] ← <Exp>
Example:
tables[3][1] ← 16
# tables is now
#[ [1, 2, 3],
#  [2, 4, 6],
#  [3, 6, 9],
#  [4, 16, 12] ]
```

In AQA pseudo-code you use the following syntax to find an array length. The red brackets < > are only to show where you add something; you don't need to put them in your code.

LEN(<Identifier>**)**

Example:

LEN(primes)

evaluates to 6 using example above

LEN(tables)

evaluates to 4 using example above

LEN(tables[0])

evaluates to 3 using example above

Let's give this array the name 'letters'. Notice that we have five rows and four columns.

The output from the array looks like this:

letters [0] [0]	returns element 'A'
letters [0] [1]	returns element 'B'
letters [0] [2]	returns element 'C'
letters [0] [3]	returns element 'D'
letters [1] [0]	returns element 'E'
letters [1] [1]	returns element 'F'

Note: This declaration will not work in all languages.

> **KEY POINT** ❗
>
> The element in the first row and second column in an array is 1, 2. Rows are first dimension. Columns are second dimension.

In AQA pseudo-code you use the following syntax for accessing an element in a two-dimensional array. The red brackets < > are only to show where you add something; you don't need to put them in your code. IntExp, means any expression which can be evaluated to an integer.

<Identifier>[<IntExp>][<IntExp>]

Example:

```
tables ← [ [1, 2, 3],
           [2, 4, 6],
           [3, 6, 9],
           [4, 8, 12] ]
```

tables[3][1]

evaluates to 8 as second element (with index 1) of
    fourth array (with index 3) in tables is 8

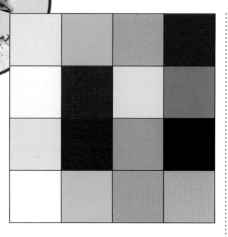

Figure 18.4 *Close-up of a colour photograph's pixels*

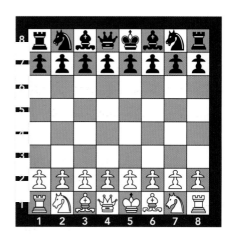

Figure 18.5 *Chess board*

We can even use this type of array to define an image. Think about the pixels in a digital photograph (Figure 18.4).

It is simply a two-dimensional array. Conceptually, the pixel values for any image would be represented as a two-dimensional array. The number of columns corresponds to the width of the image (in pixels) and the number of rows corresponds to the height of the image (also in pixels).

For example, an image that is 640 pixels wide by 480 pixels high would be stored in memory as a two-dimensional array having 640 columns and 480 rows.

These two-dimensional arrays are used extensively in gaming.

Suppose we want to store information about the chess game (Figure 18.5). We want to store information about what pieces are in which locations. The most natural way to store it would be to index locations by the row and column. This is easily done with a two-dimensional array and to access the elements within your two-dimensional array you would need to write a small looping routine.

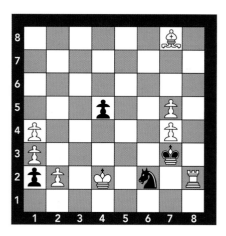

Figure 18.6 *Chess board partway through game*

Records and tuples

Records are a fundamental component of most data structures, especially linked data where the data stored in the record is related in some way so belongs together. Records are dissimilar to arrays as the number of fields is fixed and each field in a record can have a different type. For example, a record might contain three integers, a floating-point number, and a character string. Each field has a name to identify it. Records may also be stored in arrays. Many computer files are organised as arrays of logical records.

In Python, a **tuple** can be used to store several related pieces of data (a record) about a car owner and then a list to store a list of all the car owners that use a garage. This is because tuples are fixed size but lists are dynamic. In other words, a tuple can't be changed, it is immutable, whereas a list can be changed, it is mutable.

- You can't add elements to a tuple but you can to a list.
- You can't remove elements from a tuple but you can from a list.
- You can find elements in a tuple, since this doesn't change the tuple.
- You can also use the 'in' operator to check if an element exists in the tuple.

So the programmer has to decide if the data structure needs to be mutable or not. You may wonder why would you not want it to be mutable, but immutable structures can be used for things like dictionary keys, whereas lists cannot.

In relational database management systems, records are sometimes called tuples. Python also uses tuples to group items into a single value. In Python, a tuple is similar to a comma-separated sequence of values. Whilst Python tuples are not exactly the same as records, tuples in Python support the same sequence operations as strings. An index operator is used to select an element from a tuple.

Remember, whilst a tuple is similar to a list it uses different syntax and with tuples we cannot change elements. This makes programs more predictable. But once Python has created a tuple in memory, it cannot be changed.

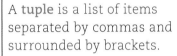

KEY POINT

A **tuple** is a list of items separated by commas and surrounded by brackets.

Tuples are easy to create in Python. You give the tuple a name, then after that the list of values it will carry. For example:

```
a = ()          #creates a zero-element tuple
print(a)
print(len(a))
```

Output:

```
()
0
```

```
b = ("one",)    #creates a one-element tuple
print(b)
print(len(b))
```

Output:

```
('one',)
1
```

```
c = ("one", "two")   #creates a two-element tuple
print(c)
print(len(c))
```

Output:

```
('one', 'two')
2
```

A tuple is a grouping of data. Packing refers to putting individual data items together into a tuple, and unpacking is the reverse.

We can easily unpack a tuple:

```
pair = ("man", "woman")
(key, value) = pair      #unpack tuple
print(key)               #display variables
print(value)
```

Output:

```
man
woman
```

Lists are extremely similar to tuples but we use different syntax as we use square brackets. Lists are modifiable (the correct term is 'mutable'), so their values can be changed.

```
cats = ['Tom', 'Cheshire', 'Tabby', 'Lion', 'Cheta']    #creates a list NOT
                                                         #a tuple

cats = ('Tom', 'Cheshire', 'Tabby', 'Lion', 'Cheta')    #creates a tuple NOT
                                                         #a list
```

CHAPTER REVIEW

In this chapter we have built upon the last chapter and explored data structures.

We have also explored arrays in more detail and how they can be used.

Remember, before tackling any computer science task or question on this topic you must:

- understand the concept of data structures
- be able to use an array
- be able to use records or equivalent
- be able to use arrays (or equivalent) in the design of solutions to simple problems.

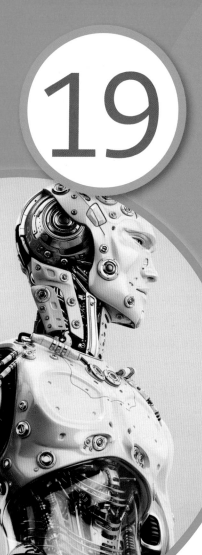

19 Data Validation and User Authentication

For any device to function correctly the input needs to be checked prior to any process and output.

KEY POINT

Input validation is commonly done with a loop that iterates as long as an input variable references invalid data.

Data validation

Validation is an automatic check performed by a computer to ensure that entered data is sensible/feasible. It does not check the accuracy of the data entered. The most common validation checks are shown in the table below.

Type of check	Explanation
Length check	Checks than an entered data value is no longer than a set number of characters. For example, checks the data isn't too long or too short.
Presence check	Checks that some data has been entered into a field.

Continued

Type of check	Explanation
Range check	For example, a user of a computer system is likely to be aged between 3 and 110. The computer can be programmed only to accept numbers between 3 and 110. However, this does not guarantee that the number typed in is correct. For example, the user could be 5 years of age but say that they are 16.
Type check	Checks that the value of data is of a particular type, for example that age data is numeric.
Format check	A format check is more advanced than a type check, for example it can be used to check a postcode format.

There are a number of other validation types that can be used to check the data that is being entered:

 Cardinality check: checks that record has a valid number of related records.

 Check digit: the last one or two digits in any code are used to check the other digits are correct.

Consistency check: checks fields to ensure data in these fields corresponds, for example If Title = "Mr", then Gender = "M".

Spell check: looks up words in a dictionary or array.

Why use validation in your code?

Your program could crash if incorrect data is input by a user, for example if the user types a string when the code expects an integer. Your code may also produce incorrect results when processing the data. Because of this, we often use validation in coded solutions, particularly when we have a user input.

For example, in Python we could use:

```
def checkingInput():
    while True:
        try:
            a = input('enter')
            if a == 'y' or 1 <= int(a) <= 10:
                return a
            else:
                print('Invalid input!')
        except ValueError:
            print('Value error! Please try again!')
```

Validating the presence of data

One common error is no data in a field where data is required. For example, id is frequently required, as is name. A pseudo-code example testing for the presence of a name is:

```
IF LEN(name) = 0 THEN
    OUTPUT 'missing name'
    invalid ← TRUE
ENDIF
```

Validating data type

Often non-numeric data is put into a numeric field. However, you can validate for character data in a character field.

Assume that myNumber is a numeric field and you want to make sure that no non-numeric data is entered in the field.

```
invalid ← FALSE
IF NOT is_numeric(myNumber) THEN
    OUTPUT 'non-numeric data in myNumber'
    invalid ← TRUE
ENDIF
```

In Python, say we want someone to enter their age but also want to stop them entering something other than an integer, as this will cause an error. We could do this using the following code:

```
while True:
    try:
        age = int(input("Please enter your age: "))
    except ValueError:
        print("Sorry, I didn't understand that.")
        #better try again... Return to the start
        #of the loop
        continue
    else:
        #age was successfully parsed!
        #we're ready to exit the loop.
```

```
        break
if age >= 18:
    print("You are able to drink alcohol!")
else:
    print("You are not able to drink alcohol.")
```

Validating uppercase characters

We will also assume that refCode should be an uppercase character field. We could write the following:

```
IF refCode < "A" OR refCode > "Z" THEN
    OUTPUT 'non-uppercase character in refCode'
    invalid ← TRUE
ENDIF
```

In Python, we could use:

```
while True:
    data = input("Please enter your first name in
    capital letters): ")
    if not data.isupper():
        print("Sorry, your response was not in
        capital letters.")
        continue
    else:
        #We have validated the name is in capitals.
        #We can now exit the loop.
        break
```

Validating data codes

The valid titleCode may be Mr, Dr, Ms and those are the only codes you want entered in that field:

```
IF titleCode ≠ "Mr" AND titleCode ≠ "Dr" AND
titleCode ≠ "Ms" THEN                #≠ used to
                                     test for items
                                     not equal
    OUTPUT 'non-valid character in titleCode'
    Invalid ← TRUE
ENDIF
```

Minimum and maximum length checks

For a maximum length check in Python, we can use:

```
input_str = input("Please provide your first name: ")

if len(input_str) > 8:    #more than 8 characters
   print("Error! Only 8 characters are allowed!")
```

Or for a minimum length check:

```
input_str = input("Please provide your full name: ")

if len(input_str) < 4:    #we use less than
   print("Error! You must enter a minimum of 4 characters!")
```

Range checks

We can use similar code for a range check. Say we want to limit the maximum age someone can enter:

```
input = input("Please provide your age: ")

input = int(input)    #we must convert the user input to an integer

if input > 120:
   print("Error! You cannot be that old!")
```

Or the minimum age:

```
input = input("Please provide your age: ")

input = int(input)

if input < 6:
   print("Error! You cannot be that young!")
```

Developing a user authentication routine

Authentication is the mechanism systems use to securely identify their users. A typical sequence for registering and logging on to a website might be the following:

The user chooses to register.

A registration form captures the following:

A user name.

An entered password.

The contact email address.

An email is then sent to the user containing an activation link.

The user clicks on the activation link.

The user can now log in to the site using their user name and password.

The user now has access to the site as an authenticated user.

We could write a simple validation routine in Python to check the password and username are correct:

```python
def validation():                              #Define our subprogram
    while True:
        UserName = input("Enter Username: ")   #Ask for username
        PassWord = input("Enter Password: ")   #Ask for password
        if UserName == 'Steve' and PassWord == 'AQA123':   #Check they match
                                                              our records
            print ("Login successful!")        #If correct send this message
            logged()                           #Run login subprogram
        else:
            print ("The username and password did not match our records!")
def logged():                                  #Define subprogram
print ("Welcome to the Hodder AQA website") #Send message to show login text
                                               #We can add other actions in
                                               #this subprogram to allow
                                               #access to the site
validation()                                   #Run our newly defined
                                               #subprogram
```

Obviously we would need to use a database or list when we have more than one user.

CHAPTER REVIEW

In this chapter we have explored data validation and user authentication.

Remember, before tackling any computer science task or question on this topic you must:

- understand the term validation
- understand how invalid data entry can cause errors in your code
- be able to write simple validation routines.

20 Reading and Writing to a Text File

Principles of writing/reading to/from a text file

To write to an external file we need to understand the term **delimiter**. A delimiter is a character used to specify the boundary between regions in a plain text file. An example of a delimiter is the comma, used in CSV (comma-separated values). The comma acts as a field delimiter in a sequence of comma-separated values. In programming, **pipe-delimited** (|) text files are also common. A delimiter is simply a character used to denote the end of one value and the beginning of the next. It is needed because the values for each variable may be in different locations on each record. The advantage of the pipe over comma or space delimiters is that the pipe is not used very often in the actual data values. In a text file the end of a line is also a delimiter. We can read the file based upon lines delimited by the line breaks.

KEY POINTS !

● Delimited data has data elements separated by a character called a **delimiter**. The most common delimiters are commas, tabs and colons.

● In **pipe-delimited** files a vertical bar (also referred to as pipe) and space is used to delimitate data. It is used as it is not commonly found in the data elements that need separating.

When you declare the variable for a text file you usually create the variable and open the file at the same time.

To return the nth line of an external file in pseudo-code:

```
READLINE(file, n)
```

If contents of file export.txt is:

This is Computer Science GCSE

Hodder Education

Steve Cushing

```
line2 ← READLINE(export.txt, 2)
```

Will set the value of a variable:

Hodder Education

To write the nth line of file with value in pseudo-code:

```
WRITELINE(file, n, value)
```

If n exceeds the previous line numbers of file plus one then the gap is filled with blank lines. If something already exists in line n it will be overwritten.

```
newLine ← "AQA"
WRITELINE(export.txt, 4, newLine)
```

Contents of export.txt is now:

This is Computer Science GCSE

Hodder Education

Steve Cushing

AQA

In pseudo-code, you use the following syntax to read in a record from a `<file>` and assign to a `<variable>`. Each READLINE and WRITELINE statement reads or writes lines of text from/to the file.

```
fname ← 'sample.txt'
content ← ['a','b','c']
FOR linecount ← 0 TO LEN(content)-1
   WRITELINE(fname, linecount+1, content[linecount])
ENDFOR
```

In Python

In most languages you are required to open and close a text file. Python has a built-in open() function. This takes a filename as an argument. Let's first create a new text file. We could name it anything we like, in this example we will name it testdoc.txt. We can also add a combination of a directory path and a filename. The open() function will only take one argument but in Python, whenever you need a filename, you can include some or all of a directory path. The directory path does not begin with a slash or a drive letter as it is a relative path.

```python
#Write to a file

with open("testdoc.txt", "wt") as out_file:

    out_file.write("This is Computer Science GCSE\
nHodder Education\nSteve Cushing\nAQA")

#Now we will read our file

with open("testdoc.txt", "rt") as in_file:

    text = in_file.read()

print(text)
```

If we now look at the output from this file:

This is Computer Science GCSE

Hodder Education

Steve Cushing

AQA

Notice how the \n command adds the text to a new line.

If we only want a few characters from our text file we can use:

```python
with open("testdoc.txt", "rt") as in_file:

    text = in_file.read(1)

print(text)
```

This outputs the first letter from the file, which is T.

If we add more letters:

```python
with open("testdoc.txt", "rt") as in_file:

    text = in_file.read(12)

print(text)
```

KEY POINT

Python has built-in methods for reading a whole file that make it easier than reading one line at a time.

Output:

This is Comp

Or, to give us more flexibility, we can read the lines of our text directly into a list:

```
with open("testdoc.txt", "rt") as in_file:

    content = in_file.readlines()

print(content)
```

Output:

['This is Computer Science GCSE\n', 'Hodder Education\n', 'Steve Cushing\n', 'AQA']

Now we have an array we can manipulate it as any other array to get the data we require from the text file.

If we want to amend a line in a text file, you can't just 'change line two' directly in a file. You can only overwrite (not delete) parts of a file, which means that the new content just covers the old content:

```
with open("testdoc.txt", "rt") as in_file:

    #read a list of lines into content

    content = in_file.readlines()

print(content)

#now change the 2nd line, note that you have to
#add a newline

content[1] = 'Exam Textbook\n'

#and write everything back

with open("testdoc.txt", 'wt') as file:

    file.writelines(content)
```

CHAPTER REVIEW

In this chapter we have explored reading and writing to an external text file.

Remember, before tackling any computer science task or question on this topic you must:

- be able to read, write and amend data in an external file
- be able to read/write from/to a text file.

21 Trees and Huffman Coding

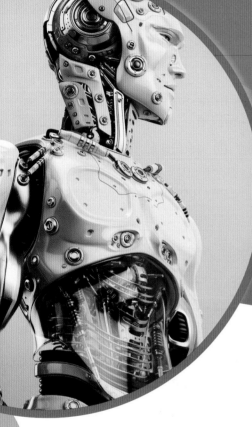

Trees are an essential structure in computing. These trees support operations such as searching, inserting and deleting, alongside other important computing operations.

Binary trees

There is a particular kind of tree, called a **binary tree**. These are very useful for storing data for the purpose of rapid access, storage and deletion. In a binary tree, the maximum number of child nodes for each parent is two. In binary trees, we also distinguish between the subtree on the left and the subtree on the right.

The tree shown in Figure 21.1 has nine nodes. Normally the root is always shown at the top of the tree.

KEY POINT

A **binary tree** is a data structure of nodes or junctions that is constructed in a hierarchy. A binary tree can only have up to two child nodes for each parent node.

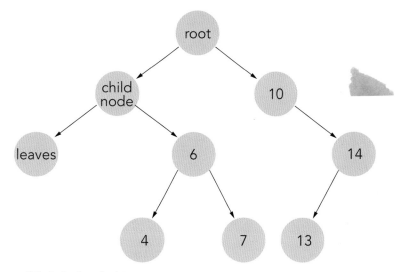

Figure 21.1 *A simple binary tree*

Letter	Frequency
A	5
R	2
B	2
C	1
D	1

Letter	Assignment
A	0
R	11
B	100
C	1010
D	1011

Huffman encoding

We can also use the binary tree to reduce the storage size of text. To **encode** English text, we would need 26 lower case letters, 26 upper case letters and some punctuation. Let's say that we could get by with 64 characters. We could achieve this with six bits but as ASCII uses seven we will also allow up to seven bits for each character.

In text, some characters are more frequent than others. We need a system where different characters can be different **bit widths**, but we also need to tell the system where each character begins and ends without using additional bits for this.

As an example of this in practice we will look at the word ABRACADABRA. If each letter requires seven bits, our 11-letter word would require 77 bits (7 × 11). This word has been chosen for our example as it has a large number of **repeated** letters in it, making it a good example. The letter A is the most common letter in our word as it is repeated five times. Some other letters are also repeated.

The frequencies of letters in our word are shown in this table.

We now assign a binary **assignment** to each letter. Each assignment must be unique and easily distinguished from the other assignments. D and C are the least frequent letters used in our word so we will give them the largest assignment of four bits. As the letter A is the most frequently used in our word, we will give it the shortest assignment of one bit. R and B are the

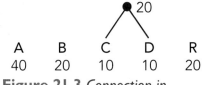

A   B   C   D   R
0   100   1010 1011   11

Figure 21.2 *A simple Huffman binary tree*

next most frequent so we will give R a two-bit assignment and B an assignment of three bits, as shown in the table.

Using these assignments we can write ABRACADABRA using our assignments as: 'A'0, 'B'100, 'R'11, 'A'0, 'C'1010, 'A'0, 'D'1011, 'A'0, 'B'100, 'R'11, 'A'0, which is 010011010100101101100110. We can find the letters as they have unique assignments. We can find each individual letter easily. This word would now only need 23 bits. We can then calculate bits saved: 77 – 23 = 54

Let's look at a simple Huffman binary tree (Figure 21.2) and how we can use it to read the code.

Looking at the tree, we can work out the word from the code, in 010011010100101101100110, the first 0 can only be an A, a 100 can only be a B, 11 a letter R, etc.

To see how we build the tree in the first place we will look at how it is constructed. In Huffman coding, we assign bits by creating a binary tree where the **children** are the encoding units with the smallest frequencies. As you are unlikely to use Huffman coding for a single word, we will examine a sentence with our word inside it. In practice, we would have many more characters used but, as an example of how the system works, we will stay with our five letters and find the assignments for these letters only.

The letter frequencies for our sentence are as follows:

Letter	Frequency
A	40
B	20
R	20
C	10
D	10

A   B   C   D   R
40   20   10   10   20

Figure 21.3 *Connection in a Huffman binary tree*

The smallest number of occurrences in our sentence are of C and D, so in Huffman coding we must connect these using a binary tree (Figure 21.3).

This creates a new node above C and D which would be called C+D as it is a connection of these two child nodes. Remember, in a binary tree there can only be two nodes. C+D now has a frequency value of 20 as there are 10 Cs and 10 Ds and the **parent** node value will be the two child frequencies added together.

The smallest frequency values now are B, C+D together, and R, all of which have a frequency value 20. We now need to connect any two of these.

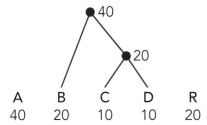

Figure 21.4 *Second connection in a Huffman binary tree*

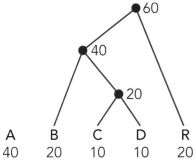

Figure 21.5 *Third connection in a Huffman binary tree*

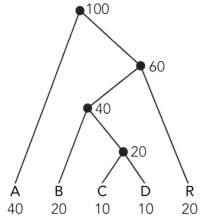

Figure 21.6 *Fourth connection in a Huffman binary tree*

Letter	Assignment
A	0
B	100
C	1010
D	1011
R	11

We will call the new node B+C+D and it will now have a frequency value of 40 (Figure 21.4): this is the frequency value of B and C+D added together. The smallest frequency value left in our table is now R so we need to connect R to either B+C+D or to A as they both have a frequency value of 40 (Figure 21.5).

We now need to connect the final two nodes (Figure 21.6).

Finally, we assign 0 to all the left branches and 1 to all the right branches (Figure 21.7).

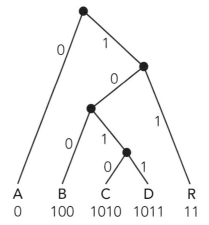

Figure 21.7 *Final assignment for Huffman binary tree*

Each encoding now shows us a path from the root and each path **terminates** at a leaf. The path to 'R' is 11, to B is 100. Our assigned values for all the letters are as shown in the table.

Each is unique, so no bit string is a prefix of any other bit string.

We have just created an example of Huffman encoding.

CHAPTER REVIEW

In this chapter we have explored Huffman coding and binary trees.

Remember, before tackling any computer science task or question on this topic you must:

- understand how Huffman coding works
- be able to explain how data can be compressed using Huffman coding
- be able to interpret Huffman trees
- be able to calculate the number of bits required to store a piece of data compressed using Huffman coding.

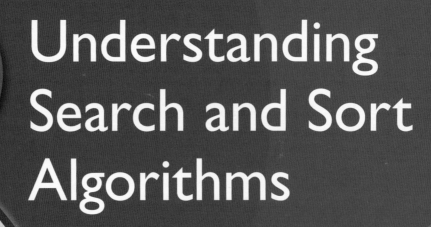

22 Understanding Search and Sort Algorithms

Let's say you have a large number of playing cards. Each card has a number written on it, and the cards have been shuffled and put in a pile we will call a **stack**. You have been asked to find the card with the highest number on it but you do not know that this is the ace of spades card.

So you would remove a card from the top of the stack and then write the number on a piece of paper. Then you would take the next card and if the number was higher than the number written on the piece of paper, you would cross it out and write the new number. You would keep doing this until the stack was empty.

We could represent this is a flowchart (Figure 22.1) or as pseudo-code.

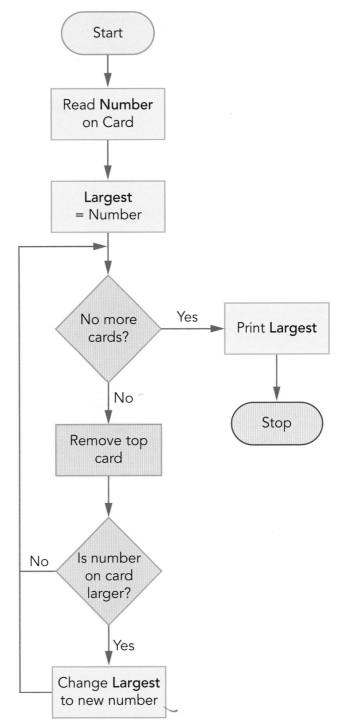

Figure 22.1 *Flowchart to find largest numbered card*

Search algorithms

Linear search

A linear search is the most basic search algorithm you can have. A linear search moves sequentially through your collection (or data structure) looking for a matching value.

22 Understanding Search and Sort Algorithms

Let's look graphically (Figure 22.2) at how a linear search works:

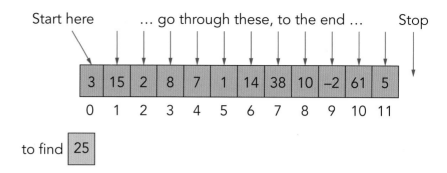

to find | 25 |

Figure 22.2 *Searching for '25'*

We will not know that there wasn't a record in the file that matched the key until the end of the search.

The number we are looking for is called the **key**. If we have a key of 3 we could show this as in Figure 22.3, where each line is the next loop in the search:

Key   List

3		6	4	1	9	7	3	2	8
3		6	4	1	9	7	3	2	8
3		6	4	1	9	7	3	2	8
3		6	4	1	9	7	3	2	8
3		6	4	1	9	7	3	2	8
3		6	4	1	9	7	3	2	8

Figure 22.3 *Searching for '3'*

When and if the code finds the key it stops. As you discovered in the first example, when it can't find the key it keeps going until the end.

In pseudo-code it could look like this:

```
key ← USERINPUT      #note this only works for
                       non-empty files

n ← 1
record ← READLINE(file, n)
WHILE record ≠ key AND NOT EOF
    n ← n+1
    record ← READLINE (file,n)
ENDWHILE
```

RESEARCH TASK

Use this book and other sources such as the internet to research searching algorithms.

```
        IF record = key THEN
            OUTPUT 'Success'
        ELSE
            OUTPUT 'There is no match in the file'
        ENDIF
```

Creating a linear search in Python:

```python
def linearSearch(myItem, myList):        #define our Linear Search function
    found = False
    position = 0
    while position < len(myList) and not found:
        if myList[position] == myItem:
            found = True
        position = position + 1
    return found

if__name__ == '__main__':
    cards = ['King Spades', 'Queen Spades', 'Ace Spades', 'King Hearts',
    'Queen Hearts' ]
        #create a list
    item = input('What card do you want to find? ')
        #ask user for card to find
    isFound = linearSearch(item, cards)
    if isFound:
        print('Your linear search has found the card requested.')
        #if found is True
    else:
        print('Your card is not in the list.')        #if found is False
```

RESEARCH TASK

Use this book and other sources such as the internet to research sorting algorithms.

Output (based upon entering Ace Spades as user input):

What card do you want to find? Ace Spades

Your linear search has found the card requested.

Let's do a **comparison** between a sorted and unsorted list.

If the order was ascending numerical or, in our next example, alphabetical on last names, how would the search for Anthony Adams on the ordered list compare with the search on the unordered list?

Unordered list	Ordered list
Carole Cren	Anthony Adams
Xian Xui	Carole Cren
Steve Cushing	Steve Cushing
Anthony Adams	Xian Xui

Unordered list:

- If Anthony Adams was in the list?
- If Anthony Adams was not in the list?

Ordered list:

- If Anthony Adams was in the list?
- If Anthony Adams was not in the list?

How about Xian Xui?

Unordered:

- If Xian Xui was in the list?
- If Xian Xui was not in the list?

Ordered:

- If Xian Xui was in the list?
- If Xian Xui was not in the list?

The search is faster on the ordered list if the item is not in the list, as the ordered list search can terminate sooner because it does not have to search to the end of the list.

Binary search

If we need a faster search, we need a completely different algorithm.

If we have an ordered list and we know how many things are in the list (i.e. number of records in a file), we can use a different **strategy**.

The binary search gets its name because the algorithm continually divides the list into two parts.

It looks at the centre value and disregards anything below or above what we are trying to find. Let's say we are looking for value 6 from seven ordered items (Figure 22.4). The orange shows the place where the list is being divided. Blue shows the active items and white the discarded items.

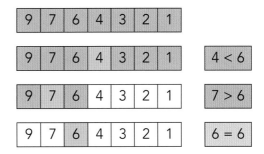

Figure 22.4 *Binary search for '6'*

So each time you get to discard half of the remaining list.

But the list has to be sorted before we can search it with binary search. To be really efficient, we also need a fast sort algorithm or to build the list in a way that maintains its order.

If we have a sorted list the following Python code performs a binary search:

```python
def binarySearch(list,element):
    if len(list) == 1:
        return element == list[0]
    mid = int(len(list)/2)
    if list[mid] > element:
        return binarySearch(list[:mid], element)
    if list[mid] < element:
        return binarySearch(list[mid:], element)
    return True
array = [1, 2, 3, 4, 5, 6]     #define our sorted array
num = 4
print(binarySearch(array, num))
```

Output: True

Comparing linear search and binary search

As long as the list is sorted, in almost all cases binary search is a more time-efficient algorithm than a linear search. A linear search looks down a list, one item at a time, without jumping. The time it takes to search gets longer at the same rate as the list gets longer. A binary search works in a similar way to how you use a dictionary. You start with the middle of a sorted list (with the first and second letter of the word you are trying to find), and see whether that's greater than or less than the value you're looking for, which determines whether the value is in the first or second half of the list. If you're looking for 'computer' you don't start off at 'A' in the dictionary. The number of search operations grows more slowly than the list does, because you're halving the 'search space' with each operation.

Because of this:

- binary search requires the input data to be sorted but a linear search does not
- binary search requires an ordering comparison; linear search only requires **equality comparisons**
- binary search requires random access to the data; linear search only requires sequential access.

Sort algorithms

There are a number of sort algorithms.

As with searching, the faster the sorting algorithm, the more complex it tends to be.

In the AQA course you need to understand two sorting algorithms:

- bubble sort
- merge sort.

Bubble sort

The simplest sorting algorithm is bubble sort.

Bubble sort works by repeating (**iteration**). The array is sorted from the first element to the last, by comparing each pair of elements in the array and switching their positions if necessary.

This process is repeated as many times as necessary, until all of the array is correctly sorted.

The worst-case scenario is that the array is in reverse order, and that the first element in the sorted array is the last element in the starting array, for example 8, 7, 6, 5, 4, 3, 2, 1 when we want a sorted list in **ascending** order.

If we look at a bubble sort in Python:

```
def bubbleSort(array):    #declaring a function called bubble sort
    for index in range(len(array)):
        #run a for loop to iterate through the array list
        for element in range((len(array) - 1) - index):
            if array[element] > array[element + 1]:
                array[element], array[element + 1] = \
                    array[element + 1], array[element]
            #we will add a print statement so we can see the progress of
            #the loop
            print('\tResolving element [', element,'] to ', array)
array = [6, 4, 3, 5, 2, 1]                #define our unsorted array
print('Bubble Sort\nArray :', array)      #output the unsorted array
bubbleSort(array)
print('Array :', array)                   #output sorted array
```

Output:

Bubble Sort

Array : [6, 4, 3, 5, 2, 1]

    Resolving element [0] to [4, 6, 3, 5, 2, 1]

    Resolving element [1] to [4, 3, 6, 5, 2, 1]

    Resolving element [2] to [4, 3, 5, 6, 2, 1]

    Resolving element [3] to [4, 3, 5, 2, 6, 1]

    Resolving element [4] to [4, 3, 5, 2, 1, 6]

    Resolving element [0] to [3, 4, 5, 2, 1, 6]

Resolving element [2] to [3, 4, 2, 5, 1, 6]

Resolving element [3] to [3, 4, 2, 1, 5, 6]

Resolving element [1] to [3, 2, 4, 1, 5, 6]

Resolving element [2] to [3, 2, 1, 4, 5, 6]

Resolving element [0] to [2, 3, 1, 4, 5, 6]

Resolving element [1] to [2, 1, 3, 4, 5, 6]

Resolving element [0] to [1, 2, 3, 4, 5, 6]

Array : [1, 2, 3, 4, 5, 6]

Merge sort

In the merge sort algorithm the idea is to take an array or list and break the data down into smaller and smaller pieces until it is broken down into individual data items, before merging the data items back together to make a sorted list.

The main elements of a merge sort are:

- **divide** the data into halves
- **conquer**: solve each piece by applying divide-and-conquer repeatedly (**recursively**) to them, and then
- **combine** the pieces together into a global solution.

Merge sort algorithms are a simple and very efficient algorithm for sorting a list.

Let's say we are given a sequence of n numbers which we will first store in an array A[1 ... n]. We want the numbers in our array sorted in increasing order. This is done by changing the order of the elements within the array.

Figure 22.5 shows an example of this:

- Divide: Split 'A' down the middle into two subsequences, each of size roughly n/2.
- Conquer: Sort each subsequence by calling MergeSort recursively (repeating) on each.
- Combine: Merge the two sorted subsequences back into a single sorted list.

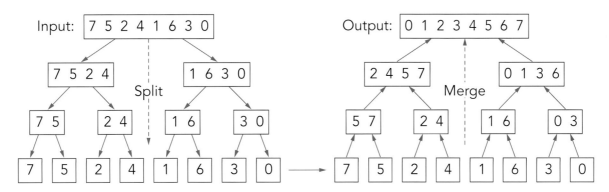

Figure 22.5 *Merge sort*

If we look at a merge sort in Python:

```python
def mergeSort(array):    #declaring a function called merge sort
  if len(array) > 1:
    middle = int(len(array) / 2)
    left = array[0:middle]; right = array[middle:]
    print('\tSplit to ', left, right)
    mergeSort(left); mergeSort(right)
#We now need to add an algorithm to divide the array elements into
#sub-sections then merge them together again
    a = b = 0
    for element in range(len(array)):
      L = left[a] if a < len(left) else None
      R = right[b] if b < len(right) else None
      if ((L and R) and (L < R)) or R is None:
        array[element] = L; a += 1
      elif ((L and R) and (L >= R)) or L is None:
        array[element] = R; b += 1
    print('\t\tMerging ', left, right)
array = [6, 4, 3, 5, 2, 1]    #define our unsorted array
print('Merge Sort\nArray :', array)
mergeSort(array)
print('Array :', array)
```

Output:

Merge Sort

Array : [6, 4, 3, 5, 2, 1]

    Split to [6, 4, 3] [5, 2, 1]

    Split to [6] [4, 3]

    Split to [4] [3]

        Merging [4] [3]

        Merging [6] [3, 4]

    Split to [5] [2, 1]

    Split to [2] [1]

        Merging [2] [1]

        Merging [5] [1, 2]

        Merging [3, 4, 6] [1, 2, 5]

  Array : [1, 2, 3, 4, 5, 6]

Comparing merge sort and bubble sort

In almost all cases, merge sort will take a lot less time than bubble sort to sort the data.

Bubble sort is not efficient in terms of time but is quite good in terms of memory as the data is sorted within the list, whereas merge sort is much more time efficient but generally uses more memory as copies of the lists are created as they are split up.

CHAPTER REVIEW

In this chapter we have explored search and sort methods.

Remember, before tackling any computer science task or question on this topic you must:

- understand basic search and sort methods
- understand and explain how linear search works
- understand and explain how binary search works
- compare and contrast linear search and binary search algorithms
- understand and explain how the bubble sort algorithm works
- understand and explain how the merge sort algorithm works
- compare and contrast merge sort and bubble sort algorithms.

23 Algorithm Efficiency

In Chapter 1 you learnt about how there are many solutions to the same problem and how algorithm efficiency becomes important. Some algorithms are more efficient than others. It is obviously better to have an efficient algorithm.

We explored briefly how there are two main measures of the efficiency of an algorithm:

- time
- space.

If it's possible to solve a problem by using what is called a brute force technique, you simply try out all the possible combinations of solutions. However, if you had to sort words with 158 characters when combined together including spaces, and you could compute 1,000,000,000 possibilities a second, you would still be left with the need for over 10^{149} seconds, which is longer than the expected life of the universe. So, to reduce time and make the algorithm more efficient, it is necessary to find a better approach.

Time measure

Time measure is a function describing the amount of time an algorithm takes in terms of the amount of input to the algorithm. 'Time' can mean the number of memory accesses performed, the number of comparisons between integers, the number of times some inner loop is executed, or some other natural unit related to the amount of real time the algorithm will take.

Space measure

Space measure is a function describing the amount of memory (space) an algorithm takes in terms of the amount of input to the algorithm. We often speak of 'extra' memory needed, not counting the memory needed to store the input itself.

Comparison

If we compare three simple algorithms for computing the sum $1 + 2 + \ldots + n$ for an integer $n > 0$ you will see that even a simple program can be programmed to work faster.

1	2	3

`sum = 0`
`for x = 1 to n`
`   sum = sum + x`
	`sum = 0`
	`for x = 1 to n`
	`   for y = 1 to x`
	`      sum = sum + 1`
		`sum = n * (n + 1) / 2`

Too many nested loops in any program can make the program take a long time to execute. Steps such as storing the length of an array in a different variable, instead of making it read the length at every iteration of the loop, will help to optimise the code. It also ensures that the code runs more efficiently. We explored some examples of this in Chapter 22 on sorting and searching. Restructuring your code (called refactoring), without changing its external behaviour, can also help make your code clear to follow.

For example, instead of this:

```
for x in a:
  for y in b:
    if x == y:
      yield (x,y)
```

it could be restructured as:

```
return set(a) & set(b)
```

It is considered bad practice to have two disjointed statements on a single line so:

```
print('one'); print('two')

if a == 1: print('one')

if <complex comparison> and <other complex comparison>:
  # do something here
```

is much better written as:

```
print('one')
print('two')
if a == 1:
  print('one')
cond1 = <complex comparison>
cond2 = <other complex comparison>
if cond1 and cond2:
  # do something here
```

as this is clearer to follow and understand.

Similarly:

```
if attr == True:
  print('True!')
if attr == No:
  print('attr is No!')
```

is better if it is written as:

```
if attr:
    print('True!')
```

Or you can just check for the opposite:

```
if not attr:
    print('attr is No!')
```

CHAPTER REVIEW

In this chapter we have explored algorithm efficiency.

Remember, before tackling any computer science task or question on this topic you must:

- understand how different algorithms can lead to faster execution and thus be more efficient.

24 Testing Your Code

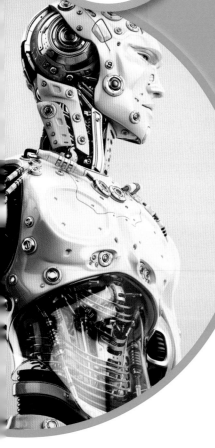

So you have now produced **well-documented**, efficient code, all laid out well with good use of white space. You may think all is well but the chances are that however hard you tried to avoid **errors**, they are inevitable in any program.

Even if you coded your program perfectly, the users of your program will always discover some problem in your application that you never even dreamed possible.

Although it's impossible to eliminate every error, this section describes errors and should help avoid most coding errors.

Types of errors in computer programming

As much as we may wish to deny it, human beings are not perfect. We make mistakes. Programmers are not exempt from this and, frequently, the mistakes we make are in the

RESEARCH TASK

Use this book and other sources such as the internet to research types of error in programmes (syntax, logic, runtime).

programs we create. These mistakes lead to issues, defects or, as they are most commonly known, bugs in the programs.

The process of fixing these mistakes, of removing the bugs, is known as **debugging**.

There are basically three types of error that computer programmers encounter when writing code:

- syntax errors
- runtime errors
- logic errors.

Syntax errors

Syntax errors or, as they are sometimes known, format errors are a big problem for those who are new to programming. A syntax error occurs when the programmer fails to obey one of the **grammar rules** of the programming language that they are writing their application in. Whilst syntax errors usually prevent the program from running in some way they are not easily found by a human.

Typically, syntax errors are down to using the wrong case, placing punctuation in positions where it should not exist or failing to insert punctuation where it should be placed within the code.

The most common syntax errors are as follows:

- The programmer forgets the quotes around a string.
- The programmer forgets to put a colon at the end of an if, elif, else, for, while, class or def statement.

This causes "SyntaxError: invalid syntax" in Python, for example:

```
if input == 8        #needs a colon

    print('Hello!')
```

- The programmer forgets to **declare** a variable.
- The programmer tries to use a keyword for a variable name.

This causes "SyntaxError: invalid syntax" in Python, for example:

```
class = 'algebra'    #you can't use a reserved name
```

- The programmer has a different number of open and close brackets in a statement or a different number of open and close quotes.

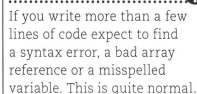

KEY POINT

If you write more than a few lines of code expect to find a syntax error, a bad array reference or a misspelled variable. This is quite normal.

QUESTION

What is a syntax error?

KEY POINT

Often programmers get errors because they use bad variable and function names, for example, a spelling mistake in a variable name. It's hard enough to remember variable names without having to remember which spelling mistake you made.

KEY POINT

Often programmers get errors because they inconsistently use uppercase and lower case letters in variable and function names. Beginner programmers often create a variable with one case, for example "myScore = 7", then later on try to reference it with a different case – "if myscore > 5:" or even "if score > 5:" – and wonder why the code doesn't run!

The programmer misspells keywords, for example:

```
fer i in range(5):     #should be 'for' not 'fer'
    print(i)
print("today)          #syntax error no "
print("today"          #syntax error no )
```

Indentation errors are also common in Python.

```
if userNum == 42:
print('Hello!')        #should be indented
```

In Python you may have:

 a **tab error** where you have used a mixture of tabs and spaces

an **indented error** where the programmer has not indented all lines in a block equally.

Remember that the indentation only increases after a statement ending with a colon, and afterwards the code must return to the previous indentation.

```
print('Steve')
    print('Cushing')     #should not be indented

if inPut == 4:
print('Hello!')      #should be indented
```

If you put the following:

```
print(Hello World!)
```

Python will say it has a SyntaxError and point with ^ to the exclamation point. The problem is that ! has no meaning in Python.

The correct code would be:

```
print("Hello, World!")     #correct code as in this instance
                           #Python would understand that the !
                           #is part of the text
```

Another example of a syntax error in Python would be:

```
class = "Computer Science"      #this syntax error is because
                                #you are using one of the special
                                #words in Python, the word "class"
```

If you had written GCSE instead of class, there would not have been a problem.

```
GCSE = "Computer Science"      #correct code
```

Name error

You may also have a name error.

This happens when you have:

- misspelt a variable, function or method name
- forgotten to import a module
- forgotten to define a variable.

But if the computer states an error message that does not contain the word 'SyntaxError' it must be a runtime error.

Some program languages that are specifically designed to introduce programming to people utilise a **drag and drop** method of writing code, where the user clicks and drags small bits of code into the place in the program where they require it. This allows them the freedom to concentrate on creating a solution to a programming problem with a robust structure without having the added distraction of satisfying syntax requirements.

You will need to be able to find errors in both your own code and the examination code so you will need to understand how to do this.

KEY POINT

If the rules of a language are broken by the program it is a syntax error. If the logical structure of the program produces unexpected results it is a logic error.

Runtime errors

Runtime errors occur whenever the program instructs the computer to carry out an operation that it is either not designed to do or will not do.

Going past the last index of a list also causes an error. ("IndexError: list index out of range")

This error happens with code like this:

```
myList = ['cat', 'dog', 'horse']
print(myList[6])   #the maximum it can be is myList[2]
```

A typo for a method name causes a run-time error or syntax error:

```
myData = 'THIS IS IN LOWERCASE.'
myData = myData.lowerr()   #should be one r not two
```

In some programs runtime errors commonly occur when programming statements are written in the *wrong order* or a programmer constructs instructions that the computer is unable to carry out.

One of the commonest runtime errors is when a program instructs a computer to divide any number by the value zero. This operation produces an infinitely large result, which consequentially is too large for a computer to accommodate. In this situation the computer will return an error message informing the user that it is unable to perform that operation.

```
a = 0            #this will cause an error as no
                 #number can be divided by 0

print(10 / a)

title = 'AQA Computer Science GCSE'

print( titel )   #should be title so in Python
                 #shows as a runtime error as
                 #code is correct

                 #In a compiled language this
                 #would be a syntax error.
```

Many runtime errors occur because the coder is using an undefined variable or function. This can also occur if you use capital letters inconsistently in a variable name:

```
callMe = 'Today or Tomorrow'
print(callme)   #run-time error should be callMe
```

This would also be classified as a syntax error in many languages as the compiler would stop the program compiling.

QUESTION

What is a runtime error?

KEY POINT

Runtime errors only appear when the program is running. Adding numbers to strings or dividing by 0 can cause them.

QUESTION

Explain the following statement:

"Run-time Error ´339´ component ´MCI32.OCX´ or one of its dependencies is not correctly registered: a file is missing or invalid"

In Python it is a runtime error because the language is interpreted.

It makes no sense in mathematics to divide by zero so this leads to a runtime error. This is because 0 times any number is 0, so there is no solution to 1 = X * 0.

```
print(1/0)          #run-time error: can't divide 1 by zero

a = input()

b = input()

c = int(a) / int(b)  #shows a runtime error when b = 0
```

Using operators on the wrong type of data also leads to a runtime error, for example you cannot add text and numbers together.

```
print("print this" + 19)     #run-time error: two different data types
                             #but could also be a syntax error
```

Logic errors

Out of the three common errors that occur in programming, logic errors are typically the most difficult kind to detect and rectify. This is usually down to the fact that there is no obvious indication of the error within the software. The code will run successfully but it will not behave in the way it was designed to. In other words, it will simply produce incorrect results.

The most common reasons for logic errors are as a result of the following:

- the programmer did not understand the manner in which the program was meant to behave
- the programmer did not understand the individual behaviour of each operation that was part of the program
- careless programming.

An example of a logic error is when a function that is supposed to return the larger of its two arguments returns the smaller argument:

```
def larger(x, y):

    if x > y:

        return y

    return x
```

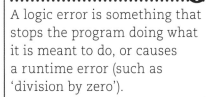

KEY POINT

A logic error is something that stops the program doing what it is meant to do, or causes a runtime error (such as 'division by zero').

KEY POINT

Out of the three common errors that occur in programming, logic errors are typically the most difficult kind of errors to detect and rectify.

KEY POINT

An argument is any piece of data that is passed into a function when the function is called.

With logic errors your code might run perfectly well without crashing, but still do the wrong thing or produce incorrect results.

In mathematics, to calculate an average of a set of numbers we add the numbers then divide by the number of numbers.

So if we have two numbers a and b:

add a + b then divide by the number of items, in this case by 2

But if we write:

```
a = 3

b = 4

average = a + b / 2

print(average)
```

we will get an answer of 5.0 not 3.5

To make the code work we would need to do the following:

```
a = 3

b = 4

average = (a + b) / 2

print(average)
```

```
if age < 5 and age > 70:      #Age cannot be less than 5 and
                              #greater than 70 at the same time

    print('Free entry!')
```

Let's look at another example of a logic error. Say we want to find the sum of 2 + 8 = 10 multiplied by a variable of 5. We could write the following Python code:

```
num = 5

print('Result:', num * 2 + 8)
```

Output: Result: 18

The code will run but the answer will not be what we want, we have another example of a logic error.

To get the output to be what we wanted we need to add brackets:

```
num = 5

print('Result:', num * (2 + 8))
```

Output: Result: 50

Now we have a correct output, the logic error has been fixed.

Often logic errors will remain undetected until an angry user contacts the programmer to say that the program has performed some calamitous operation, such as paying all the employees of a company too much in their monthly salary!

So how can logic errors be prevented? Well, the following rules should prevent most of the errors occurring. Programmers should:

- fully understand how a finished program is meant to behave
- have thorough knowledge of the behaviour of every operation that is written into the program
- avoid careless programming
- implement a thorough and rigorous testing strategy.

Testing for errors before and during the coding stages

It is important to thoroughly test a system in order to ensure that it is **robust** and not likely to **malfunction**. It should be understood, however, that a program is very unlikely to work perfectly the first time it is executed. Therefore testing is carried out on the code to try and make it fail and reveal the presence of errors. If software is not tested effectively in extreme circumstances the consequences could:

- ruin the reputation of the company that has written the program
- cause an accident if the code is part of a program that runs a system on an aircraft or within a nuclear power station, for example.

In the next section we will look at **debugging**, which is the process of detecting and correcting errors during execution of the program. However, in this section we will look at how errors can be detected prior to running the program.

Dry-run testing

Dry-run testing is usually carried out on the algorithm which is written in pseudo-code or as part of a flowchart. This form of testing is usually done prior to the program code being written.

The process involves the stepping through of the algorithm one instruction at a time with purposely chosen example test data. A **trace table** is used by the programmer to keep track of the test data, its purpose being to demonstrate what went wrong within an algorithm and pin-point exactly where the problem is. It should be understood that this form of testing is usually done on a small scale as it is quite hard work and very repetitive.

KEY POINTS

- A **trace** is a method of using data to check that a flowchart or code covers all possibilities correctly.
- A **trace table** is a technique used to test algorithms. They are used to make sure that no logic errors occur whilst the algorithm is being processed.

QUESTION

Describe three methods that a programmer can deploy to test for errors when programming.

Trace tables

A **trace table** is a technique used to test algorithms to see if any logic errors are occurring whilst the algorithm is being processed.

Within the table, each column contains a variable and each row displays each numerical input into the algorithm and the resultant values of the variables.

Trace tables are particularly popular with people who are learning to program.

We will look at this in more detail using a Python example:

```
1  y = 2         #variable y = 2
2  x = 2         #variable x = 2
3  y = y + x
```

Trace table:

Line	y	x
1	2	
2	2	2
3	4	2

Now we will use this in a simple WHILE loop:

```
1  number = 1              #line 1
2  y = 2                   #line 2
3  x = 2                   #line 3
4  while number < 4:       #line 4 start of the loop
5      number = number + 1 #line 5 the variable called number increases by 1
6      y = y + x           #line 6 the variable y increases by variable x
7      print(y)            #added so we can see the value of y as an output
```

Output:

    4

    6

    8

Trace table

Line	number	y	x
1	1		
2	1	2	
3	1	2	2
4	1	2	2
5	2	2	2
6	2	4	2
4	2	4	2
5	3	4	2
6	3	6	2
4	3	6	2
5	4	6	2
6	4	8	2
4	4	8	2

KEY POINT

The main advantage of dry-run testing is it enables programmers to spot errors even before they start writing code.

QUESTION

What is a trace table?

Checking code using unit testing

If a programmer has only to check the code within a small program they may just go literally through the program line by line checking for errors manually. Now, this is tedious enough with a small program and is also open to human error so you can imagine that with large programs this process of checking code is completely unfeasible, so professional program developers use software tools called unit tests.

Unit testing is a popular practice that consists of writing additional programs that test individual functions of a main program under development. Unit tests are small pieces of code whose purpose is to prove the software modules are correct.

Unit testing is an important process as it is an automatic tool that can uncover **regressions** – unwanted changes in previously working code, which may have inadvertently been introduced during development.

Like other software, there are effective and ineffective unit tests. A poor unit test will focus on a scenario that is not relevant for the application, whilst a good quality unit test is one that is written to catch cases such as a scenario where someone enters a negative value as a salary figure.

Code coverage is a term that is used to describe the percentage of lines of code that are covered by unit tests.

Testing for errors during the execution of code

The process of testing a program for errors during its execution is a cyclic activity called debugging. To debug code effectively, two things are needed:

- the ability to test each of the instructions provided by a program
- the capability to retrieve the information back about:
  - the results of those instructions
  - any changes in the program when the tests were carried out
  - the error conditions
  - what the program was doing when the error occurred.

Fortunately, there are software tools that can assist in the debugging process. These tools are called debuggers and the source code of a program is run through these in order to detect syntax, runtime and logic errors. The debugger produces a report on-screen which highlights and lists the above information to the program tester.

KEY POINT

The process of testing a program for errors during its execution is a cyclic activity called debugging.

Debuggers

There are a number of specific features within debuggers which can assist the program tester in detecting errors, such as:

- breakpoints
- watcher
- steps.

KEY POINT

Make sure parts of your programs work as you work on them. Do not write massive files of code before you try to run them. Code a little, run a little, fix a little.

Breakpoints

Breakpoints are breaks that can be manually inserted into code by the tester in order to halt the execution of the program at specific points to allow the tester to inspect the values of variables at those points. Usually, code on the line where a breakpoint has been inserted will be highlighted in red or yellow. Any number of breakpoints can be inserted into a program, although a point is reached when there really is no reason to insert any more break points.

Watch

A watch is usually in the format of a table and display of the values of specified fields and variables relative to the particular line that the debugger is currently on. To add a watch, the tester usually types the name of the variable they are interested in within an area of the user interface of the debugging program.

Also, expressions that require evaluation, such as x + 1 or array accesses, can be typed in to a watch.

Steps

Once the program is paused (for example, by a breakpoint), the debugger allows the tester to continue the execution of the program one line at a time, effectively stepping through the program. This allows a programmer the capability to see exactly how many variables and objects are impacted when a particular line is executed.

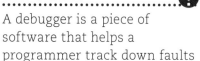

KEY POINT

A debugger is a piece of software that helps a programmer track down faults in a program.

How do you document your tests?

For most programs, it is practically impossible to *prove* that the program is correct on all machines and systems with any input. What you do need to do is demonstrate that your program works as stated in the specification. You do this by producing a testing document (Figure 24.1) saying how you intend to test the program and then showing the results of these tests.

This documentation is called a **test plan**, and you should provide one with each program. The test plan shown is an example of one used by a software company. Yours will be simpler, but remember to record the tests you carry out.

But remember to only list measurable things in your test plan.

Software test plan

1. Identifier (Test Plan ID)	
2. Brief introduction (testing objective)	
3. Test items (modules)	
4. Features to be tested	
5. Features not to be tested	
6. Test approach	Which test type (func/non-func/code)
7. Entry/exit criteria	
8. Suspension and resumption criteria	
9. Test environment	Hardware and software needed
10. Testing tasks	
11. Test deliverables	
12. Roles and responsibilities	List of all major tasks to complete the testing effort
13. Staffing and training needs	
14. Schedule	Test estimation

Figure 24.1 *Software test plan*

When should testing take place?

If a basic software development **lifecycle** is considered, testing is usually carried out between the development period and the application launch or handover to the client. For you this would be before you pass your finished program to the teacher. But this is not a good way to do it as testing should be an ongoing process as the software is developed.

Types of testing

There are three types of test data:

1. Under normal conditions: the application is tested under normal working conditions and the data that a coded solution is supplied with is within the anticipated range.
2. Under extreme conditions: the coded solution is provided with data that is within the operating range but at its limits of performance.

3. Under erroneous conditions: an application or program is provided with data that is outside its limits of performance. These particular tests try to break the application and to investigate if things occur when they shouldn't or vice versa.

Choosing the test data

Before performing a test, you need to decide what data you intend to use to carry out the test. It is not normally possible to perform tests with every single possible piece of data. Developers need to choose from a limited range of test data. In making this choice, the developer considers the following:

- valid data: selecting the most common data that should work under normal conditions
- extreme data: data that is always valid, but is on the limit of what is accepted
- boundary data: data that is on either side of the boundary, so it might be valid or invalid
- erroneous data: invalid data, i.e. data that is expected to fail, for example data that is clearly the wrong data type and should fail.

Tests should find that the program works as expected with the correct data and rejects erroneous data without crashing.

For example, if you are developing a game where the user must select a whole number between 1 and 20, you could try a range of inputs to see what happens:

3, 14, (valid data) 1, 20, (valid extreme), the string "three", –12 (erroneous), 20.01111 (invalid extreme data)

Testing under normal conditions is about testing valid data that should be accepted.

Testing extreme behaviour involves being subjected to tests on the borderline of failure but within the acceptable range to understand how the software behaves. With limits of 0 and 20 being subjected to tests, we need to explore values such as 1 and 20.

Testing invalid extreme behaviour involves being subjected to tests on the borderline of failure, but just outside the acceptable range to understand how the software behaves.

With limits of 0 and 20 being subjected to tests we need to explore values such as 0.5 and 20.5.

Lastly, testing erroneous invalid behaviour involves the variable with limits of 0 and 20 being subjected to tests where the returned results should be clearly wrong to understand how the software behaves.

CHAPTER REVIEW

In this chapter we have explored types of errors and how to test your code.

We have also explored test plans and how to record your tests.

Remember, before tackling any computer science task or question on this topic you must:

- understand how to use a debugger
- understand common errors and how to find them
- be able to select suitable test data
- understand how to draw up a test plan.

25 The Computer System's Architecture

Hardware is a name given to a collection of physical 'things' that, when put together in a certain way, form a **system**. The hardware is the machine. To be able to write programs you must understand the function of hardware components of a computer.

The human body could be looked upon as a collection of hardware. First you have your brain – not the thought processes that go on inside it but the physical organ. Then you have the internal hardware that keeps your body working, such as your heart, lungs and digestive system.

You also have 'devices' for taking on board different information, such as the eyes for visual data, your hands that use the sense of touch for tactile information, your ears for sound information and not forgetting your tongue for your sense of taste.

All this information is processed and stored in your brain but only whist you are still alive.

Your body has ways of outputting information too. This involves using speech as well as movements, expressions and gestures that you can make with your face and body.

So hardware basically refers to parts or components of a system that can be physically touched – although there are not many of us that could truly say that they would like to touch someone's brain or internal organs.

Now let's now take a look at the hardware components of a computer and how they fit together to form a system.

The main components are shown in Figure 25.1:

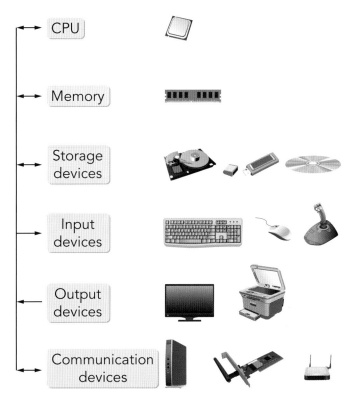

Figure 25.1 *Computer hardware components*

Input/output

Inputs and user interfaces

Every interactive device has to have an input process and output. In computer science, we are interested in the interaction between the computer and the human brain (Figure 25.2).

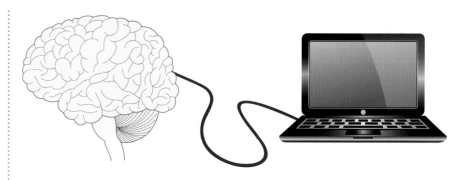

Figure 25.2 *The brain and the computer*

Inputs to humans are via our receptors. We have a very wide range of input receptors, such as eyes and ears.

Computers need **input** and **output** devices too. A keyboard and a mouse are input devices. Most screens on desktop computers are output devices. Screens on mobile phones and tablet computers are both output *and* input devices as they have a touch screen. A camera is an input device and a printer an output device. A games controller can be just an input device, but if it can vibrate it is an output device too.

Of course any input device is only of use if it can link to the user in some way. The user needs to show the computer what it wants it to do.

A **user interface**, 'UI', is the means by which a user can control a software application or hardware device. A good user interface provides a 'user-friendly' experience, meaning it is easy to use. The user interface is one of the most important parts of any program because it determines how easily you can make the program or device do what you want it to do.

Input can be from physical devices such as the mouse, game controller, keyboard, etc. But it can also be from virtual devices within the software.

 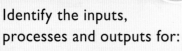
Nearly all software programs now have a graphical user interface, 'GUI'. This means the program uses graphical controls, accessed via a mouse, touchpad, touchscreen or keyboard.

A typical GUI includes a menu bar, toolbar, windows, buttons, and other controls.

Macs and Windows PC operating systems have very different user interfaces, but they share many of the same elements, such as a desktop, windows, icons, pop-ups, etc.

Hardware devices also include a user interface. A typical TV remote has a numeric keypad, volume and channel buttons, mute and power buttons. The remote is a user interface.

While user interfaces can be designed for either hardware of software, most are a combination of both.

Output devices

Humans can also output data and information. We can do this with physical pressure and movement using our hands, feet, head and eyes. We can output noise by clapping, speech and singing.

The most popular output devices for a computer used to be the screen/monitor, printers and speakers. Today we have a plethora of new output devices from 3D virtual glasses and heads-up displays to electronic paper and voice synthesisers.

Of course, these components must work together. They are all connected via the motherboard.

Von Neumann architecture

In the 1940s, a mathematician called John von Neumann described a basic **architecture** arrangement of a computer.

Most of today's computers follow the concept that he described.

Von Neumann architecture relates to the relationship between the hardware that makes up a computer system.

A von Neumann-based computer:
- uses one memory for both instructions and data
- cannot distinguish between data and instructions in a memory location
- executes programs by doing one instruction after the next in a serial manner using a fetch-decode-execute cycle.

Advantage of von Neumann architecture

The largest advantage is that it simplifies the micro-controller chip design because only one memory is accessed.

In micro-controllers, the most important thing is the contents of RAM (random access memory) and in the von Neumann system it can be used for both variable (data) storage and program instruction storage.

Another advantage is that it allows greater flexibility in developing software, particularly in the development of operating systems

Disadvantages of von Neumann architecture

Whilst the advantages far outweigh the disadvantages, the problem is that there is only one bus (pathway) connecting the memory and the processor. Because of this only one part of an instruction or a data item can be fetched at a time. This means the processor may have to wait longer for the data/instruction to arrive. This is referred to as the von Neumann bottleneck.

Motherboard

Within a computer the hardware within the system includes the **CPU** (central processing unit), which is situated on a **printed circuit board** called the **motherboard**. The motherboard links the CPU to the memory and other hardware.

There is the hard disk drive, the RAM (random access memory), optical drive and other circuit boards such as the graphics and sound cards.

These are all regarded as hardware (Figure 25.3) because if you removed the case you could physically touch the devices; however, you should not do that unless you know what you are doing! The hardware refers only to the electronic and electro-mechanical parts of the computer, not the casing.

RESEARCH TASK

Use this book and other sources such as the internet to research the von Neumann model.

QUESTION

What is the purpose of the CPU?

KEY POINT

The **motherboard** is the central printed circuit board (PCB) that holds all the crucial components of the system.

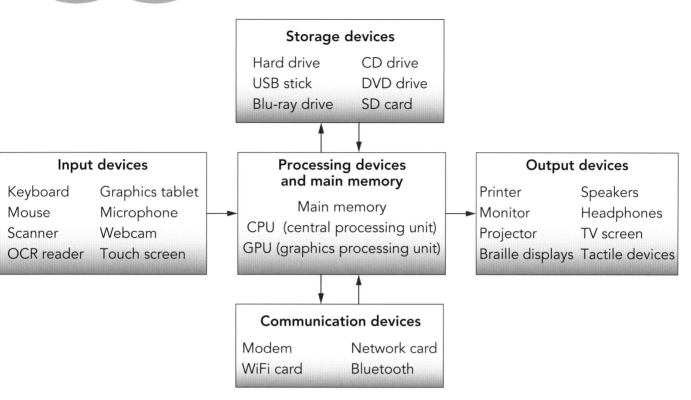

Figure 25.3 *A summary of a computer system's hardware*

QUESTION

What is a motherboard?

QUESTION

Define a system.

RESEARCH TASK

Use this book and other sources such as the internet to research the function of the hardware components of a computer system.

The motherboard (Figure 25.4) is like your nerves, the essential connections that send and receive signals throughout your body. The CPU computes data and uses the motherboard to receive and send signals to things like the hard drives (storage). A chip on the motherboard is also responsible for holding all of the computer settings, such as Time and Date. Both the CPU and the motherboard have speeds associated with them.

Figure 25.4 *A motherboard*

Bus

A **bus** is a collection of parallel wires used for data transmission. The bus is the part of the circuit that connects one part of the motherboard to another. The more data the motherboard's bus can handle at any one time, the faster the system. The speed of the bus is measured in megahertz, as is the speed of the CPU (see below). Motherboards have buses for data, address and control, and each one transfers data from one computer component to another.

The CPU – Central Processing Unit

This internal device is often referred to as the 'computer's brain' and it is the piece of hardware that is responsible for the 'compute' in computer. If you did not have the **CPU**, you would not have a computer.

Just like our brain, the CPU's purpose is to process data and it does this by performing functions such as searching and sorting data, and calculating and decision-making using the data.

What this means is that every task that you carry out on a computer, whether it is designing a spreadsheet, writing an email, playing a game or searching the internet, the CPU deals with all of the data-processing associated with those and many more tasks which makes them possible.

The history of the CPU is very interesting. People define CPU in different ways: some people include the main memory in the CPU and some just use CPU as an alternative word for processor.

The first CPU chip was invented in November 1971. It was basically a 4-bit processor designed for a calculator. Its instructions were eight bits long. Program and data were separate.

Since these early days of CPUs with a **single-core** processor there have been many changes to the 'brain' in our computer.

Processor speed doubled every few years. One big change to the CPU was the addition of a second core, resulting in **dual-core** processors. Each core has its own cache and controller. The benefit of this is that each core functions as efficiently as a single processor. Because the two cores are linked together, they can perform operations twice as fast as a single core can.

Imagine making your breakfast, which includes buttered toast and a cup of tea. However fast you work, some tasks will need your full attention. For example, you cannot butter the toast and pour the tea at the same time. But if you had a second person to help you, and they made the toast and you made the tea, the process would be much faster. Providing you were each given the correct instructions, of course.

Figure 25.5 *Quad-core processor*

But the technology has not stopped there. The next step was **quad-core** processors (Figure 25.5). You may be thinking that each addition multiplies the processing power of a single-processor machine, but it does not always work like this. The software running on the machine has to be designed to take full advantage all the processors.

Some ARM processors designed for mobile devices can even interpret Java bytecode directly.

The CPU undertakes instructions it receives from programs in what is called a **cycle**. If we go back to the making the toast and tea example, obviously, if you worked faster, you could produce the breakfast quicker. Maybe the addition of a faster kettle would help too. The CPU not only has a number of cores, it also has speed. The speed of the CPU is measured in how many cycles it can perform in a second. The name given to one cycle per second is a hertz. A CPU that processes one million cycles per second is said to have a speed of a megahertz, and a CPU that can handle one billion cycles per second is said to have a clock speed of one gigahertz.

Therefore, to have a very high CPU speed is a good thing, because more instructions per second get executed. The problem is that the faster it is the hotter it gets, and the more power it needs.

Most CPUs now are at least 2 GHz.

But most people cannot notice the speed difference between one processor speed and the next speed higher unless they play the very latest computer games. And, if we go back to our breakfast analogy, however fast you work and however many friends you have to help you, if the instructions are not clear and the things you need are not available you will not be any faster. With CPUs, programmers have a part to play in maximising the speed and use of the cores they have.

Components of the processor

A processor contains the following components:

- arithmetic and logic unit – performs arithmetic and logical operations on data
- control unit – fetches, decodes, executes instructions
- internal buses – to connect the components
- internal clock – derived directly or indirectly from the system clock.

Arithmetic logic unit

The **arithmetic logic unit** (called the ALU) is a major component of the central processing unit of a computer system.

The ALU routinely performs the following:

- logical operations: these include AND, OR, NOT
- logical comparisons
- bit-shifting operations: this pertains to shifting the positions of the bits by a certain number of places to the right or left, which is considered a multiplication operation
- arithmetic operations: this refers to bit addition and subtraction.

Control unit

The **control unit** (called the CU) handles all processor control signals. It directs all input and output flow, fetches code for instructions from microprograms and directs other units and models by providing control and timing signals.

CU functions are as follows:

- controls sequential instruction execution
- interprets instructions
- guides data flow through different computer areas
- regulates and controls processor timing
- sends and receives control signals from other computer devices
- handles tasks, such as fetching, decoding, execution handling and storing results.

QUESTION

What does the arithmetic logic unit (ALU) do?

Internal buses

An internal bus is a type of data bus that only operates inside the computer or system. It carries data and operations as a standard bus, however it is only used for connecting and interacting with internal computer components.

The CPU bus is internal to the CPU and is used to transport data to and from the ALU.

Internal clock

A clock is a signal used to synchronise things inside the computer. The beginning of each clock cycle is when the clock signal goes from '0' to '1', marked with an arrow in Figure 25.6. The clock signal is measured in a unit called Hertz (Hz), which is the number of clock cycles per second. A clock of 100 MHz means that in one second there are 100 million clock cycles.

Figure 25.6 *The clock cycle*

In computing all timings are measured in terms of clock cycles.

Factors affecting processor performance

There are a number of things in the computer architecture that can affect the processor performance. We discuss the most important factors here.

Number of cores

A CPU can contain one or more processing units. Each unit is called a core. Each core contains an ALU, control unit and registers.

Today, processors often have two (dual-core), four (quad-core) or more cores. CPUs with multiple cores have more power and can therefore run a number of programs at the same time.

You may think that a dual-core processor will have double the speed of a single core but it does not work like that because each CPU has to communicate with the other and this uses up some of the extra speed. Added to this, some tasks cannot be split up effectively so do not benefit from more cores.

Clock speed

The clock speed of a processor is stated in megahertz (MHz) or gigahertz (GHz). Basically, the faster the clock, the more instructions the processor can complete per second, but there are limits to how fast a CPU can run. If the clock tells the CPU to execute instructions too quickly, the processing will not be completed before the next instruction is carried out. It can also overheat.

On-board cache

The on-board **cache** is a type of high-performance RAM built directly into the processor. Cache has both size and type. It enables the CPU to access repeatedly used data directly from its own on-board memory. We will explore this in more detail in chapter 27 when we explore memory.

Instruction sets

The user has no control over the instruction set. It is built in to the CPU and cannot be changed or updated. But, together with processor architecture, the built-in instruction set does affect the CPU's performance. Some instruction sets are more efficient than others, enabling the processor to do more processing. Processor benchmark tests can be used to measure the speed the processor can carry out instructions.

CHAPTER REVIEW

In this chapter we have explored the computer system architecture.

We have also explored the von Neumann architecture.

Remember, before tackling any computer science task or question on this topic you must:

- understand how the architecture works together
- define the terms hardware and software and understand the relationship between them (More on this topic in chapter 34.)
- be able to explain the von Neumann architecture
- be able to explain the role and operation of main memory and the following major components of a CPU:
  - arithmetic and logic unit
  - control unit
  - internal buses
  - internal clock
- be able to explain the effect of the following on the performance of the CPU:
  - number of cores
  - clock speed
  - on-board cache
  - instruction sets.

26 Embedded Systems

RESEARCH TASK

Use this book and other sources such as the internet to research the item embedded system.

An embedded system is a system that has computer hardware with software embedded in it as one of its components. As embedded systems are small, low cost and simple they have become very popular and are now indispensable in our lives. They are found everywhere, from kitchens to hospitals.

Consider this list of embedded systems that are being used every day:

- aircraft (flight landing gear systems and many other systems from sensors to controllers)
- all gym equipment from treadmill to cycling equipment
- ATMs
- car systems (pressure monitoring system, airbags, power windows and GPS systems)
- microwave ovens
- military applications

- mobile phones
- pace makers
- robots
- toys
- TV remotes (and all other remote control devices)
- vending machines
- washing machines (including dishwashers and drying machines)

and many more …

Every embedded system consists of custom-built hardware built around a micro-controller. The hardware contains memory chips onto which the software is loaded. The software residing on the memory chip is called 'firmware'. Not all embedded systems have an operating system. Small appliances, such as toys and remote control units, do not need an operating system and we can write only the software specific to that application.

Programming microcontrollers

Often you can program a microcontroller using the BASIC programming language.

Standard basic instructions include:

for...next (the normal looping statement)

go sub (go to a subroutine)

goto (goto a label in the program)

if...then (the normal if/then decision statement)

end (end the program and sleep)

BASIC logic statements include:

=	>
<>	>=
<	AND
<=	OR

The Raspberry Pi (Figure 26.1) can be used as a microcontroller and you may have come across one. It is only the size of a credit-card but it is in fact a fully functioning single-board computer. It was developed in the UK by the Raspberry Pi Foundation to help promote the teaching of computer science in schools.

KEY POINT

Embedded systems frequently have more limited resources than PCs. Embedded systems usually focus on dedicated tasks but PCs are general-purpose computers.

KEY POINT

Embedded systems usually require minimal human intervention.

QUESTION

Briefly describe the term embedded system.

QUESTION

What is a programming language?

Figure 26.1 *Raspberry Pi*

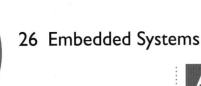

Actuators and sensors

Micro-processors use actuators and sensors to function (Figure 26.2).

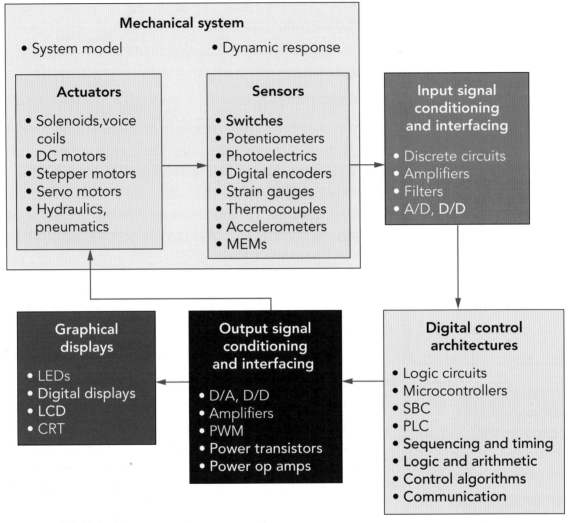

Figure 26.2 *Architecture of actuators and sensors*

Actuators

An actuator is used to move or control the output. It is a type of motor for moving or controlling a mechanism or system. To operate it needs a source of energy, usually in the form of electric current, hydraulic fluid pressure or pneumatic pressure. The actuator converts that energy into motion.

Sensors

A sensor is a converter that measures a physical quantity and converts it into a signal. The microcontroller uses this signal to make a decision. For example, a mercury thermometer converts the measured temperature into expansion and contraction of a liquid, which indicates the temperature via markings on the tube. Of course, this is not digital but analogue and microcontrollers need digital signals. For microcontrollers a thermocouple converts temperature to an output voltage which can be read.

A sensor is therefore a device which responds to an input quantity by generating either an analogue output, which would need converting into a digital signal by an analogue–digital convertor (ADC) or a digital output in the form of an electrical or optical signal.

KEY POINT

The term analogue refers to continuously changing values without steps.

Sensors in everyday objects

Modern mobile phones have a wide variety of sensors that automate many of our daily tasks.

Accelerometers

An accelerometer measures linear acceleration of movement. An accelerometer sensor will measure the directional movement of a device but cannot measure lateral orientation or tilt; for this a gyroscope sensor is needed.

Gyroscopes

Gyroscope (gyro) sensors are used in mobile phones to detect the orientation of the phone. A gyro sensor measures the angular rotational velocity. As such, the sensor tracks the phone's rotation or twist.

Digital compasses

The digital compass sensor in a mobile is usually based on a sensor called a magnetometer. This sensor provides mobile phones with a simple orientation in relation to the Earth's magnetic field. This way the phone always knows which way is North and can auto-rotate digital maps.

Barometers

A barometer sensor measures altitude. The barometer is there to help the phone's GPS chip lock onto GPS signals by delivering altitude data.

Wearable technology

Wearable technology, also called wearables, is clothing and accessories incorporating computer and advanced electronic embedded technologies. Wearables contain sensors, and also often make use of web connection and bluetooth networking to connect wirelessly to other devices and the connected world. They also use their inbuilt sensors to connect to your body and can be used to help to achieve goals such as fitness, weight loss or to be better organised.

Most of the early generation wearables were wrist worn but now an increasing number are clipped to the body, hung around the neck, built into things such as glasses or implanted into the body. The main types of wearable include:

- **smartwatches**: wrist-worn devices that connect to things like mobile phones and PDAs to tell the user about:
  - call notifications, email and social media messages
  - fitness tracking by keeping track of the activity the user does such as the number of steps taken or distance travelled, calorie count, etc.
  - where the user is, using GPS, sometimes with maps or breadcrumb trails to help them find their way

- **head-mounted displays**: objects such as glasses that are designed to either block out the rest of the world or add to it via virtual reality in order to:
  - present a computer-generated virtual reality
  - act as an overlay of information

- **smart clothing:** where the sensors are built into things you can wear

- **smart jewellery:** with sensors built into things like rings

- **implantables:** wearables that you have no choice but to carry with you wherever you go as they are surgically attached under your skin. They provide things such as:
  - insulin pumps
  - heart stimulation
  - contraceptive devices
  - validation for door entry and device control
  - brain stimulation.

Comparing embedded and non-embedded systems

An important difference between most embedded systems and non-embedded systems, is that an embedded operating system does not load and execute other applications. This means that the system is only able to run a single application. Embedded systems are often embedded in a large device or system. For example, a computer used to control a car is embedded, the microprocessor controlling a washing machine is embedded.

In embedded systems, the software typically resides in firmware, such as a flash memory or read-only memory (ROM) chip. In general-purpose computers this loads programs into random access memory (RAM) each time. The coding on an embedded system is, therefore, totally focused on controlling and managing the system (or hardware). The code is written to fully use the potential of the connected hardware and manage it for the benefit of the user. Though there is still data and algorithms in embedded systems, they only control and manage the specific connected hardware.

CHAPTER REVIEW

In this chapter we have explored embedded systems.

We have also explored microcontrollers.

Remember, before tackling any computer science task or question on this topic you must:

- understand the term embedded systems and where they could be found
- understand how an embedded system differs from a non-embedded system.

27 Memory

A computer has to store both programs and data whilst they are being used and when the computer is turned off. It does this using a storage device which stores data and programs either temporarily or permanently. The main storage or memory (often called primary storage) is the area in a computer in which data is stored for quick access by the computer's processor.

There are two fundamentally different types of storage:

● main memory (often just called memory)
● secondary store (also known as backing store).

The main memory is where the operating system resides. The main memory is divided into two types:

● read-only memory (ROM)
● random access memory (RAM).

QUESTION

What is an array?

KEY POINT

On modern computers, memory is usually composed of semiconductors known as RAM (random access memory).

KEY POINT

There are two technologies for RAM chips: dynamic RAM and static RAM.

KEY POINT

Volatile memory is a type of storage whose contents are erased when the system's power is turned off or interrupted.

KEY POINT

Non-volatile memory is typically used for the task of secondary storage, or long-term persistent storage. Examples: ROM and hard drive.

KEY POINT

ROM retains data when the computer is turned off. Its contents are permanently embedded and thus will not be erased when power is turned off.

KEY POINT

Firmware is programming that's written to the read only memory (ROM) of a computing device. It is added at the time of manufacturing and is used to run user programs on the device.

Data within a computer's main memory is actually stored in individually addressable memory cells. Structures such as arrays, lists and trees are simulated to make the data more accessible to the data's users. The computer is capable of determining what an individual memory cell contains by a process referred to as 'reading'. The contents of a memory cell can also be changed (a process referred to as 'writing') but when something is written to a memory cell its former contents are lost.

Main memory has the following characteristics:

- Its contents can be accessed directly by CPU.
- It has very fast access times.
- It has relatively small capacity.

Contents of RAM are lost when a computer is turned off (**volatile**) but contents of ROM are retained (**non-volatile**).

Secondary store is always non-volatile. Secondary store can be external devices like CDs, magnetic disks, etc. We will explore this in more detail in chapter 28.

Contents in secondary store cannot be accessed directly by CPU. The data must be transferred into main memory to be used through a process of loading and saving. This makes it slower but is does have much higher capacity.

ROM

ROM is memory that cannot be changed by a program or user. ROM retains its memory even after the computer is turned off. ROM is used to store the instructions for the computer to boot up when it is turned on again.

ROM is also used to store software that needs to be available when the computer is turned on (such as the instructions for booting the computer) or software that will 'never' change, such as the BIOS.

With von Neumann architecture, the program(s) being run are kept in the computer memory as well as the data that is currently being processed.

RESEARCH TASK

Use this book and other sources such as the internet to research the role and operation of main memory.

27 Memory

RAM

RAM is a fast, temporary type of memory in which programs, applications and data are held.

RAM holds things while they are running:

● the operating system
● applications software.

If a computer loses power, all data stored in its RAM is lost.

Cache memory

Cache memory is a special type of RAM and is part of the primary store. The cache is almost always located on the same microchip as the CPU. This means it can be accessed much more quickly than ordinary RAM. Processors often have separate caches for data and instructions. By executing a program from cache memory, a program also runs more quickly.

The basic purpose of cache memory is to store program instructions that are frequently re-referenced by software during operation. Fast access to these instructions increases the overall speed of the software program. But cache memory is much more expensive than ordinary RAM, so computers don't have much of it.

The CPU has to decide which parts of a program to keep in the cache to gain maximum performance improvements.

The cache only stores a copy of the data also stored in RAM but as the microprocessor processes data, it looks first in the cache memory. If the data was used previously it often finds the data there and does not have to do a more time-consuming reading of data from larger memory or other data storage devices.

Traditionally, cache is categorised in 'levels' that describe its closeness and accessibility of the cache to the microprocessor:

● Level 1 (L1) cache is extremely fast but relatively small, and is usually embedded in the processor chip (CPU), which is why it is called level 1: it is closest to the processor. Level 1 cache usually ranges in size from 8 kB to 64 kB.

- Level 2 (L2) cache is often larger than L1 but one stage further from the processor although still on the same chip.

- Level 3 (L3) cache is typically specialised memory that works to improve the performance of L1 and L2. It can be significantly slower than L1 or L2, but is usually double the speed of RAM.

The size of the cache refers to the size of the data store. A typical level 2 cache is either 256 kB or 512 kB, but can be as small as 64 kB, or as high as 2 MB.

Most programs use very few resources once they have been opened and operated for a time. This is because frequently re-referenced instructions will be cached. The more cache the system has the more likelihood that a particular memory fetch will find the data that it requires in the cache, leading to less main memory accesses and better performance. Computers with slower processors but larger caches tend to be faster than (using measurements taken of a system performance) computers with faster processors but less cache.

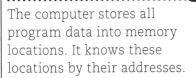

KEY POINT

The computer stores all program data into memory locations. It knows these locations by their addresses.

CHAPTER REVIEW

In this chapter we have explored computer memory.

Remember, before tackling any computer science task or question on this topic you must:

- understand the terms RAM and ROM
- understand cache
- understand memory speeds
- understand the differences between main memory and secondary storage
- understand the differences between RAM and ROM
- be able to explain the effect of the following on the performance of the CPU:
  - cache size
  - cache type.

28 Secondary Storage

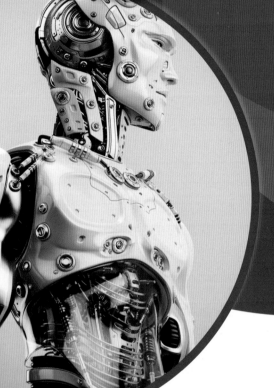

The majority of secondary storage devices are used for long-term storage. They are also used to:

- back up data
- add more storage space for files/pictures/videos, etc.
- easily transport files
- share files over a network.

Different types of non-volatile secondary storage include:

- magnetic storage
- optical storage
    - compact disks (CDs)
    - digital versatile disks (DVDs)
    - Blu-ray disks
- solid state disks: USB flash drives (pen drives) and flash memory cards.

Magnetic storage devices (MSD)

In **magnetic storage**, a magnetic hard disk drive (HDD) uses moving read/write heads that contain electromagnets (Figure 28.1). These create a magnetic charge on the disk's surface, which contains iron particles that can be given a magnetic charge in one of two directions. Each magnetic particle's direction represents 0 (off) or 1 (on). As you will remember, these represent a bit of data that the CPU can recognise.

On a magnetic hard disk, the data is stored in thin, concentric bands. A drive head is used to read or write a circular ring, or band, which is called a track. There can be more than a thousand tracks on a 3.5-inch hard disk. The sections within each track are called sectors. A sector is the smallest physical storage unit on a disk, and is almost always 4,096 bytes in size.

The head can move to any given sector to read or write data from/to that sector. It is best if the data is stored in groups of sectors that are next to each other. The name given to a group of sectors is a cluster. A cluster can consist of one or more consecutive sectors. But sometimes the next sector is unavailable so the second cluster may need to be written elsewhere on the same disk. It will be written wherever the file system finds another sector available. A file stored in this non-contiguous manner is said to be fragmented. Fragmented files can slow down system performance as the file system needs to direct the drive heads to several different addresses to find all the data in the file.

Advantages of magnetic storage

- Very large data storage capacity.
- Stores and retrieves data much faster than an optical disk.
- Data is not lost when you switch off the computer as it is with RAM.
- Cheap per MB compared to other storage media.

Disadvantages of magnetic storage

- Hard disks have moving parts which can fail.
- Crashes can damage the surface of the disk, leading to loss of data.

KEY POINT

In **magnetic storage**, magnetic material is given a polarity. That polarity is then read and depending on the direction is output as a binary 1 or a 0.

Magnetised data on disk

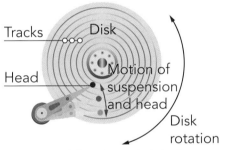

Figure 28.1 *A hard disk drive*

RESEARCH TASK

Use this book and other sources such as the internet to research how data is stored on physical devices (magnetic, optical, solid state).

- Easily damaged if dropped.
- Uses a large amount of power compared to other media.
- Can be noisy.

Optical storage devices (OSD)

An optical drive uses reflected light to read data (Figure 28.2). Writing to the disk is achieved using a laser beam to record digital (binary) data. In **optical storage** technology, this laser beam encodes digital data onto an optical, or laser, disk in the form of tiny pits arranged in concentric tracks on the disk's surface.

Once written, the optical disk's surface is covered with tiny dents (pits) and flat spots (lands). When an optical drive shines light onto the disk the light is reflected back from a pit or land but scattered by the transition between the two. Continuing with a pit or land is therefore used to represent a bit value of 0 (off) but a change between the two represents a bit value of 1 (on).

The polycarbonate disk layer contains the tiny dents (pits) and flat spots (lands) which cause light to be reflected back off them. To make a recordable disk, you start with a polycarbonate layer that has blank grooves rather than a pattern of pits and lands. The blank grooves keep the drive on track before the data is written. The disk includes a thin layer of dye or other modifiable surface. Pulsing at high power, the laser in the drive 'burns' the pits and lands into the dye. So, in effect, a higher power laser is used to modify the reflective properties of the disk.

To read the data back, the laser works at normal, lower read power. For reading the disk the laser beam that reads and writes to the disk is reflected back to a sensor, which then converts it into electronic data

The reflective layer is there to reflect the laser.

A layer of lacquer covers the reflective layer to protect it from the artwork.

Artwork can be either screen printed or written onto this surface.

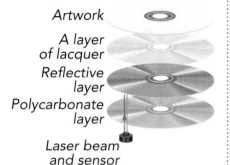

Artwork

A layer of lacquer

Reflective layer

Polycarbonate layer

Laser beam and sensor

Figure 28.2 *The layers of an optical disk*

KEY POINT ❗

In **optical storage**, pits and grooves in a flat surface provide a reflection for a laser, a light sensor then assigns a binary 1 or a 0 depending on the light intensity.

KEY POINT ❗

CD, DVD and Blu-ray disks are all the same physical size and use the same spiral track layout for placing data on the platter.

CD-R (CD-Recordable), DVD-R (DVD-Recordable) and BR-R (Blu-ray-Recordable) discs can, with minor exceptions, be written to only once. Data, once recorded, cannot be overwritten or deleted. Disks with the -RW (Rewritable) suffix can be written to repeatedly, by deleting or overwriting old data to make room for new data.

DVD led to an increase in storage capacity of up to five to ten times compared to CD. Blu-ray Disc increased DVD capacity by five to ten times. This was achieved mainly by using a blue laser rather than a red laser, and improved lenses. This allowed for a much smaller focus laser beam which enabled the recording of much smaller and higher density pits on the disc.

Advantages of optical storage devices

- Easy to store and carry.
- Read in a number of devices such as audio and TV systems.
- Long lasting if looked after properly.

Disadvantages of optical storage devices

- Data on write-once disks (CD-R, DVD-R) are permanent and cannot be changed.
- Require special drives to read/write.
- Expensive per GB/TB in comparison to other methods.
- No standards for longevity tests.
- Can easily be broken, scratched or damaged by heat and light.

Solid-state disks (SSD)

Solid-state disks contain no moving parts and are found in three common formats: hard disk replacements, memory cards and USB flash drives. They record data using special transistors that retain their state even when there is no power to them. Because there is no moving actuator arm, like on a hard disk drive, they are faster in reading and, in some cases, writing data. They are also more rugged so are not as easily damaged when dropped.

Solid-state disks are constructed of transistors and other components you'd also find on a computer chip. There are two

types of flash memory: NOR and NAND. Both contain transistors formed in a grid, but the wiring between the cells differs. In NOR flash, the cells are wired in parallel. In NAND flash, the cells are wired in series. These grids are separated into sections called 'pages', and these pages are where all the data is stored. Pages are then formed together to form what are called 'blocks'.

SSDs can't overwrite data directly. Instead, the SSD must first find an empty page in a block and then write to that empty page. Whenever data is written, it must be written to a new block even if it is just a write that updates part of the data in an existing block.

Advantages of solid-state disks

- Read speeds are faster than normal hard drives.
- Lightweight.
- Very durable.
- Free from mechanical problems.
- Require less power than magnetic drives.
- Silent in use.

Disadvantages of solid-state disks

- Limited storage capacity when compared to normal magnetic hard drives.
- Cost per MB stored is higher than magnetic drives.

Cloud storage

Cloud storage means 'the storage, of data online in the cloud'. In cloud storage, data is stored and is accessible from multiple distributed and connected resources that comprise a cloud via the internet.

In cloud storage, data is stored on servers and can be accessed across the internet. The data is stored across multiple servers that can be in many locations. The physical environment where the servers are is usually owned and managed by a hosting company.

Cloud storage systems are increasing in popularity as a cost-effective back-up for businesses and individuals. Some modern software even backs up the data to remote cloud-based servers automatically, sometimes every few seconds.

KEY POINT

Solid-state drives do not require physical motion so they have shorter response times. They also do not suffer from physical wear.

KEY POINT

An SD card uses solid-state storage.

QUESTION

Describe the benefits and drawbacks of a using traditional magnetic hard drive in a laptop computer when compared to a solid-state hard drive.

KEY POINT

Cloud storage uses magnetic and, increasingly, solid-state storage at a remote location.

QUESTION

List five criteria that you would need to consider in developing a policy for backing up your data.

Figure 28.3 *Cloud computing*

RESEARCH TASK

Use this book and other sources such as the internet to research what is meant by the World Wide Web (www).

RESEARCH TASK

Use this book and other sources such as the internet to research the storing of data in the cloud.

Companies providing cloud storage systems include dropbox. Amazon Web Services even allow the user to map a drive in the cloud and format it. Other examples of cloud storage include Google Drive, Xdrive and Microsoft Cloud.

Cloud computing now lets users access all their applications and documents from anywhere in the world.

Cloud computing has led to a major change in how we back up data and store information (Figure 28.3).

Given the many advantages, Apple, Google and Microsoft have all developed cloud-based data services.

A growing number of people want to access the latest version of their documents on a range of devices, but the benefit of shared documents in businesses, where a number of people work together on a single project, is driving this cloud-based technology forward even faster.

But, as with all computing, there are advantages and disadvantages of cloud storage.

Advantages of cloud storage

- Unlimited storage capacity: cloud storage offers limitless storage.

RESEARCH TASK

Use this book and other sources such as the internet to research the security issues associated with the cloud and other contemporary storage.

- Automatic backup: on a computer a hard disk crash can destroy all your valuable data if it is stored on the device, but if it is in the cloud a computer crash shouldn't affect any of your data.
- Universal access: you don't carry your files and documents with you on the cloud; they stay in the cloud and you access them whenever you have a computer or mobile and an internet connection. All your documents are instantly available wherever you are.
- Device independence: the user is not limited to working on a document stored on a single computer or network. You can change computer and even change to your mobile device, and the documents follow you through the cloud.

Disadvantages of cloud storage

- Cloud storage requires a reliable internet connection. Cloud storage is impossible if you can't connect to the internet.
- Cloud storage will not work as well with low-speed connections. Web-based apps and large documents and images require a lot of bandwidth.
- Even on a very fast connection, web-based storage can sometimes be slower than accessing a data stored on a desktop or laptop computer.
- The user loses control over what happens to the data as this is managed by the cloud service provider.

CHAPTER REVIEW

In this chapter we have explored secondary storage.

Remember, before tackling any computer science task or question on this topic you must:

- understand different secondary storage media
- understand why secondary storage is required
- be aware of different types of secondary storage (solid state, optical and magnetic)
- explain the operation of solid-state, optical and magnetic storage
- discuss the advantages and disadvantages of solid-state, optical and magnetic storage
- be able to explain the term cloud storage
- be able to explain the advantages and disadvantages of cloud storage when compared to local storage.

29 Fetch-Execute Cycle

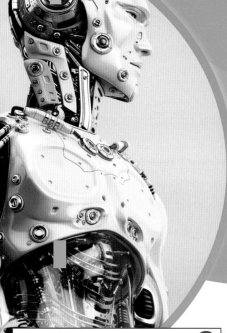

The **fetch-execute cycle** is sometimes called the instruction cycle. It is the basic operation cycle of a computer, as it is the process by which a computer retrieves a program instruction from its memory, then determines what actions the instruction requires in order to carry out the instruction.

First, the processor fetches the instruction from the main memory. The instruction is sent to the memory buffer register via what is called a data bus (Figure 29.1) and then copied to the current instruction register for decoding and execution. Next the decoder interprets the instruction.

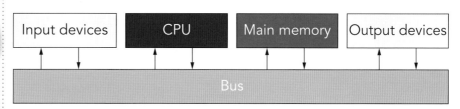

Input devices	CPU	Main memory	Output devices
		Bus	

Figure 29.1 *The CPU (computer's brain) is connected to the other hardware components by a bus*

Let's look at each of these steps in more detail.

Fetch-execute cycle and memory

The process starts with the address in memory of the first instruction being stored in the program counter.

Fetch-execute cycle – fetch the next instruction

The program counter contains the address of the next instruction to be executed, so the control unit goes to the address specified in the program counter, makes a copy of the contents, and places the copy in the current instruction register.

At this point the current instruction register contains the instruction to be executed. Before going on to the next step in the cycle, the program counter must be updated to hold the address of the next instruction to be executed when the current instruction has been completed.

Because the instructions are stored contiguously in memory, adding 1 to the program counter puts the address of the next instruction into the program counter. So the control unit increments the program counter up 1.

Accessing memory takes one cycle. Most computers can access memory at a minimal rate of 133,000,000 cycles per second, so one access takes 7.5 nanoseconds or 7.5 billionths of a second.

Fetch-execute cycle – decode the instruction

In order to execute the instruction in the current instruction register, the control unit has to determine what the instruction is, for example an instruction to perform some operation on a data.

At this phase, the instruction is decoded. The logic of the circuitry in the CPU determines exactly which operation is to be executed. The instructions themselves are built into the circuits. This is why a computer can only execute instructions that are expressed in machine code.

Fetch-execute cycle – get data if needed

The instruction to be executed may require additional memory accesses in order to complete its task.

Fetch-execute cycle – execute the instruction

Once an instruction has been decoded and any operands (data) fetched, the control unit is ready to execute the instruction. Execution involves sending signals to the arithmetic logic unit (ALU) to carry out the processing. In the case of adding a number to a register, the operand is sent to the ALU and added to the contents of the register.

Prior to the execute cycle, much is transferred but nothing gets done. After each fetch cycle the next clock pulse initiates an execution phase. The instruction is decoded and then acted upon. What happens in the execute stage is automatic. Every instruction consists of a number of parts or fields. Exactly how many and what type depends on the processor's architecture, but there are usually at least two. This consists of a simple binary value that specifies what the instruction must do. Each instruction has a unique code that causes the computer to carry out the required operation.

When the execution is complete, the cycle begins again.

CHAPTER REVIEW

In this chapter we have explored the fetch-execute cycle. Remember, before tackling any computer science task or question on this topic you must:

● understand and explain the fetch-execute cycle.

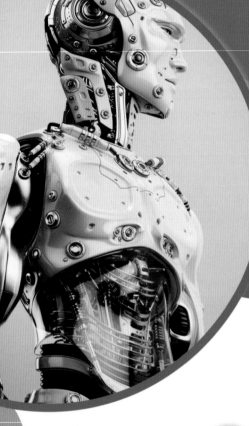

30 Encryption

QUESTION

Briefly describe the term encryption.

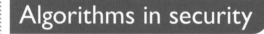

Algorithms in security

If you program anything that works over the internet and needs to handle confidential information, you will have to use what are called 'cryptographic' algorithms to keep the system secure.

Cryptographic algorithms are sequences of rules that are used to encrypt and decrypt code. They are algorithms that protect data by making sure that unwanted people can't access it.

Most security algorithms involve the use of encryption, which allows two parties to communicate but uses coded messages so that third parties, such as hackers, cannot understand the communications.

Encryption algorithms are used to transform plain text into something that cannot be understood. The encrypted data is then decrypted to restore it, making it understandable to the intended party.

There are hundreds of different types of cryptographic algorithms.

Caesar cipher

Whilst you don't need to remember how a Caesar cypher works for the exam, it illustrates how a cypher works.

In a **Caesar cipher** there is one shared key. With a Caesar cipher, an algorithm replaces each letter in a message with a letter further along in the alphabet using a number key.

The cipher simply shifts the alphabet and is therefore also called a shift cipher. You need to know what the number key is to decipher the message. The number key is simply the number of letters you shift.

Caesar cipher is one of the oldest types of ciphers. It is named after Julius Caesar, who is said to have used it to send messages to his generals over 2,000 years ago.

> **KEY POINT**
>
> A **Caesar cipher** is a type of substitution cipher in which each letter in the text is 'shifted' a number of places along the alphabet.

> **QUESTION**
>
> If a shift key of two has been used, decipher the following Caesar cipher.
>
> gzco swguvkqp

> **EXAMPLE**
>
> Let's look at an example with a shift key of one.
>
> **Riddle:** What is the clumsiest bee?
>
> **Answer:** B C V N C M J O H C F F
>
> *The answer is a bumbling bee!*
>
> Each letter in the encrypted message is just the next letter along in the alphabet because the key is one.

If we look at this mathematically the encryption formula is:

$$E_n(x) = (x + n) \bmod 26$$

And here is the decryption formula:

$$D_n(x) = (x - n) \bmod 26$$

1 The alphabet we are working with contains 26 letters (English).
2 n is a number less than or equal to 25.

You may be puzzled by what the mod function is and why you would ever want to use it. Mod is short for modulo and the mod operator gives the remainder after integer division.

30 Encryption

Integer division functions/operators are found in nearly all programming languages. Once you start to write real code you will certainly meet it.

If we consider a clock face with numbers from 0 to y–1 then counting mod y would be a process of advancing from number to number until you reach y – 1 then you 'roll over' to 0 and start the sequence again. So counting mod 6 would be 0, 1, 2, 3, 4, 5, 0, 1, 2, … etc. Notice that in counting mod 6 the integer 6 doesn't ever occur.

These assumptions can also be modified for any alphabet language of your choosing. If the alphabet contains m letters, then n has to be less than or equal to m – 1. Here is a general outline and picture of how the algorithm above works (Figure 30.1). You should be aware that for this example the key n is set to 3, but it will work with any number.

For example, if we decide to shift the letters by 3 positions:

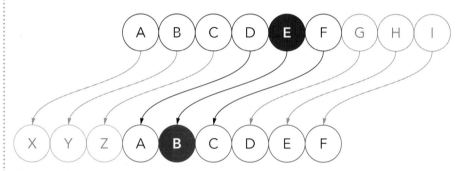

Figure 30.1 *Decrypting text*

Mathematically you would do this by numbering the letters of the alphabet from 0 to 25, as follows:

A	B	C	D	E	F	G	H	I	J	K	L	M	N	O	P	Q	R	S	T	U	V	W	X	Y	Z
0	1	2	3	4	5	6	7	8	9	10	11	12	13	14	15	16	17	18	19	20	21	22	23	24	25

Transform the letters of the plaintext in numbers:

MYCOMPUTER becomes 12 24 2 14 12 15 20 19 4 17

Do the shift for every letter:

12 + 3 mod 26 = 15 (P)

24 + 3 mod 26 = 1 (B)

2 + 3 mod 26 = 5 (F)

14 + 3 mod 26 = 17 (R)

12 + 3 mod 26 = 15 (P)

15 + 3 mod 26 = 18 (S)

20 + 3 mod 26 = 23 (X)

19 + 3 mod 26 = 22 (W)

4 + 3 mod 26 = 7 (H)

17 + 3 mod 26 = 20 (U)

The plain message MYCOMPUTER becomes PBFRPSXWHU

TASK

Write a program in your chosen code to encrypt and decrypt using a Caesar cipher. The user should enter the key and the text.

TASK

Re-write the code shown on this page in your chosen language to use a conditional statement, not the break command to exit the loop.

Encryption and networks

The main purpose of encryption is to protect the confidentiality of digital data stored on computer systems and that is to be transmitted via the internet or any other computer networks. Modern encryption algorithms play a vital role in security as they provide not only confidentiality but also the following essential elements of data security:

- **Authentication**: the origin of a message can be verified.
- **Integrity**: proof that the contents of a message have not been changed since it was sent.

Most data transmitted over a network is sent in clear text, making it easy for unwanted persons to capture and read the sensitive information. By using encryption algorithms, networks can protect data from intruders and make sure that only the intended recipient can decode and read the information.

CHAPTER REVIEW

In this chapter we have explored encryption.

We have also explored the Caesar cipher.

Remember, before tackling any computer science task or question on this topic you must:

- be able to perform encryption using the Caesar cipher
- understand how encryption can be used
- understand why data on networks need to be encrypted.

31 System Security

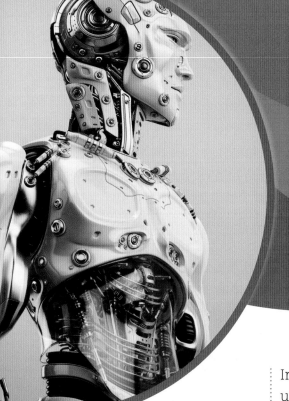

In the next two chapters we will explore why it is essential to use strong passwords, keep anti-virus software and security patches up to date, log out of services when we finish using them, and be careful with the information we send in emails, texts or instant messages.

Issues

With all the benefits technology brings it also brings issues. The only time anything is private in computing is when the computer is off-line. We all put private information onto the internet but in the hands of people who we believe will look after it. Never put any private information on the open public internet. When using online banking, make sure the connection is encrypted (**HTPPS**).

File sharing

The illegal sharing of music and films over the internet has become more and more of a problem as internet speed has grown faster. Famous court cases based upon intellectual property rights and privileges have hit the news.

Software piracy

With the growth of the use of the internet more and more people are using illegal, sometimes borrowed, software. Billions of pounds are lost as a result of pirated software.

Hacking

Hacking refers to accessing data without authority. It has become more and more of a problem over the years. Sometimes hackers unlawfully access data, but do not damage it. But often hackers hack into data either to steal from it or to cause malicious damage. Either way, it is illegal to hack into someone else's data.

Web content

The World Wide Web has revolutionised communication. It is a wonderful place for information exchange and self-expression. Anyone can gain an extensive global audience. But in recent years this has led to a rapid growth in everything, including negative materials such as pornographic material, instructions for making bombs, and hate propaganda.

Invasion of privacy

The chances are that the more you use the internet the easier it is for someone to invade your privacy. Your data is probably stored around the world in a wide range of databases. Your activity, and life, is probably being monitored. And it is not just the internet where this is a problem. When someone goes shopping with a loyalty card, details of what they have purchased will be recorded. Critics of the system argue that these loyalty cards compromise the privacy of customers, but the retailers who use them argue that they are a way of offering special offers targeted to the right customers.

Computer viruses

It is estimated that over £10 million of damage can be the result of a single computer **virus**. With so many viruses about, even in email attachments or in downloadable files and screen-savers, the issue of computer viruses is a growing problem.

Cookies

Internet cookies are very small text files. They are downloaded from the web server to a web browser. They record the activities on the browser and then send it back to the server. Whilst cookies can be very useful for auto-completing forms, they can also be used by advertisers and less scrupulous users.

Deep linking

Users of the World Wide Web often move from page to page following hyperlinks, which can appear as images or text. Often the hyperlink takes them away from the website they are on to another website. Originally, hyperlinks were at the heart of the World Wide Web. Deep linking occurs when one web page includes a hyperlink to a webpage that is buried deep within another site. This can give an appearance that the hyperlinked pages are part of the original website. A growing number of companies are concerned that their content will be stolen.

Unlicensed computer professionals

Plumbers and electricians, doctors and most people who provide a service to the public are usually licensed. Computer professionals are not. This makes it almost impossible to know whether the person who is fixing your computer is both competent and reliable. Remember that people accessing your computer have full access to all of the data on it.

Downloadable components

There are a growing number of cases in the news of young children starting to play a free game, and downloading extra characters and plug-ins, not realising that these are all charged for. The use of a free game followed by purchasable components is a growing issue, particularly with mobile phone use. Free games also provide a good method of delivering worms and malware.

Bluetooth vulnerability

The use of bluetooth on mobile phones and tablets has led to security vulnerabilities. Many vulnerabilities have been found over the years in the technology, and many successful attacks have been demonstrated against it.

Like many other secure channel protocols, bluetooth works using an initial phase called pairing, where two devices establish short shared keys of a few numbers, followed by a data protection phase, where data is encrypted and authenticated with those shared keys.

The problem is eavesdroppers were able to obtain enough information to guess the pairing PIN, which opened up the data on the paired device. New protocols have now been put in place to attempt to stop this.

Security measures

MAC address filtering

Media access control (MAC) addresses identify every device on your network. A MAC address is an alphanumeric string separated by colons, like this: 00:03:D1:1A:2D:14. Networked devices use this address as identification when they send and receive data over the network.

In MAC address filtering you find the MAC address of every device you want to allow on your network, and then you fill out a table in the router's user interface so that any device on the list can join your network and any device not on the list will be blocked from joining the network.

The problem is, a hacker using a wireless network analyser will be able to see the MAC addresses of every computer you've allowed on your network, and can change their computer's MAC address to match one that's in that table. However, this is not an easy thing to do.

Firewalls

A firewall is a network security system that monitors and controls all incoming and outgoing network data transfer

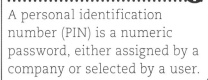

based upon a set of what are called security rules. Firewalls can be either hardware or software:

- **Hardware firewalls** can be purchased as stand-alone hardware but they are also often found in broadband routers.
- **Software firewalls** are software based and must be installed on the computer. The software can then be customised.

There are a number of techniques that firewalls use to prevent harmful information from getting through the security wall and these include:

- **packet filtering**: looking at the data in each packet entering or leaving the network
- **application gateway filtering**: applying security mechanisms or blocking services such as FTP
- **proxy server filtering**: intercepting all messages entering and leaving the network and hiding the true network address.

In addition to limiting access to computers and the networks they are connected to, firewalls can be used to allow remote access to a private network using secure authentication.

Authentication

Authentication is the process of identifying the identification of a user (or in some cases, a machine) that is trying to log on or access resources. This is often achieved using a username and password, but there are many different ways to achieve this including:

Passwords and Smart Cards

Most systems require that a user be authenticated in order to log on to the system or service. This can be done by entering a password, inserting a smart card, and entering the associated PIN, or by using a fingerprint.

Network access authentication

Network access authentication verifies the user's identity to each network service that the user attempts to access. It differs in that this authentication process is, in most cases, transparent to the user once he or she has logged on.

KEY POINT

The term backdoor refers to an undocumented, unauthorised method of gaining remote access to a system, bypassing normal authentication methods.

Single Sign-On (SSO)

Single Sign-On (SSO) is feature that allows a user to use one password (or smart card) to authenticate to multiple servers on a network without re-entering their details.

Whatever the method, authentication is always designed to check that the individual is who he or she claims to be. Authentication is therefore an absolutely essential element of a typical security model.

Encryption

When we are using networks, for example for ordering something online or completing forms, we often have to send others our personal information. A typical transaction might include our names, email addresses and physical address and phone numbers, passwords and even our personal identification numbers (PINs). Information security is provided on computers and over the networks by a variety of methods but many of these methods use encryption. Encryption is a way to enhance the security of a message or file by scrambling the contents so that only someone with a secret code or key can read it.

There are two main types of encryption but the most common is what is called symmetric encryption. Basically this just means that the same key, or secret, is used to encrypt and decrypt the data. The second main type of encryption is called Asymmetric encryption and this uses two interdependent keys, one to encrypt the data, and the other to decrypt it.

Encryption is required when someone enters personal information or banking information on the internet to make a purchase. But the same encryption that can be of benefit can be of use to a terrorist. Even the information that you enter through an encrypted connection could be accessible at the other end by a criminal.

QUESTION

Explain the term encryption.

Importance of Network Security

We use computer networks to send, receive and store information. Whether it's sending emails, storing documents, or obtaining information through a web server, network security is vital. Without it we allow others access to our sensitive, confidential and personal information.

We need network security for protection against many external and internal threats such as email based network security problems, denial of service network security attacks, worms and trojans, and wireless network security attacks.

CHAPTER REVIEW

In this chapter we have explored system security.

Remember, before tackling any computer science task or question on this topic you must:

- be able to explain different security threats
- understand the need for, and importance of, network security (More on this topic in chapter 32.)
- be able to explain the following methods of network security:
  - authentication
  - encryption
  - firewall
  - MAC address filtering. (More on this topic in chapters 30, 32.)

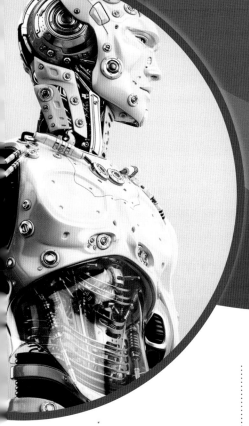

32 Social Engineering and Cyber Security

Social engineering

Social engineering is a non-technical method used by hackers to gain access to data and to systems. It relies heavily on human interaction and often involves tricking people into breaking normal security procedures:

- Virus writers use social engineering to persuade people to run malware-laden email attachments.
- Phishers use social engineering to convince people to give them sensitive personal information.
- Scareware hackers use social engineering to frighten people into running software that is useless at best and dangerous at worst.

Someone could use social engineering to break into a computer network by trying to gain the confidence of an authorised user.

People often do not realise how valuable the data they have on their systems is to a hacker. Social engineers often rely on the natural helpfulness of people as well as on their weaknesses. Other typical social engineering techniques include appealing to a user's vanity, authority or greed, alongside old-fashioned eavesdropping.

It's easy to identify the people around us that could gain physical access to our files, legitimately or not; they include our family, friends and others. But identifying those who can gain access to our information and computers remotely is impossible. This is why using technology safely and securely is so important.

If you practise secure computing practice, you can at least limit the risk of an unauthorised individual accessing your files and confidential information or installing malicious software on your computer.

Two of the easiest things you can do to keep others from accessing your account or information are using a strong password and locking your computer when you walk away from your desk.

Examples of social engineering

Remember that in a social engineering attack, an attacker uses human interaction to obtain or compromise information about an organisation or its computer systems. Social engineering tactics involve acts such as deception, manipulation and intimidation. The table below shows some of these threats:

Phishing	Phishing is attempting to encourage users to enter confidential data, for example usernames, passwords and credit card details, by pretending to be from a trustworthy source. It is usually carried out by email spoofing or instant messaging. Users are often asked to enter details at a fake website which *looks* just like the proper version.
Shouldering	Shouldering, also sometimes called 'shoulder surfing', is using direct observation techniques, such as looking over someone's shoulder, to get passwords, PINs, security codes and similar personal data.
Blagging	Blagging is the act of creating and using an invented scenario to engage a targeted victim in a manner that increases the chance the victim will divulge information or perform actions that would be unlikely in ordinary circumstances.

QUESTION

Describe three main security measures required when using an internet connected computer.

KEY POINTS

- **Phishing** is a technique for fraudulently obtaining sensitive information by asking users for their passwords, credit card numbers, etc. This is achieved by sending an email or SMS while masquerading as a legitimate entity, such as the user's bank.

- **Shouldering** is observing a person's private information over their shoulder, for example cashpoint machine PIN numbers.

Pharming	Pharming is a scamming practice in which malicious code is installed on a personal computer, server or DNS. Records are modified, misdirecting users to fraudulent websites without their knowledge or consent.

Cyber security

Cyber security relates to the protection of information systems from theft or damage. There are many cyber security threats including those listed in the table below:

Adware	Also known as advertising-supported software. This is any software package that automatically shows adverts, such as a pop-up. They may also be in the user interface of a software package or on an installation screen. The main object of adware is to generate revenue for its author. Adware, by itself, is harmless. However, some adware may include spyware such as keyloggers.
Computer virus	A computer virus is a self-replicating program that attaches itself to existing programs and can then easily spread from one computer to another. Viruses can increase their chances of spreading to other computers by linking to files on a network system. A virus attempts to make a computer system or data files unreliable.
Denial of service (DoS) attacks	This is an attempt to make a computer or network system unavailable to its users. A DoS attack is usually focused on preventing an internet site or service from functioning efficiently, or at all, temporarily or indefinitely. The attacks usually target sites or services hosted on high-profile web servers such as banks and payment websites (for example, PayPal).
Hacking	Hacking means finding out weaknesses in an established system and exploiting them. A computer hacker is a person who finds out weaknesses in a computer system to gain unauthorised access. A hacker may be motivated by a multitude of reasons, such as profit, protest or challenge.
Keyloggers	A keylogger is a type of spyware that logs the keys used and can collect data from an infected computer, including personal information such as websites visited, user logins and financial information.

Physical threats (for example loss/theft of devices)	Computer systems consist of physical items such as keyboards, monitors, memory sticks/removable storage devices, base units and servers. These can be lost or stolen very easily – especially memory sticks and portable storage devices.
Spyware	A type of malware (malicious software) installed on a computer system that collects information about users without their knowledge. Spyware is usually hidden from a user and can be difficult to detect. Spyware is often secretly installed on a user's personal computer without their knowledge. Spyware can also install additional software or redirect web browsers to different websites. Some spyware can change computer settings, which could lead to slow internet connection speeds or changes in web browser settings.
Trojans	A Trojan often appears to be something which is wanted or needed by the user of a PC but is a stand-alone malicious program designed to give full control of a PC infected with a Trojan to another PC. They can be hidden in valid programs and software. Trojans can steal information or harm their host computer systems.
Worm	A worm is a stand-alone computer program that replicates itself so it can spread to other computers. Like a computer virus, a worm can use a computer network to spread. But unlike a computer virus, it does not need to attach itself to an existing program. Worms almost always cause some harm to a network, even if only by consuming bandwidth.

Malicious code

Viruses, keyloggers, worms and many of the items in the table above are different types of malicious code. They are often confused and thought of as being the same thing. They are pieces of code that are able to replicate themselves. However, they are distinctly different with respect to the techniques they use and their host system requirements. This distinction is due to the way they attack the host systems.

Measures for protecting your personal data from cyber attacks

The following preventative measures can help a user protect themselves from cyber attacks:

- Do not give out personal information over the phone, on the web or in an email unless completely sure of the recipient. Always verify the authenticity of requests for any personal information.
- Encrypt your data.
- Keep your operating system, browser, anti-virus and other critical software up to date.
- Never click on links in emails. Even if you do think the email is legitimate, go to the website and log on directly. Be suspicious of any unknown links or requests sent through email or text messages.
- Never open email attachments unless you know it is from a reliable source and turn off the option to automatically download attachments in emails.
- Set secure passwords and don't share them with anyone. Also avoid using common words, phrases or personal information in your passwords.

Measures for protecting a network and computers from cyber attacks

- Encrypt the data.
- Ensure that any HTTP open sessions time out after a reasonable time.
- Ensure that TCP connections time out after a reasonable time.
- Install a firewall.
- Install anti-malware and anti-virus protection.
- Lock the network. Many cyber attack victims are compromised via WiFi networks. The best defence against this is to have no wireless network at all. Wired networks, while less versatile due to the need for cables, are more secure. If you use WiFi, update it regularly to the latest encryption standard.

KEY POINTS

- A secure site is a website that uses encryption techniques to secure its data.
- A programmer at any computer or other device connected to a computer network could easily modify the software at that host. This is why sensitive data should be encrypted.

KEY POINT

A time-out is where the server is set to think that there has been too long an interval of time between (1) the establishment of a connection, and (2) the receipt of any data, so the server drops the connection.

KEY POINT

Cyber security consists of the processes, practices and technologies designed to protect networks, computers, programs and data from attack, damage or unauthorised access.

279

- Secure the hardware. Physically locking computers to a desk using the small metal loop found on most laptop and desktop devices prevents theft and access to network login data.
- Use tracking software on all networked mobile devices.

Automatic updates and patches

If your device seems to be working fine, you may wonder why you should apply a **patch** or software update. By not applying a patch you might be leaving the door open for malware to come in. Malware exploits flaws in a system in order to do its work, and updates and patches are designed to close these doors as they are found. The time frame between an exploit and when a patch is released is continually getting shorter.

Passwords

Passwords are inconvenient, but necessary to protect your personal data. If you use the same password on all your devices and accounts, your data and your devices will also be vulnerable to malware and hackers. So how do you ensure the security of devices and data with effective passwords?

First you must change any default passwords that have been provided by external sources and not set by you. Passwords should not be easy to crack, which they will be if the password is simply personal data, such as your postcode, a phone number or a significant date such as a birthday, or if you use the same password on all your accounts and devices.

The characteristics of a good password include having a password that:

- cannot be found in a dictionary
- contains special characters and numbers
- contains a mix of upper- and lowercase letters
- cannot be guessed easily based on user information (birth date, postcode, etc.)
- is changed whenever you feel there has been a breach of security.

Make passwords complex but memorable:

- You can replace letters with numbers or special characters, for example Johns becomes J0hn5.

KEY POINT

A **patch** is a piece of software designed to update a computer program to fix things like security vulnerabilities.

KEY POINT

A power-on password is a password entered on computer startup, before the OS loads.

KEY POINT

Make passwords complex but memorable.

- You can also use a phrase and turn it into a password, for example pick a sentence and reduce it to the first letters of each word only, for example, "I Like Computer Science" becomes ILCS.
- Take a word and reverse spell it, for example Today becomes yadoT.

Choosing a strong password lowers the chance of a security breach with your accounts and devices. The advice on passwords used to be to change them regularly, but this has become more difficult as the number of devices and different access sites people use is ever growing. If a user changes all their passwords every few months, they often end up using weaker passwords and reusing them across multiple networks and devices. It is now considered to be more important to use strong, unique passwords everywhere than to change passwords regularly, although doing both obviously leads to greater security.

Biometric devices

A **biometric device** is a device that authenticates a person's identity by translating a personal characteristic, such as a fingerprint, into a digital code that then is compared with a digital code stored in a computer, thus verifying a physical or behavioural characteristic. These are used on a wide range of mobile devices.

Security misconfiguration vulnerabilities

Security misconfigurations are simply incorrectly configured safeguards for a system. These misconfigurations typically occur when holes are left in the security framework due to misconfigured access rights.

Security misconfigurations can include things likes:

- Default accounts not being changed
- Directory listings being enabled
- Failure to secure directories
- Misconfigured firewalls
- Missing OS security patches
- Unsecured third party applications being installed
- Web-serving source files being left open

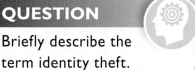

QUESTION

Briefly describe the term identity theft.

KEY POINT

A **biometric device** identifies the person seeking access to a computing system by their physical characteristics, for example fingerprints, voice or retina patterns.

KEY POINTS

- Unauthorised access is the use of a computer or network without permission. Unauthorised use is the use of a computer or its data for unapproved or possibly illegal activities.
- Computer crime is any illegal act involving a computer.

Security misconfigurations can occur at any level, including the client, web server, application server, user databases or custom code. Attackers find these misconfigurations through unauthorised access, and this results in a partially or even totally compromised system. If a system or network is compromised through faulty security configurations, data can be stolen or modified.

When any of the components that make up a web application are configured badly there is a target for attackers. Security misconfiguration vulnerabilities can happen at platform level, web server level, application server level and through custom code. In order to provide a secure system all of the component parts of a network application need to be configured correctly.

There are many ways that misconfiguration can lead to security vulnerabilities. To protect from these vulnerabilities there are a number of steps that need to be taken:

- Keep software up-to-date by installing the latest updates and security patches.
- Remove unused features including the removal all the sample applications that come with content delivery systems.
- Disable default accounts and change passwords. You should also change usernames, passwords and ports for default accounts.
- Develop a strong application architecture that effectively isolates components and encrypts data. Ensure security settings are set to secure values.
- Run tools, such as automated scanners, to check for vulnerabilities.
- Secure all layers individually and don't rely on one layer in a web application providing security for layers lower down in the stack.
- Make sure folder permissions are set correctly on the server.

Unpatched and/or outdated software vulnerabilities

Software vulnerabilities, like malware, have serious security implications. The companies that sell software are aware of these security vulnerabilities and regularly release security

RESEARCH TASK

Use this book and other sources such as the internet to research how to protect software systems from cyber attacks.

QUESTION

Briefly describe the term biometrics.

updates to address these flaws. Microsoft, Adobe, Oracle, Firefox and Apple are just some software companies that regularly release security updates. Some software companies, like Google Chrome and Flash, even release updates automatically and many of these are invisible to users.

Outdated and unpatched devices present a major security risk as the unpatched software remains weak, leaving the user open to cyber-crime attacks. Updating systems with the latest security patches protects against attacks that exploit vulnerabilities. Applying security updates often also addresses technical issues with the software and often improves the software's performance.

MAC address filtering

Each device you own also comes with a unique media access control address called a MAC address. This is what identifies it on the network. Normally, a router allows any device to connect to the network providing it knows the appropriate passphrase. Without **MAC address filtering**, any wireless client can join and authenticate with a WiFi network providing they know the network name and encryption keys. When MAC address filtering is enabled the access point, or router, performs additional checks using a different parameter. A router first compares a device's MAC address against an approved list of MAC addresses and only allows the device onto the WiFi network if its MAC address has been specifically verified and approved by the administrator of the network.

This provides an additional level of security but it is still not totally secure, as MAC addresses can be spoofed in many operating systems. This is where a device pretends to have one of those allowed. This is because MAC addresses are relatively easy to get, as they are sent over the WiFi with each packet going to and from the device. This is necessary as the MAC address is what is used to ensure that each packet gets to the right device. All an attacker has to do is monitor the WiFi traffic, examine a packet to find the MAC address of an allowed device and then change their device's MAC address to that allowed MAC address. However, this not an easy thing to do whereas changing an IP address is much simpler.

KEY POINT

MAC address filtering allows devices to access, or be blocked from accessing, a network based on their physical address embedded within the device's network adapter.

CAPTCHA

CAPTCHA stands for Completely Automated Public Turing test to tell Computers and Humans Apart. It is a program used by some websites to provide further protection for a user's password by verifying that user input is not computer generated. There are now a wide number of different CAPTCHA systems using images, numbers and even simple calculations, but basically the idea is to create something humans can read but that current computer programs can't.

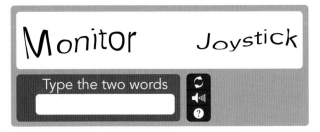

Figure 32.1 *Human readable (distorted) security text*

In Figure 32.1, an example is shown with distorted text used.

Email verification

Email confirmation and CAPTCHA are used to solve different problems. Email verification is used to check that users are using their real email address in the registration process. Email verification is where an email is sent to the user's email address and they have to click on a link in it to confirm that the email address is theirs. Email confirmation also protects from identity theft. For example, the user cannot register a government email address and pretend that they are someone from the Cabinet Office as they will not be able to click on the confirmation link sent by the email as they are not the owner of this address. Email confirmation allows the system to link each user to a specific email address.

Email verification proves that the email address is valid but automating a response to an email is fairly easy, and thus cannot be taken as assurance that the client is not a bot. Email confirmation therefore doesn't protect from the bots (as CAPTCHA does).

Mobile phone verification

With mobile phone verification, you ask the user to enter their mobile phone number, then you send them an SMS (text message) with a code and they must enter this code into a web form on the website.

Removable media

For many years one of the most common ways to deliver a virus has been through removable media. This has become even more of an issue since the development of AutoRun. This is similar to AutoPlay, which automatically starts playing video when you put a DVD or Blu-ray disk into a media player. But unlike AutoPlay, which only plays the media file, AutoRun starts automatically and can then start installing malware. The best option is not to use any removable media unless it has been verified as being clean, but it is also possible to disable AutoRun.

Penetration tests

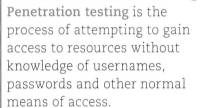

KEY POINT

Penetration testing is the process of attempting to gain access to resources without knowledge of usernames, passwords and other normal means of access.

A **penetration test** is an authorised attempt to evaluate the security of an IT infrastructure by safely attempting to hack into the system to find vulnerabilities. These tests also explore how effective defence systems are. Penetration tests can be performed using manual or automated technologies.

They are carried out on a wide range of systems, including servers, web applications, wireless networks, network devices, mobile devices and other potential points of risk.

There are two types of penetration test, called black-box testing and white-box testing.

White-box penetration tests versus black-box penetration tests

White-box testing is a penetration test that uses detailed insider knowledge of the target system to improve the tests. In application penetration tests the source code of the application is usually provided along with design information. The test can also make use of interviews with developers. In infrastructure penetration tests all the network details are provided. The goal of a white-box penetration test is to provide the tester with as much information as possible.

QUESTION

Briefly describe the term black-box testing.

White-box penetration testing has some clear benefits:

- It leads to deep and more detailed testing.
- It requires less testing time.
- It also tests things like quality of code, application design, etc.

But there are also some disadvantages. It is not a realistic attack, as the penetration tester is not in the same position as an uninformed attacker.

Unlike white-box penetration tests, a black-box penetration test requires no previous information and takes the approach of an uninformed attacker.

The benefits of this type of attack:

- It simulates a realistic scenario.

The disadvantages of a black-box penetration test:

- Tests can take much longer to perform.
- Some areas of the infrastructure and software may remain completely untested.

Networked computers are more vulnerable. A stand-alone computer is a self-sufficient system. There is no connection to any other computers. Because of this, it is more secure than computers that are part of a network. A stand-alone lessens the possibility that hackers, spyware or viruses can compromise confidential information by accessing it.

CHAPTER REVIEW

In this chapter we have explored social engineering and cyber security.

Remember, before tackling any computer science task or question on this topic you must:

- be able to explain different security threats
- understand the need for, and importance of, network security (More on this topic in Chapter 31.)
- understand and be able to explain the following security measures:
  - biometric measures (particularly for mobile devices)
  - password systems
  - CAPTCHA (or similar)
  - using email confirmations to confirm a user's identity
  - automatic software updates (More on this topic in Chapter 31.)

- be able to explain the following methods of network security:
  - authentication
  - encryption
  - firewall
  - MAC address filtering (More on this topic in Chapters 30, 31.)
- understand and be able to explain the following cyber security threats:
  - malicious code
  - weak and default passwords
  - misconfigured access rights
  - removable media
  - unpatched and/or outdated software.
- be able to explain what penetration testing is and what it is used for
- be able to define the term cyber security and be able to describe the main purposes of cyber security
- be able to describe what social engineering is and how it can be protected against
- be able to explain the following forms of social engineering:
  - blagging
  - phishing
  - pharming
  - shouldering (or shoulder surfing). (More on this topic in Chapter 31.)
- be able to define the term 'malware'. (More on this topic in Chapter 31.)
- be able to describe what malware is and how it can be protected against. (More on this topic in Chapter 31.)
- be able to describe the following forms of malware:
  - computer virus
  - Trojan
  - spyware
  - adware. (More on this topic in Chapter 31.)

33 Ethics, the Law and the Environment

Much is written about using computers safely, but alongside safety is the law and ethics when using computers, particularly when you start to learn to code.

Ethical use

If you access, view or collect confidential material and/or personal information, it is your responsibility to maintain confidentiality. Do not share this information with unauthorised individuals. But ethics and the law are not the same thing.

Ethics relates to the rules and standards governing the conduct of an individual with others. As technology and computers became more and more a part of our everyday lives the definition of ethics evolved, called computer ethics. Computer ethics is concerned with standards of conduct as they relate to computers.

QUESTION

Briefly describe the term intellectual property.

Ethics	The law
Ethics are a guideline to computer users and are not legally enforceable.	The law consists of rules to control computer users that are legally enforceable.
Computer users are free to follow or ignore a code of ethics.	Computer users must follow the regulations and law for the country they live in.
Ethical rules are universal and can be applied anywhere, all over the world.	Laws depend on the country and state where the crime is committed. There are many examples of laws in one country allowing things that are illegal in others. This is a big issue with the internet.
Ethics aims to create ethical computer users.	Laws aim to prevent misuse of computers.
If you don't follow ethical rules you are deemed to be immoral.	Not obeying laws is referred to as crime.

KEY POINT

Computer ethics are moral guidelines that govern the use of computers and information systems.

KEY POINT

Computer addiction is a growing health problem that occurs when the computer consumes someone's entire social life.

Basically, **computer ethics** are about knowing the difference between what is ethical and what is unethical. It may be possible to access someone's personal information on a computer system but this action is unethical. It is also easy to copy and duplicate digital content, but ethics suggests that it is wrong to do so without gaining the author's approval.

The digital divide

Over the past few years society dependence on computer technology has increased. The ability to communicate via email and access the internet has become an essential part of everyday life. But there are many people in the world who do not have access to the internet and this has led to a disparity called the digital divide.

This gap is of growing concern. Rural communities, low-income families, people with disabilities and areas of the wider world do not have the same advantages as more privileged households and communities. To many people this is a major ethical issue.

EXTENSION TASK

How would your life be different if there were no computer systems?

Online gambling

Online gambling is becoming a real problem in the Western world and leads to many ethical questions. The internet opens up opportunities to lose large amounts of money while staying in the comfort of one's own home.

Cyber squatting

Cyber squatting is when someone purchases a domain knowing that it will be useful to a well-known company. They then sit on the name until they can sell it at a higher price. Often companies with well-known trademarks are unable to purchase their domain name as it is owned by a cyber squatter. Common names are also subject to cyber squatting, raising questions about, even though it is legal, how ethical this practice is.

Email privacy

People often write important messages in their emails. But, increasingly, email security has been compromised. Email was once only available to the computer literate. Today email has become a standard means of communication for millions of people. Many of these people wrongly assume that only they and the recipient of their email will be able to read the communication. This illusion of privacy is a big area of concern. Email travels from server to server and can be read easily by a hacker with some technical knowledge. Recently email privacy has become a big ethical debate about individual rights, corporate rights and the use of technology.

Facial recognition

Facial recognition is now used in train stations, airports and a number of public places. It is no longer in the realm of science fiction. But many people are concerned at the lack of privacy, and how the captured data could be used by unscrupulous companies and individuals.

Facial recognition has even found its way into social media sites.

> **KEY POINT** ❗
>
> Domain names are used by companies and individuals to identify one or more of their IP addresses. For example, the domain name hodder.co.uk

Cyber ethics	Cyber ethics is a system of moral standards or moral values that can be used as guidelines for all computer users to follow.
Code of ethics	These are guidelines that help determine whether a specific computer user's actions are ethical or unethical.
Intellectual property	Anything created by inventors, authors and artists that is their own idea or work becomes known as their intellectual property.
Copyright	This protects the form of expressions of ideas, not the ideas themselves.
Privacy	This refers to the right of all individuals and companies to deny or restrict the collection and use of information about them.
Cyber crime	Cyber crime is any illegal act involving computers or computational devices, usually over the internet or other networks.
Cyber law	Cyber law is any law relating to protecting the internet and other online communication technologies.

Legal use

You will know all the warnings against illegally downloading copyrighted material like films, music, publications, software and video games. What you may not realise is that when you begin downloading illegal copies of this type of material, you can also inadvertently begin sharing these files with others. The IP address of the computer used to download materials is also easy to track, making it possible to identify who the responsible individuals may be.

Getting caught is not the only reason to stay away from downloading illegal files. There is also a chance these files contain viruses, Trojans or other malicious files that can cause problems on your computer.

There are laws relating to copyright and intellectual property:

- Intellectual property is about creations of the intellect (hence the name): inventions, artistic works, names, images and designs. Intellectual property also relates to industrial property, such as inventions, trademarks, etc. The word property means a possession, something in which the owner has legal rights.

- Unlike intellectual property, copyright law only protects the form of expressions of ideas, not the ideas themselves. So copyright laws do not protect ideas or systems, only how they are expressed. This means that nothing in copyright laws prevents others from developing another work based on the same idea.

KEY POINT

The IP address is a number that identifies a device on a TCP/IP network.

QUESTION

Briefly describe the term pirated software.

Software cracking

Software cracking is the modification of software to remove or disable features which are considered undesirable by the person cracking the software. Crackers often illegally remove or overwrite copy protection features, nag screens and adware.

The term 'crack' refers to the means of achieving software cracking. This can include stolen serial numbers or a tool that performs the act of cracking, such as keygens used to generate an activation key, patching which involves adding a patch so that the software cannot conduct security checks, and loaders to load the software without these security checks.

A cracker (also known as a black hat hacker) is an individual who breaches or bypasses security to gain access to software without paying royalties. Cracker refers to anyone who reverse engineers software or illegally modifies software.

Software and source code theft

Computer source code is the most important asset of a software company. The term source code refers to the programming instructions that are compiled into the executable files that are sold by the software development company.

Most people would agree that a company or individual should be allowed to receive a return from the investment needed to develop quality software. To allow for this, software developers need a level of protection for the ownership over the software they produce, to protect them from **software theft**. In legal terms this is in the form of intellectual property law, which comes under the principles of copyright and patent law.

The rights of the developer are formally agreed in legal terms in a software licence. When you buy a piece of software you normally have to agree to a software licence by clicking 'I Agree' or by opening the package. This is a legal agreement between the owner and user of the software. It gives the user permission to use the software but does not transfer ownership rights to the intellectual property. Any act of reverse engineering or cracking the software is illegal.

> **KEY POINT** !
>
> **Software theft** occurs when someone; (1) steals software media, (2) illegally copies a program, or (3) illegally registers and/or activates a program.

> **KEY POINT** !
>
> Product activation is a process that attempts to prevent software piracy by requiring users to provide a software product's identification number in order to receive an installation identification number.

Open source and proprietary software

Open source software is software where you can see and access the source code. You can also modify and improve it. The internet is built on open source technologies including the Linux operating system and the Apache Web server application. Applications software such as Star Office are also open source software.

Whilst open source software is free, the term 'free software' is not a good term for it, as the purpose of the open source movement it to allow for open development and improvement. Apple provides free upgrades for its operating system but it is not open source.

Proprietary software is software that is owned by a company or the programmer. Usually the owner is the company that developed the code for the software. Proprietary software is restricted in its use, and its source code is almost always kept secret. The restrictions include aspects such as that the software cannot be copied or distributed without complying with stated licensing agreements.

Plagiarism

Whilst plagiarism is not a recent problem, the internet has led to an explosion in the copying of other people's work. In schools, colleges and universities, tutors now have a real problem in identifying and discriminating between original work and plagiarised work.

Plagiarism is also theft.

Personal versus private

Laws on data use relate to some types of personal information. A distinction is made between personal data and *sensitive* personal data. A leak of sensitive personal data is treated more seriously in the law. Sensitive personal data includes data relating to a person's race, sexuality, health, criminal record or affiliations (such as political persuasion or trade union membership). A person's name or phone number may be personal, but in the law it is not covered as sensitive personal data. Compiling all the names and phone numbers of residents of a town in a single book is not viewed as particularly

KEY POINT

Source code is the original program code of software, it is the part most computer users don't ever see.

KEY POINT

Copyright is exclusive rights given to authors and artists to duplicate, publish and sell their materials.

KEY POINT

Information privacy is the right of individuals and companies to deny or restrict the collection and use of information about them.

threatening by most people, whereas compiling lists of socialists would be viewed as sensitive.

Differences between Europe and the USA

Under EU law, personal data can be collected only under strict conditions and for a legitimate purpose. The main law in the EU protecting users is the Data Protection Directive. In the USA, the attitude towards data protection is governed mainly by market forces, so there is no all-encompassing law regulating the collection and processing of personal data. Instead, data protection is regulated separately by each state.

Security versus privacy

It is now common practice for companies, such as Google, to collect personal information such as data about the services you use and how you use them. They keep server logs of location information, data about the software you use, storage data and other identifying information. Giving them access to this data enables us to better exploit the internet. Doctors can track public health risks using this type of data. As soon as we voluntarily shared it with others, the information stopped being truly private.

There is a big debate about what is private and what is not, and a similar debate about how secure individuals should be allowed to make their data. If it is possible to make data totally secure these secure systems would also be used by people such as terrorists, so governments want to limit security levels below what they can break into! Governments need to access data to keep their citizens safe.

The environmental impacts of technology

When you use computer electronics, you are participating in one phase of that product's life (Figure 33.1). Before the product makes it to you, raw materials (resources) are taken (extracted) from the environment. These are then processed and manufactured into a product. The product is packaged and transported, again using valuable resources. The next stage is the use of the product and the energy needed for this use. The final stage is how you dispose of the device when you change it.

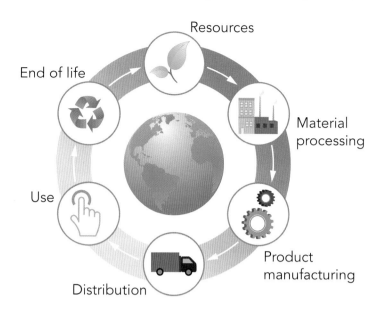

Figure 33.1 *The technology cycle*

Resources and material processing

The life of most computing devices starts in an open-pit mine in South America. They will then cross nearly all continents from the time the raw materials are collected to the time the product is manufactured. Technology devices often use copper from Chile processed in Sweden, tantalum from Australia or Congo, beryllium from Kazakhstan, platinum from South Africa and a semiconductor chip built by workers in Ireland or Israel.

Energy use

You may think that your computer-based technology uses the most energy when you use it and that by switching devices off, and using power-saving modes, you can reduce this. Whilst this is true, eighty-one per cent of the energy a computer device uses is used when it is made. It actually takes more energy to create the device than it takes to run it for its entire working lifetime. This makes computer devices different to all other household appliances, most of which use the most energy during their lifetime. So, however good the user is at turning off their systems, they will be involved in using large amounts of energy just by owning the device, especially if they are updating the hardware regularly.

End-of-life management

Consumer electronics are increasingly treated as disposable items. We throw away televisions, computers and mobile phones. Globally, we throw away over 40 million metric tons of electronic waste (e-waste) every year, and only about 13 per cent of that weight is recycled. Most e-waste recycling occurs in China, India, Pakistan, Vietnam and the Philippines, where they shred, burn and dismantling the products in 'backyards'. Emissions from these activities damage human health and the environment due to exposure to toxic metals, such as lead.

Manufacturers are starting to take responsibility for changing the way they manufacture electronics. This involves using fewer natural resources during production. Users can also make a difference by buying products that use recycled materials or that can be updated rather than thrown away. Donating or recycling used electronics helps too.

The disposal of computer devices is unlike most other consumer goods because they are usually disposed of before they become useless. The main reason for purchasing new computer devices is not to replace a non-functioning system but to keep up-to-date with the rapidly changing technologies. One way of reducing the amount of computer waste would be to reuse systems that may be out of date, but remain fully functional.

Waste disposal

Disposal of IT equipment comes under the WEEE Directive (waste electrical and electronic equipment).

The main objectives of the WEEE Directive are:

- to increase reuse, recycling and other forms of recovery, leading to a reduction in the amount of waste going to landfill or incineration
- to improve the environmental performance of all operators involved in the life cycle of electrical and electronic equipment
- to set criteria for the collection, treatment, recycling and recovery of WEEE

RESEARCH TASK

Use this book and other sources such as the internet to research the environmental impacts of technology.

- to make producers responsible for financing most of these activities – private householders are to be able to return WEEE without charge.

What can individuals do?

Everyone has a responsibility to reduce their individual carbon footprint. Completely powering off computing devices when not in use is good for your devices and for the planet. Other things that could be done include:

- changing power settings so that devices power down after 15 minutes of inactivity
- considering end-of-life management for all computing devices
- dimming the screens on computing devices as this saves power
- disabling screensavers as they don't actually conserve energy, some even use more energy than normal use
- not having too many programs running at the same time and change the system settings to reduce programs that auto-start
- shutting down all devices at the end of the working day
- turning off printers, scanners and other peripherals when not using them
- unplugging all computing devices when they are fully charged, otherwise they will be using power to keep topping themselves up throughout the day
- unplugging chargers when they're not in use to save on power consumption
- using hibernate instead of sleep mode.

RESEARCH TASK

Use this book and other sources such as the internet to research the ethical impacts of using technology.

QUESTION

Compare the terms legal and ethical use related to computer software.

CHAPTER REVIEW

In this chapter we have explored ethical, legal and environmental issues relating to computer use.

Remember, before tackling any computer science task or question on this topic you must:

- be able to explain the current ethical, legal and environmental impacts and risks of digital technology on society. Where data privacy issues arise these should be considered.

34 Software

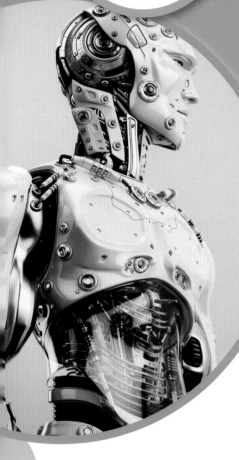

So far we have looked at code and the hardware that makes up a computing device. We have even looked at how code is written, but computing devices need both hardware and software infrastructures to function (see Figure 34.1). In this section we will explore some of the software infrastructures, including **system software** and **application software**.

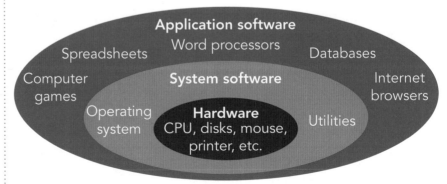

Figure 34.1 *Link between hardware and software*

System software

The term 'system software' refers to the operating system and all utility programs that manage the computer resources at a low level. They are types of computer programs that are designed to run a computer's hardware and application programs. If we think of the computer system as a layered model, the system software is the interface between the hardware and user applications.

Understanding the operating system

At the very heart of the computer is the **operating system** (often called the OS). The operating system is one of the most important 'parts' of any computer. Almost every type of computer, which includes mobile phones, notepads, video game systems and e-book readers, needs an operating system in order to operate properly.

The operating system is actually not one but a collection of programs that control the system (Figure 34.2). The operating system is responsible for the management and control of all the computer's resources. This includes memory, processors, hard drives, monitors, I/O devices, etc. It not only handles the system resources, but also the application software that users run, security and file management. It also provides a link between the hardware and software.

Recognises and installs peripheral devices

Handles inputs and outputs

Manages files and folders

Loads and runs other software applications

Shares out system memory

Handles system errors and alerts user

Moves data to and from the hard disk

Allows software to communicate with hardware

Manages system security

Figure 34.2 *Tasks of the operating system*

Some of the most popular operating systems are:

- Windows
- Windows CE
- Macintosh OS X (Mac OS X)
- iOS (iPhoneOS)
- Linux
- Android Phone
- Blackberry (RIM OS)
- Solaris (SunOS)
- AIX
- IOS (Cisco)
- XOS (Extreme Networks)
- IronWare OS (Foundry).

QUESTION

State three examples of operating systems which are used in different computer devices.

QUESTION

What is operating system software?

Handling and managing all of the system resources

The operating system handles the computer's memory and the sharing of the central processing unit (CPU). Its job is to make sure that each application gets the correct and adequate resources. The operating system is the most important program that runs on a computer. Every general-purpose computer must have an operating system. Operating systems send output to the display screen, keep track of files and directories on the disk and control all the peripheral devices like disk drives and printers.

It is the operating system that brings life to the computer and is the first program loaded into memory when the computer is turned on.

The functions of the operating system include the following key functions:

- memory management
- processor management
- I/O management
- file management
- security
- error handling
- program management
- interaction with the user.

Memory management

The operating system is totally responsible for memory management. It keeps tracks of memory use and decides which process will get memory, when and how much.

The operating system memory management functions include:

- controlling the allocation of memory and dealing with the transfer of programs in and out of memory when the process no longer needs it or when the process has been ended.

Processor management

The operating system processor management functions include:

- carrying out a process called scheduling where it manages the CPU
- organising processing time between programs and users
- keeping track of processors and the status of any process running.

I/O management

The operating system manages all the input and output devices, including controlling the backing store and all peripherals such as scanners and printers. It does this using what are called drivers.

Software	Use
Driver	Specially written program which translates the commands from the operating system into commands that the hardware will understand.

The operating system does the following activities for device management:

● translates instructions sent by application software into a format that I/O devices can understand, and vice-versa

● decides which process gets the device, when and for how much time.

File management

The operating system handles the organisation and tracking of files and directories (folders). It also saves or retrieves these from a computer disk.

The operating system does the following activities for file management:

● allows the user to perform tasks including the creation of files and directories

● allows the user to save files to a backing store

● allows the user to rename, copy, move and delete files

● keeps track of where files are located on the hard drive through either a File Allocation table (FAT) or the New Technology File system (NTFS).

Security

Computer systems often have multiple users. These users are often running multiple processes and these processes must be secure. The operating system maintains security and access rights of users.

The operating system does the following security activities:

● controls the access of programs, processes and users to the computer resources

● ensures that all access to system resources is controlled

- ensures that external I/O devices are protected from invalid access attempts
- provides an authentication feature for each user by means of a password.

Error handling

In any computer, the operating system deals with errors and user instructions. Errors can occur anytime and anywhere including errors in CPU, in I/O devices or in the memory hardware.

The operating system does the following error management activities:

- monitors the system for any errors that occur
- takes appropriate actions to ensure correct operations
- closes the program if errors are terminal.

Application management

It is the operating system that provides information about all user programs running on your computer. It does this by handling everything from user programs to system programs, including everything from the printer spooler to the servers.

The application packages the user uses, such as word processors and spreadsheets, are what most users buy a computer for. Without an operating system these applications could not execute (run). The OS also provides these applications with tools and services such as printing and fetching data from a hard disk. Without an operating system, you cannot use your word-processing software, spreadsheet software, or any other applications.

With graphical operating systems, the application also manages the menu facilities and windows supported and provided with the operating system.

The operating system does the following application management activities:

- loads a program into memory
- allows the application software to communicate with the hardware
- provides a mechanism for processing all internal communication.

Abstraction

We have looked at this term before, as it is a very important term in computer science, but it is worth revisiting it here. In simple terms, the idea of abstracting is the idea of hiding or ignoring details that are unimportant in any context. You are reading this book. You are not thinking about each individual letter or how they have been made with blobs of ink. You are seeing words and sentences.

In the same way, an operating system hides away certain details that are not needed at any particular time.

An example from real life is money. Originally, everyone had to barter, to swap a cow for the eight chickens they wanted, etc. It was hard if you could not find someone with what you wanted who would exchange it for what you had to offer. Money came about because it provided a common way to exchange things with one another. You pay money for what you want and they don't care about what you sold to get the money; money is therefore a good example of an abstraction.

Operating systems provided a common way to access a variety of hardware when it is needed. They offer another level of abstraction.

But you may be asking the question that, if an OS is trying to keep programs from having to worry about hardware differences why are there different operating systems? Each OS was developed by different companies and to suit different hardware systems. It is like all countries having money but using different currencies. Most currencies can be exchanged for one another. In a similar way, virtual machines can run another OS inside of a parent OS, it's just yet another level of abstraction.

Utility software

Other types of system software include **utility software**. Utility software is used to help to manage, maintain and control computer resources. Operating systems usually contain all the necessary tools for this, but separate utility programs can be used to provide enhanced functionality.

KEY POINT !

Utility software is programs that provide additional capabilities to manage the computer beyond those provided by the operating system.

QUESTION

What is a defrag?

TASK

Use this book and other sources such as the internet to research the purpose and functions of utility software.

Examples of utility programs are antivirus software, disk defragmenter, backup software and monitoring tools. Let's look at a few of these in a bit more detail:

Software	Use
Virus scanner	To protect your system from Trojans and viruses
Disk defragmenter	To speed up your hard disk
System monitor	To look at your current system resources

Translation software

We looked at translation software, a system software, in chapter 14, but in summary the purpose of translator software is to convert program source code into machine code that can be executed on the processor.

Translation software includes:

- assemblers
- compilers
- interpreters.

Each performs a different task:

Assembler	An assembler (meaning one that assembles) is a computer program which translates assembly language to an object code or machine language.
Compiler	A compiler translates the whole program (source code) into object code that can be stored and re-used. A compiler makes faster, more secure code. A compiler also produces object code that is difficult to read, meaning competitors won't easily be able to steal or users hack the code.
Interpreter	Interpreters allow for code to run on multiple platforms. You can also debug and test code without having to re-compile the entire source code.

Application software

Application software is computer software that causes a computer to perform useful tasks beyond the running of the computer itself. Such software is often called a software application, a program, an application or an app.

The word 'application' is used because each program has a specific application for the user. For example, a word processor can help a user write a document.

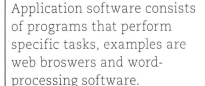

KEY POINT

Application software consists of programs that perform specific tasks, examples are web broswers and word-processing software.

34 Software

Application software programs are designed to run under an operating system; they are a further abstraction from the hardware. They range from word processors and web browsers to video games and media players.

Examples of application software include:

- Animation software
- Audio editing
- Data manipulation (databases and spreadsheets)
- Digital audio editor
- Graphic art software
- Graphics editing
- Image editing software
- Image organisers
- Media content creating/editing
- Music sequencer
- Presentation software
- Sound editing software
- Text editors (word processors, desktop publishing)
- Vector graphics editor
- Video editing software
- Web browser

At the time of writing this book, the most popular application software were:

- Microsoft Word, Google Chrome, Windows Media Player, World of Warcraft, Adobe Photoshop, iTunes, Skype and WordPerfect.

Mac programs were always called applications, but Windows programs were referred to as executable files. This is why Mac programs use the .APP file extension, while Windows programs use the .EXE extension. But whatever the extension, both Mac and Windows programs serve the same purpose so both should be called software applications.

> **KEY POINT** !
> ⋯⋯⋯⋯⋯⋯⋯⋯⋯⋯⋯
> Never use brand names in exams, use generic descriptions such a 'word processor'.

CHAPTER REVIEW

In this chapter we have explored software.

Remember, before tackling any computer science task or question on this topic you must:

- be able to explain the differences between system software and application software and understand the relationship between them
- define the term software (More on this topic in chapter 25.)
- be able to explain what is meant by:
  - system software
  - application software
- be able to give examples of both types of software
- understand the need for, and functions of, operating systems (OS) and utility programs
- understand that the OS handles management of:
  - processor(s)
  - memory
  - I/O devices
  - applications
  - security.

35 Networks

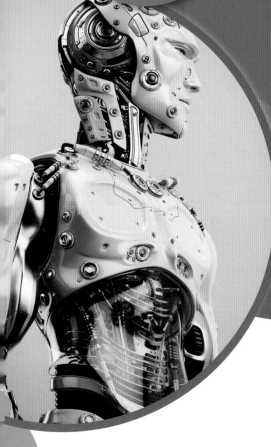

Definition of a computer network

A computer network can be described as two or more computers connected together to communicate. The purpose of connecting computers together in a network is to exchange information and data. Also, networked computers can use the resources of other computers.

There are a number of basic components of computer networks and these are described below.

QUESTION

What is a network?

KEY POINT !

The server provides services to a client.

Servers

These are powerful computers that provide services to the other computers on the network.

Clients

Clients are computers that use the services that a server provides.

Communication media

The communication media is the physical or wireless connection between the devices on a network. This could be through cable in an organisation's local network, wireless signal or the internet. Network data speeds are measured in bits per second either using the terms megabits per second (Mbps) or gigabits per second (Gbps).

Network adapter

The network adapter or, as it is often referred to, the network interface card (NIC), is a circuit board that is equipped with the components necessary for sending and receiving data. It is usually either plugged into one of the available slots on a computer or is built onto the motherboard. A transmission cable is attached to the connector on the NIC.

Resources

The term 'resources' refers to any peripheral device that is available to a client on the network, such as printers, fax devices and other network devices; however, the term also refers to data and information.

User

A user is basically any person that uses a client to access resources on the network.

Protocols

The protocols of a network are formal, written rules used for network communications. They are essentially the languages that computers use to communicate between each other on a network. We will explore these in more detail in chapter 37.

QUESTION

Briefly describe the term network.

RESEARCH TASK

Use this book and other sources such as the internet to research the different ways that computers can be connected in a network.

Advantages of computer networks

There are a number of advantages to using networks:

- Networks allow users to share software stored in a main system.
- Files can easily be shared between users over a network.
- Network users can communicate via email, instant messenger and VoIP (voice over IP).
- Within networks, it is much more straightforward to back up data as it is all stored on file servers.
- Networks allow data to be transmitted to remote areas that are connected within local areas.
- Networked computers allow users to share common peripheral resources such as printers, fax machines, etc., therefore saving money.

Disadvantages of computer networks

There are also a number of disadvantages to using networks:

- The cost of purchasing cabling to construct a network as well as the file servers can be costly.
- The management of a large network is complicated, which requires training, and a specialist network manager usually needs to be employed.
- In the event of a file server breaking down, the files contained on the server become inaccessible, although email might still work if it is stored on a separate email server. The computers can still be used but are isolated.
- If a virus gets into the system, through a network it can easily spread to other computers
- With networks, there is a risk of hacking, particularly with wide area networks. Stringent security measures, such as a firewall, are required to prevent such abuse.

Types of network

Local area networks (LANs)

LANs are characterised by high-speed transmission over a restricted geographical area. If the LAN is too large, signals need to be boosted. A LAN is usually owned by a single person/ organisation.

Wide area networks (WANs)

While LANs operate where distances are relatively small, WANs are used to link LANs that are separated by large distances that range from a few tens of metres to thousands of kilometres. The internet is the biggest example of a WAN. WANs are often under collective or distributive ownership.

Personal area networks (PANs)

A PAN is a computer network organised around an individual person. PANs often involve mobile computers, cell phones and/or handheld computing devices, such as PDAs, and use bluetooth.

Network topologies

Bus topology

Bus networks (Figure 35.1), which have absolutely nothing to do with the system bus of a computer, use a common backbone to connect all devices.

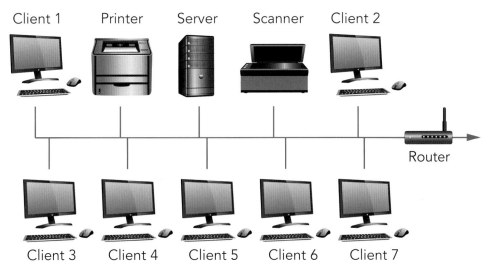

Figure 35.1 *A bus topology*

A single cable that functions as the backbone of the network acts as a shared communication medium that devices connect to via an interface connector. When a device wishes to communicate with another network device, it transmits a broadcast message onto the backbone wire that all the devices see; however, only the intended device actually accepts and processes the message.

Bus topologies are easy to install and require only a relatively small amount of cabling when compared to alternative topologies. Bus networks are the best choice of topology when the network has only a limited number of devices. If the network grows so that there are more than a few dozen computers connected to the backbone bus, then it is probable that performance issues will start occurring. Finally, if the backbone cable suffers a catastrophic failure, then the entire network effectively becomes unusable.

Advantages of bus topology

● It is easy and cheaper than other wired types of network to install as a consequence of requiring only a small quantity of cable.

● The lack of dependency on a central device, which is present in a star topology.

Disadvantages of bus topology

● This network topology performs well only for a limited number of computers because as more devices are connected the performance of the network becomes slower as a consequence of data collisions.

● The impact of a single cable failure makes this type of wired network less reliable than other wired networks.

Star topology

Nearly all wired home networks use the star topology (Figure 35.2). This topology is therefore better understood than many other networks. The router on its own cannot be the hub node of your network. It needs to be linked to a switch, although in practice they are usually in the same box. The star topology has a central connection point, referred to as a 'hub node', that could be a device such as network hub, switch or router. Devices are usually connect to the switch with network cable that is referred to as an unshielded twisted pair (UTP) Ethernet.

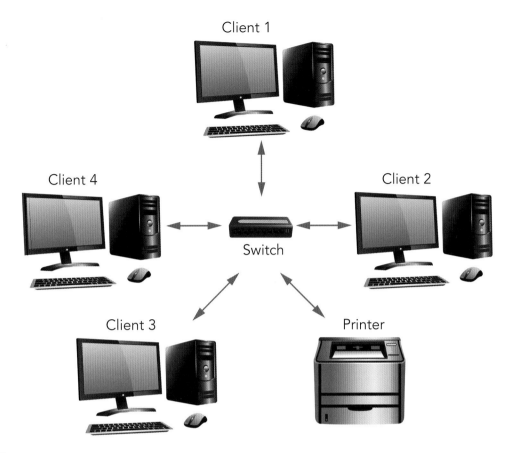

Figure 35.2 *A star topology*

Star topologies generally require more cable than bus topologies. However, a failure in any star topology cable will only restrict access to the computer that is connected via that cable and not the entire network. It should be realised, however, that if the switch fails, the entire network also goes down.

Advantages of star topology

- Compared to bus topology, star topology is better in terms of performance, as signals don't necessarily get transmitted to all the workstations, although performance does depend upon the capacity of central switch.

- As the transmission medium is not shared, there can be multiple simultaneous communications.

- Failure of one node or link doesn't affect the rest of network and it is easy to detect a failure and troubleshoot it, as it allows isolation of each device within the network.

Disadvantages of star topology

- The network operation ultimately relies on the correct functioning of the central switch. So if the central switch crashes, it will lead to the failure of the whole network.
- The use of a router or a switch as the central device and the additional cabling costs increases the overall cost of the network.
- Performance, and the number of nodes which can be added in star topology depends upon the capacity of the central device.

KEY POINTS

- WiFi is a family of related protocols rather than a single protocol.
- WiFi is a trademark and the generic term for networks of this nature is WLAN.

Wireless networks

A wireless network (WiFi) uses radio waves to communicate (Figure 35.3). Radios, mobile phones and televisions also use radio waves.

Router

Figure 35.3 *A wireless network*

This is what happens: a computer's wireless adapter translates data into a radio signal and transmits it using an antenna and receives radio signals and converts them into data (remember, data has to be 1s and 0s).

Advantages and benefits of wireless networks

KEY POINT

The Ethernet is a family of related protocols rather than a single protocol.

The primary benefit of a wireless network is the freedom from cables, providing the device connecting to the network is within range of the wireless router. It is also very convenient.

The wireless nature of WiFi networks allows users to access network resources from nearly any convenient location.

With the growth of public wireless networks, users can also access the internet outside their normal work or home environment. For example, most public places, such as chain coffee shops, airports, libraries, etc. offer their customers a wireless connection to the internet at little or no cost.

The initial setup of an infrastructure-based wireless network is relatively low cost, as it requires no expensive cabling and for a small network it is just a single access point.

Wireless networks are also easily expanded.

Risks and disadvantages of wireless networks

Any time data is sent wirelessly, there is a chance that it can be intercepted. The security used to encrypt the information determines how easy or hard it is to intercept the data. Some of the more commonly used encryption methods have known weaknesses. If a user sets up a wireless router without any security, they are asking for trouble. People standing outside their home with a laptop or mobile phone would be able to use their internet connection and possibly even access the files on other networked computers.

A WiFi range, whilst sufficient for a typical home, can be insufficient in a larger building. To obtain additional range, repeaters or additional access points have to be purchased. Wireless networking signals are subject to a wide variety of interference, and thick walls, metal used in building construction and static interference all cause networking problems.

The speed on most wireless networks is much slower than the slowest common wired networks. In some situations, where speed is essential, a user may need a wired network.

Personal area networks (PANs)

A PAN is a computer network that is used for data transmission between different personal devices, such as computers, telephones, tablets, etc. Many such networks use

bluetooth technology that allows the user to create an Ethernet network with wireless links.

A PAN is the interconnection of information technology devices within the range of an individual person, typically within a range of 10 metres. For example, a person travelling with a laptop, a phone and a portable printer could interconnect them together without having to plug anything in.

CHAPTER REVIEW

In this chapter we have explored different types of network.

Remember, before tackling any computer science task or question on this topic you must:

- understand that networks can be wired or wireless
- be able to explain the following common network topologies:
  - star
  - bus
- explain the benefits and drawbacks of a range of networks
- be able to define what a computer network is
- be able to discuss the benefits and risks of computer networks
- be able to discuss the benefits and risks of wireless networks as opposed to wired networks
- be able to describe the main types of network including:
  - personal area network (PAN)
  - local area network (LAN)
  - wide area network (WAN).

36 Network Data Transfer

Any electronic communications process requires the following components:

- a source of the information
- a transmitter to convert the information into data signals compatible with the communications channel
- a communications channel
- a receiver to convert the data signals back into a form the destination of the information can understand.

The transmitter encodes the information into a suitable form to be transmitted over the communications channel.

The communications channel moves this signal as electromagnetic energy from the source to one or more destination receivers.

The channel may convert this energy from one form to another. This could be electrical or optical signals. It must maintain the integrity of the information so the recipient can understand the message sent by the transmitter.

The communication medium can be either cable or wireless. When wired copper cable is used, the copper cable can be either coaxial or twisted pair. The alternative wired solution is fibre optic.

Coaxial	Twisted pair	Fibre optic
Electrical signal communication via the wires	Electrical signal communication via inner conductor of the wires	Optical signal communication via the glass fibres
High noise contamination	Medium noise contamination	Very low noise contamination
Can be affected by external magnetic interference	Less affected by external magnetic interference	Not affected by magnetic interference
Low bandwidth	Medium bandwidth	High bandwidth
Lowest cost of the three communication media	Moderately expensive compared to coaxial cable	Most expensive of the three communication media

Benefits and drawbacks

Using existing copper cable would be less expensive, as most PCs come with copper NIC cards. Replacing these with optical ones can work out as quite expensive. Also, traditional systems were built to run on copper infrastructures. Fibre can be used to replace these; however, the electronics needed to make it work are also relatively more expensive as is the cost of replacing all the existing cables.

Fibre has a higher bandwidth than copper, but the electronics that it requires to transmit data are expensive. An optical fibre cable also weighs less than a comparable copper wire cable. Fibre can retain a higher bandwidth over greater distances than comparable copper cabling and eavesdropping on a LAN using copper cables is easier, making fibre more secure. Copper cable is suitable for most applications as it is cheaper, but optical fibre is more suitable for high bandwidth uses such as cabling a public WAN or high definition video streaming.

Noise

All transmission media generate some **noise**. As the signals pass through a communications channel the atomic particles and molecules in the transmission medium vibrate and emit random electromagnetic signals, as noise. When the wanted signal is not significantly higher than the background noise, the receiver cannot separate the data from the noise and communication errors occur. Fibre optic cable has the least noise of all the transmission media used in networks.

Network protocols

A protocol is, in one sense, nothing more than a set of rules that govern data transmission so that a particular type of data will be formatted in a particular manner.

The importance of these protocols is that they provide a standard way to interact among networked computers.

Addressing

In many ways, internet addressing is similar to the postal addressing system.

The address system on the internet is called Internet Protocol (IP) addressing. In IPv4, an IP address assigned to a host is 32 bits long and is unique.

An IP address has two parts: one part that is similar to the postal code and the other part that is similar to the house address. They are known as the net id (netid) and the host id (hostid).

The host is the end point of communication on the internet and where a communication starts. It could be a web server, an email server, or the desktop, laptop or any computer we use for accessing the internet.

The netid identifies a contiguous block of addresses and is used to identify which particular network the host is located on.

Another popular form of address is the media access control (MAC) address. MAC addresses are six bytes (48 bits). The computer's own hardware configuration determines its MAC address. The configuration of the network it is connected to determines its IP address.

The first half of a MAC address contains the ID number of the adapter manufacturer. The second half of a MAC address represents the serial number assigned to the adapter by the manufacturer.

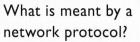

QUESTION

What is meant by a network protocol?

QUESTION

What is an address?

TCP/IP

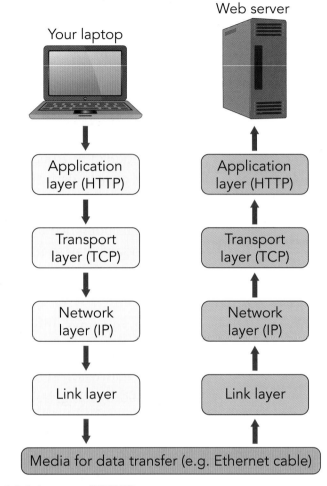

Figure 36.1 *Layers of TCP/IP*

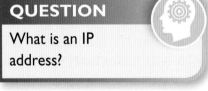
KEY POINT

A protocol is a set of rules or standards that control communication between devices.

KEY POINT

TCP/IP is Transmission Control Protocol/Internet Protocol, consisting of a set of standards that control how data is sent across networks including the internet.

When we meet someone in business we shake their hand as a greeting. This is true in computing too, when two computers connect in a network they first use a 'handshake'.

For computers to work together they have to use what are called protocols. A protocol is a set of rules which governs the transfer of data between computers.

Protocols are essential for any communication between computers and networks. They determine the speed of transmission, size of bytes, error-checking methods, and even whether communication will be asynchronous or synchronous.

Like any delivery system, in networks we need a delivery model. When you use the postal system you can ask for guaranteed delivery. On the internet, TCP/IP (Transmission

Control Protocol/Internet Protocol) is the most common delivery model. TCP is in charge of the reliable delivery of information, while IP is in charge of routing, using the IP addressing mechanism.

All networked computers communicate through what are called protocol suites. The most widely used and most widely available protocol suite is the TCP/IP protocol suite. TCP/IP is a four-layer system, as shown in Figure 36.1.

The application layer

The application layer provides applications for file transfer, remote control and internet activities.

> **KEY POINT**
> The application layer is where the network applications, such as web browsers or email programs, operate.

Some of the most common application layer protocols are:

FTP (File Transfer Protocol)

The File Transfer Protocol (FTP) is a standard network protocol that is used to transfer computer files from one host to another host over a TCP-based network, including the internet.

HTTP (Hypertext Transfer Protocol)

HTTP is the underlying protocol used by the world wide web. HTTP controls how messages are formatted and transmitted. It also controls the actions web servers and browsers should take in response to received commands. When you enter a URL in your browser it sends an HTTP command to the web server instructing it to fetch and transmit the requested web page.

IMAP (Internet Message Access Protocol)

The Internet Message Access Protocol (IMAP) is an internet standard protocol used by email clients to retrieve email messages from a mail server over a TCP/IP connection.

IMAP, POP and SMTP protocols are discussed more fully later in this chapter.

HTTPS

The Hyper Text Transfer Protocol (HTTP) is an application protocol for data communication on the World Wide Web. It delivers the web page. Hyper Text Transfer Protocol Secure

(**HTTPS**) is a secure version of HTTP. It is HTTP that is used for the data that is sent between your browser and the website that you are connected to. The 'S' at the end of HTTPS stands for 'Secure'. It means all communications between your browser and the website will be encrypted.

HTTPS uses one of two secure protocols to encrypt the data communications – SSL (Secure Sockets Layer) or TLS (Transport Layer Security). Both the TLS and SSL protocols use an 'asymmetric' public key infrastructure (PKI) system.

When your browser requests an HTTPS connection, the website will first send its SSL certificate to your browser. This certificate contains the public key needed to begin a secure data session. Based on this initial exchange, your browser and the website then initiate the 'SSL handshake'.

SMTP (Simple Mail Transfer Protocol)

Simple Mail Transfer Protocol (SMTP) is a TCP/IP protocol used in sending and receiving email. SMTP can only send data to a computer that is turned on, so it is only used to send data from the sender to mail servers, and then on to other mail servers. POP3 and IMAP are used to fetch email/manage a mailbox when the receiving computer is turned on.

SNMP (Simple Network Management Protocol)

Simple Network Management Protocol (SNMP) was created as a way of gathering information from different networked systems in a consistent way. It can be used in connection with a wide array of systems. The method of querying information and the paths to the relevant information are standardised. There are many versions of the SNMP protocol, and most networked hardware devices implement some form of SNMP access.

The transport layer

Below the application layer is the transport layer. It is the main interface for all network applications.

The most commonly used transport layer protocols are:
- TCP (Transmission Control Protocol)
- UDP (User Datagram Protocol).

Differences between TCP and UDP	
TCP	**UDP**
Data is read as a byte stream. No distinguishing indications are transmitted to signal the message (segment) boundaries. TCP is a connection-oriented protocol. If a connection is lost, the server requests the lost part.	UDP is a connectionless protocol. When data or messages are sent, there is no guarantee they will arrive. There may also be corruption while transferring a message. Packets are sent individually and are guaranteed to be whole if they arrive. There is one packet per one read call.
TCP is more complex but reliable.	UDP is faster but provides no reliability mechanism.
TCP is suited for applications that require high reliability, and transmission time is relatively less critical.	UDP is suitable for applications that need fast, efficient transmission, such as games. UDP is also useful for servers that answer small queries from huge numbers of clients.
If two messages are sent along a connection, one after the other, the first message arrives first. Data cannot arrive in the wrong order.	Messages are not ordered. When two messages are sent out they may arrive in a different order. If ordering is required, it has to be managed by the application layer.
Data is read as a 'stream', with nothing distinguishing where one packet ends and the next begins. There may be multiple packets per read call.	There is no tracking of connections, etc. UDP is faster because there is no error-checking for packets and the network card/OS has less work to do to translate the data back from the sent packets.

Data packets

QUESTION

What is a packet?

Anything sent between computers has to be divided up into what are called **packets**. Even a PowerPoint or spreadsheet has to be divided into packets to be transmitted (Figure 36.2). Imagine an object built of LEGO, where each brick is a packet. Packets are small data units. Of course, once transmitted, the packets have to be put back together in the correct order. These protocols wrap each data packet with a set of instructions. The computing name for this is encapsulation. Once all the packets have been received, the client needs to know they have all arrived so the very last packet is a special one called a frame.

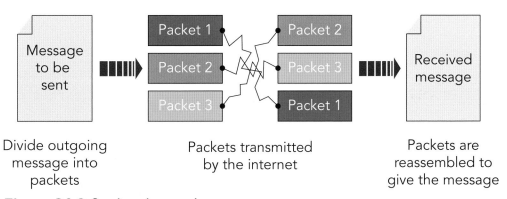

Divide outgoing message into packets   *Packets transmitted by the internet*   *Packets are reassembled to give the message*

Figure 36.2 *Sending data packets*

The network layer

The network layer is considered the backbone of the OSI Model. It selects and manages the best logical path for data transfer between nodes. The network layer addresses and packages data for transmission and it then routes the packets across the network, the name given to packets at this level is IP datagrams. The network layer is also sometimes referred to as the internet layer because the source and destination IP addresses are added to the packets. The layer is responsible for taking routing decisions, based on the destination IP address to determine which route to send the datagram along. This layer contains hardware devices such as routers, bridges, firewalls and switches, but it actually creates a logical image of the most efficient communication route and implements it with a physical medium. Network layer protocols exist in every host or router. The router examines the header fields of all the IP packcts that pass through it.

The link layer

This layer is also sometimes known as network interface layer. The link layer is where most LAN (local area network) and wireless LAN technologies are defined.

This layer normally consists of device drivers in the OS and the network interface card attached to the system. The link layer is the protocol layer in a program that handles the moving of data in and out across a physical link in a network.

The device drivers and the network interface card control all communications with the media being used and transfer the data over the network.

The most commonly used link layer protocols are:

- ARP (Address Resolution Protocol)
- PPP (Point-to-Point Protocol).

The link layer is responsible for encoding bits into packets prior to transmission and then decoding the packets back into bits at the destination. The link layer is also responsible for logical link control, media access control, hardware addressing, error detection and handling and defining physical layer standards.

KEY POINTS

- The link layer is where the network hardware, such as the NIC (network interface card), is located. OS device drivers also sit here.
- The link layer is sometimes referred to as the network interface layer.

Network routing and data rate

So we know that packets are routed from a source to a destination. These packets may need to travel via lots of cross-points, similar to traffic intersections in a road transportation network. Cross-points in the internet are known as routers. A router's function is to read the destination address marked in an incoming IP packet, to identify an outgoing link where the packet is to be forwarded and to forward the packet.

Similar to the number of lanes and the speed limit on a road, a network link that connects two routers is limited by how much data it can transfer in any given amount of time This is called the bandwidth or capacity and it is represented by a data rate, such as 1.54 megabits per second (Mbps).

Suppose that traffic suddenly increases, for example because of many users trying to download from the same website. The packets generated can be queued at routers or even dropped. Routers only have a limited amount of space, known as a buffer, to store backlogged packets. It is possible to reach the buffer limit. Since the basic principle of TCP/IP allows the possibility of an IP packet not being delivered, the limits of the buffer is not a problem. On the other hand, from an efficient delivery point of view, it is desirable not to have any packet loss (or at least to minimise it).

IMAP, POP and SMTP protocols

When you send and receive an email there are three different protocols that can be used to handle the email:

- IMAP (Internet Message Access Protocol)
- POP (Post Office Protocol)
- SMTP (Simple Mail Transfer Protocol).

IMAP and POP are used to receive email. SMTP is used to send an email (Figure 36.3).

Receiving emails

The software you use on your local machine is called a client and this is connected to what is called a mail server. When someone sends you an email, it travels from the sender's email client to their mail server using SMTP. Their mail server then uses the recipient email address to determine where the mail should be sent and then delivers it to the receiver's mail server.

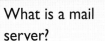

QUESTION

What is the purpose of a router on a network?

QUESTION

What is a mail server?

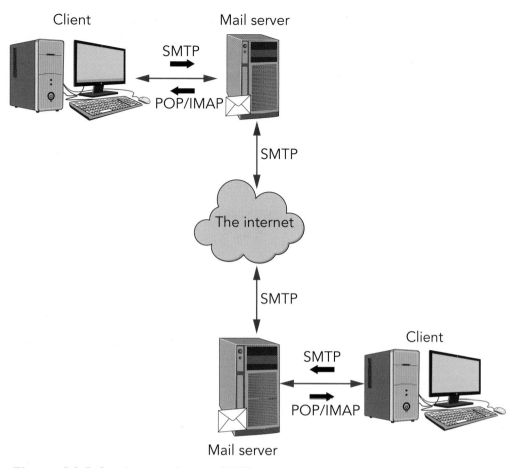

Figure 36.3 *Sending email using SMTP*

The receiver's mail server stores the received email in a mailbox until the receiver's mail client asks for it. IMAP and POP are the two main protocols used for retrieving email from a mail server. Both protocols are supported by almost all popular mail client programs, including Outlook and Apple Mail.

When a mail client reads an email it can do one of two things.

The IMAP protocol, by default, allows the user to keep all messages on the server. It constantly synchronises the email client program with the server and displays what messages are currently there. All the actions performed on the messages are carried out directly on the server.

The POP protocol is set by default to download all the messages from the email server onto the client device. This means that all the actions performed on the messages (reading, moving, deleting, etc.) are performed on the client machine. Because everything is kept on the client machine, the user cannot reopen messages from any machine other than where the messages have been downloaded. There is, however, an option to setup the POP protocol to save a copy of the message on the server after downloading them on the client device.

Sending emails

When you send an email you will always use some form of SMTP, which is a totally different protocol to IMAP and POP.

When you click on send on an email message the mail client contacts the SMTP server. The server authenticates who the user is using the login id and password and then receives the email message from your client. SMTP is used to pass the email on to the receiver's email server.

CHAPTER REVIEW

In this chapter we have explored different ways that data is transferred over networks. Remember, before tackling any computer science task or question on this topic you must:

- be able to define the term 'network protocol'
- be able to explain the purpose and use of common network protocols including:
    - Ethernet
    - WiFi
    - TCP
    - UDP
    - IP
    - HTTP
    - HTTPS
    - FTP
    - email protocols:
        o SMTP
        o IMAP
        o POP
- be able to describe the four-layer TCP/IP model:
    - application layer
    - transport layer
    - network layer
    - link layer.
- understand that the HTTP, HTTPS, SMTP, IMAP and FTP protocols operate at the application layer
- understand that the TCP and UDP protocols operate at the transport layer
- understand that the IP protocol operates at the network layer.

37 Aspects of Software Development

You will also have to complete practical tasks during your course, including a set task in the form of a single project which will be undertaken in a period totalling 20 hours. In preparation for this you should learn how to follow good design procedures.

When you complete the practical task for assessment you will be expected to work independently and produce a unique piece of work, but during the course you may also work in teams. Whatever the method of working, to be complete any solution must be designed, implemented, tested and evaluated. We will explore each of these concepts in more detail in this chapter. Remember that someone else needs to follow what you do so always give evidence for each stage in a way that ensures a third party can understand exactly what you have done.

Design

When you design a solution to any problem you need to consider all of the component parts needed to solve the problem. For most non-trivial problems, you're going to need to do some thinking to figure out how things are going to work and how things are going to fit together. You will also need to document what you do in a report.

This will include:

- thinking about inputs, outputs and how your solution will work
- planning the data structures needed to achieve a workable solution
- designing and testing all the algorithms
- designing an appropriate modular structure for the solution
- designing the user interface to enable the user to interact with your system in an effective way.

You will need to articulate your designs in a way that is appropriate to the task you are undertaking, but keep in mind that someone else needs to see what you have done and how. Show all the key aspects of your solution and how these are structured.

The start of the design process is always to identify the requirements of the problem. You can then make valid judgements so that you can decompose the problem into sub-problems. One way to do this is to first identify all the nouns in the set task. A simple example of how this could help would be:

Write the **code** to calculate the **area** of a **rectangle** when a **user** enters its **width** and **height**.

We can now easily identify the inputs. These are the **width** and **height**.

The output needed is also easy to identify it is the **area**

The verbs tell you what the actions are:

Write the code to calculate the area of a rectangle when a user enters its width and height.

37 Aspects of Software Development

The processes are writing the code, (what we have to do), and the calculation based upon what the user enters (the process our code needs to do).

Once you have fully understood the task and its inputs, outputs and processes you can start to develop your code.

As you will need a user input for this small task for the width and height you need to remember that users do not always enter data correctly, so your algorithms should also be robust enough to deal with invalid inputs. You may wish to add some sort of validation routine to make sure that they do!

Your algorithms for this small task perform the calculation and output the answer to the screen. You code should always be well designed and free of errors in logic and in the use of programming constructs, leading to an overall solution which works and produces the correct output.

You could communicate your design to this task using many of the tools covered in this book including:

- reports
- diagrams
- pseudo-code
- flowcharts
- annotation to your code.

You may also want to provide designs for the layout of actual screens for the input and output.

Remember when you undertake a design you will need to show:

- a comprehensive design which could be used as the basis for an effective implementation of the complete solution
- a good understanding of variables, data types and structures
- all of the main blocks of the proposed solution, including data validation where it is used as in this small task
- that your design choices are justified with reference to user requirements and the task set.

You will need to articulate your designs in a manner appropriate to the task and with sufficient clarity for a third party to understand, showing how the key aspects of your solution are structured. You should show that you have clearly identified the requirements of the problem and made valid judgements for decomposing the problem into sub-problems that show good application of key concepts to the problem.

Your algorithms should be well designed and free of errors in logic and in the use of programming constructs, leading to an overall solution which is fully functional. Algorithms should also be robust enough to deal with invalid inputs.

All requirements of the problem must be fully addressed.

Implementation

You will be expected to implement your designs, including:

- implementing the data structures and code so that a computer can understand your solution.

Again, drawing upon the contents of the book, you will need to use your coding skills to work at an appropriate level. You will be expected to provide program listing(s) that demonstrate your technical skill. You will also be expected to use appropriate annotation. Your code should be well structured. Again, remember that you are presenting your work to a third party.

You should:

- include explanations of particularly difficult-to-understand sections of your code
- provide a carefully divided presentation of the code
- provide appropriately labelled sections, to make navigation as easy as possible for a third party reading the code listings
- show how your program fully addresses all the requirements of the problem set
- show that your program runs with few or no logic errors
- show how your program has been fully decomposed into subprograms.

Your code needs to:

- be applied sufficiently to demonstrate proficiency
- be annotated to show a successful solution to the problem that utilises exception handling, data use validation and subroutine interfaces as appropriate
- use meaningfully named variables (local and/or global)
- be appropriately structured for ease of maintenance.

When developing your code you should:

- use subroutines complete with appropriate interfaces
- use effective and cohesive subroutines
- demonstrate good exception handling
- incorporate self-documenting code
- demonstrate modularisation of your code
- show that you can use appropriate local variables
- demonstrate minimal use of global variables
- show the appropriate use of data validation
- show the appropriate use of constants
- demonstrate a consistent style throughout
- always use meaningful identifier names
- ensure that you use appropriate indentation
- add annotation, using it effectively wherever it is required to help someone understand your solution.

Testing

You will be expected to test your designs against the original task requirements, including:

- testing your solution for errors
- choosing and using test data covering normal (typical), boundary (extreme) and erroneous data.

You will need to develop a comprehensive test plan that includes:

- test data that enables the testing of all requirements
- coverage of normal, erroneous and boundary data types
- the expected outcomes for each test.

Your test plan should show how each component will be tested to meet the requirements of the problem.

Testing is asking the questions, 'Does the solution work?' and 'How well does it work?' You will need to plan a series of tests to show that the different sections and elements within your solution work as intended, that your solution is successful. It is best to test your designs both during the coding process and after the system has been fully coded. When carrying out tests it is important that normal (typical), boundary (extreme) and erroneous data should be used as appropriate.

You will need to present your results in a structured way, for example in tabular form, showing clear evidence of testing. You should also explain the reasons for the tests carried out alongside the evidence for them.

This could take the form of:

- the test performed
- its purpose if not self-evident
- the test data
- the expected test outcome
- the actual outcome with a sample of the evidence.

You will need to demonstrate that:

- a thorough representative range of tests has been planned and carried out
- all the requirements of the problem have been achieved
- your test data includes normal (typical), boundary (extreme) and erroneous data and shows that you have included:
  - a comprehensive application of programming concepts and principles, including changes as a result of testing (debugging)
  - constructs, data validation and a choice of data types and structures and how these have led to an overall solution which is fully functional as a result of effective testing
- you have produced a test plan which is clear and unambiguous.

Evaluation/refining

You should evaluate your solution to the task throughout the design process, including:

- refining your solution as a result of testing
- assessing how well the solution meets the requirements of the problem
- suggesting how your solution could be improved if the problem were to be revisited.

Evaluation is considered to be, 'How well does the solution work, and how could it be better?'

Overall quality of your report

You must show a thorough analysis and real quality in your completed report, this means using the correct terminology and sequencing the report so that someone can follow the stages that you went through.

The report should consist of the following sections:

- how you designed the solution to the problem
- how you tested the solution to the problem
- how you tested your solution, including the test data you used
- how you created your solution, including all the code with annotations so that others can understand what you have done
- any potential enhancements and refinements to your solution that you carried out as a result of testing.

You should try to use a range of technical terms, but make sure that they have been used accurately. There should also be a consistent approach to the structure and layout of your report which enables easy cross referencing between sections and between different parts of the solution.

Key Point Index

Key Point Index

Generalisation Generalisation means adapting a solution that solved one problem to solve another. It also means replacing many things with one. First decide what similar problems have in common, then write code that by using variables and functions can be called when you need these similar features. — 116

Hexadecimal Hexadecimal is a number system based on 16, where the numbers 10 to 15 are represented by the letters A to F. — 132

High-level language A high-level language is a programming language designed to allow people to write programs without having to understand the inner workings of the computer. — 138

HTTPS HTTPS provides an encrypted version of HTTP for more secure web transactions. — 322

Immutable An immutable object is an object whose state cannot be changed after it is created. — 64

Import To import is to bring in from an outside source. — 110

Indefinite loop Iteration is the process of repeating a particular action. In an indefinite loop, the number of iterations is not known when we start to execute the body of the loop, as it depends on when a certain condition becomes true. — 74, 92

Integer An integer is a data type for representing whole numbers. — 167, 176

Interpreter An interpreter is a program that executes a source program by reading it one line at a time and doing the specified operations immediately. — 138

Iteration Iteration is the process of repeating a particular action. For examples FOR; WHILE. — 77

Library A library is a collection of files, computer programs or subroutines. — 110

Logical A logical data type has one of two values (True/False, 0/1). — 46

Loop A loop is part of a program that repeats itself (to prevent the need for the same piece of code to be typed out multiple times). — 74, 104, 184

Low-level language A low-level language is a programming language that provides little or no abstraction from a computer's instruction set. — 138

MAC address filtering MAC address filtering allows devices to access, or be blocked from accessing, a network based on their physical address embedded within the device's network adapter. — 283

Machine code Machine code is a set of instructions that a computer can execute directly. Machine code is written in a binary code, and each statement corresponds to one machine action. — 125, 137, 139

Magnetic storage In magnetic storage, magnetic material is given a polarity. That polarity is then read and depending on the direction is output as a binary 1 or a 0. — 255

Memory Just like humans, computers rely a lot on memory. They need to process and store data, just like we do. However, computers store data in digital format in a reserved location and of a set location size. — 69

Memory location The computer memory is made up of partitions (much like a set of drawers). The memory location is the address which uniquely identifies every location in the memory. — 68

Menu A menu is an element displayed on the screen that gives the user a choice of options. — 99

Modularity Modularity is writing and testing parts of the program separately, then combined these parts with other modules to form the complete program. The name given to this process is top-down programming. — 12

Module A module is a section of code that forms a part of an overall program. — 12

Motherboard The motherboard is the central printed circuit board (PCB) that holds all the crucial components of the system. — 236

Nested loops Nested loops consist of an outer loop and one or more inner loops. Each time the outer loop is repeated, the inner loops are re-entered and started again as if new. — 97

Key Point Index